The Chartered
Institute of Marketing

# CIM Companion:

# strategic marketing management:
# planning & control

CIM Publishing

**CIM Publishing**

The Chartered Institute of Marketing
Moor Hall
Cookham
Berkshire
SL6 9QH

www.cim.co.uk

First published 2002
© CIM Publishing 2002

Series Editors: Mark Stuart and John Ling.

Applications for the copyright holder's written permission to reproduce any part of this publication should be addressed to the Editors at the publisher's address.

The publishers believe that the contents of this book contribute to debate and offer practical advice. No responsibility will be taken by the publishers for any damage or loss arising from following or interpreting the advice given in this publication. No sexism is implied by the use of the pronoun 'he' or 'his', which is used to avoid ungrammatical or clumsy language.

It is the publisher's policy to use paper manufactured from sustainable forests.

**British Library Cataloguing in Publication Data**
A CIP catalogue record for this book can be obtained from the British Library.

ISBN 0 902130 88 9

Printed and bound by The Cromwell Press, Trowbridge, Wiltshire.
Cover design by Marie-Claire Bonhommet.

# contents

# Study guide

This Companion is designed to complement the core texts recommended in the syllabus for this module: Strategic Marketing – Planning & Control (2nd Edition) by Drummond and Ensor, Marketing Strategy & Competitive Positioning (2nd Edition) by Hooley, Saunders & Piercy, and Strategic Marketing Management (5th Edition) by Aaker. It aims to offer you support as either an individual learner or a group learner as you travel the road to becoming a competent and proficient marketer. This is a process of learning that has two important elements:

## Understanding marketing concepts and their application

The study text in the following Sessions has been written to highlight the concepts that you will need to grasp as you start to understand the principles of strategic marketing, what strategic marketing can achieve, and how it is implemented. The material is described briefly and concisely, to enable you to cover a range of key material at the entry point to strategic marketing. It does not attempt to be fully comprehensive and you should read widely from other sources. To develop your understanding of the concepts introduced here, your reading should include:

- Recommended course texts (readings are shown in Table 2 for each of the Sessions in this book).

- Marketing press and quality national newspapers.

- More comprehensive marketing textbooks detailed on the module reading list in the syllabus, which provide a wider context for the concepts explained in this Companion and more Case Studies and examples to illustrate strategic marketing in practice.

## Developing the skills to implement marketing activity

Equally important in the journey towards marketing excellence is the acquisition, development and refining of a range of skills that are required by marketers across all industries and sectors. These transferable skills hold the key to the effective implementation of the marketing techniques explored in the study text.

## Using the Companion

You should familiarise yourself with the syllabus for this module, which is shown in Appendix 2. For this Companion, it has been broken down into fifteen Sessions, each of which covers approximately the same proportion of the content. Every student brings with them to their studies different levels of experience – as a customer, from previous studies, and from working in marketing or sales. You should therefore be aware that, whilst you may need to spend considerable time on an unfamiliar area of the syllabus, you may make up this time when studying another area with which you are more familiar.

Each Session has a series of short Activities, which you should try to complete as you work your way through the text. These will help you to check your understanding of the material, and brief feedback is provided at the end of each Session, so that you can compare your answers. Some of these are exam questions from past papers, so you can use them to practise your exam technique.

Each Session also contains a Case Study and a series of related questions. Many of these have been taken from past examination papers, so you can use them to help prepare you for the mini case within your exam. Try to complete these without reference to your notes, or the Session text, and then compare your answers with some key points that are given at the end of the Companion, in Appendix 1.

At the end of each Session you will also find a number of Projects. These are designed to help you to extend and apply your understanding of the subject covered in the Session. These often take the form of practical activities undertaken in your own organisation or an organisation of your choice. While not all participants in CIM programmes are working in an organisation, these Projects can still provide valuable learning if interpreted rather than followed to the letter or applied to organisations that you are aware of.

Finally, you will see that there is a past Examination paper in Appendix 3. This can help you with your revision, examination technique, and preparation. Nearer to your actual examination, allow time to complete the paper under examination conditions – that is, allow three hours of uninterrupted time, and complete the paper without reference to your notes or the study material. When you have completed the exercise, you can compare your answers to the notes in Appendix 4. If either your approach to the exercise or the comparison of your answers highlight areas of particular weakness, you should refer back to the text and re-read the relevant Session, together with the chapters of the supporting textbook.

This Companion's structure and content follows the syllabus order, as this module follows a standard 'process' which in itself is logical in its 'flow'.

# Table 1 – Web sites

| CIM www.connectedinmarketing.com | |
|---|---|
| www.connectedinmarketing.com/cim/index.cfm | |
| www.cimvirtualinstitute.com | |
| www.adslogans.co.uk | Online database of advertising slogans enabling marketers to check whether a slogan is already in use. |
| www.ipa.co.uk | Institute of Practitioners in Advertising. |
| www.asa.org.uk | Advertising Standards Agency. |
| www.new-marketing.org | Research updates into new marketing issues, customer segmentation and repercussions for marketing practitioner. |
| www.europa.eu.int | European Union online. |
| www.wapforum.org | Industry Association responsible for creating the standards for WAP (Wireless Application Protocol). |
| www.prnewswire.co.uk | UK media monitoring service – reviews mentions in all media types (print, online publications and broadcast). |
| www.keynote.co.uk | Market research reports. |
| www.verdict.co.uk | Retail research reports. |
| www.datamonitor.com | Market analysis providing global data collection and in-depth analysis across any industry. |
| www.store.eiu.com | Economist Intelligence Unit, providing country-specific global business analysis. |
| www.mintel.com | Consumer market research. |
| www.royalmail.co.uk | General marketing advice and information. |
| www.ft.com | Financial Times online newspaper and archives (subscription based). |
| www.afxpress.com | Business news plus industry trends. |
| www.statistics.gov.uk | Detailed information on a variety of consumer demographics from the UK Government Statistics Office. |

| | |
|---|---|
| www.worldmarketing.org | World Marketing Association. |
| www.accountingweb.co.uk | Provides the latest financial news, company information, taxation guides and other financial matters. |
| www.financewise.com | Specialist index of web sites providing links to information on all aspects of finance (registration required). |
| http://web.utk.edu/~jwachowi/wacho_world.html | Exhaustive listing of web financial resources presented with a student perspective. |
| www.bized.ac.uk | Contains a complete example of a company called Cameron Balloons complete with finances. Can be used to illustrate all the basic principles of financial decisions made in this Companion. |
| www.amazon.co.uk | Classic example of groundbreaking online customer service and marketing orientation in practice. |
| www.johnsonandjohnson.com | An example of a 'credo' and its documented influence on the activities of this global corporation. |
| www.mckinseyquarterly.com | Free full text articles on strategy issues from one of the world's premier business journals. |
| www.strategy-business.com | Online journal on the topic of business strategy, with good search facilities. |
| www.virgin.com | A well-known successful example of unrelated diversification. |
| www.cbi.org.uk/innovation/index.html | Information on innovation in industry. |
| www.marketing.haynet.com/keynote/index.html | Useful notes on the preparation of marketing plans, and access to research data. |
| www.hbsp.harvard.edu | Free abstracts from Harvard Business Review articles. |

# Table 2 – Background reading

The following references are suggested background readings for each Session. It is suggested that the student undertake this reading before studying the relevant Companion Session.

| Session | Reading from Core Text:<br>**1. Drummond & Ensor – *Strategic Marketing – Planning & Control* (2nd Edition) – Butterworth-Heinemann**<br>**2. Hooley, Saunders & Piercy – *Marketing Strategy & Competitive Positioning* (2nd Edition) – FT Prentice-Hall.**<br>**3. Aaker – *Strategic Marketing Management* (5th Edition) – Wiley.** |
|---|---|
| **Session 1** | 1. Chapter 1 – The strategic perspective.<br>2. Chapter 1 – Market-led strategic management. |
| **Session 2** | 1. Chapter 1 – The strategic perspective.<br>2. Chapter 2 – Strategic marketing planning. |
| **Session 3** | 1. Chapter 5 – Internal analysis.<br>2. Chapter 3 – Portfolio analysis.<br>2. Chapter 5 – Assessment of corporate capabilities. |
| **Session 4** | 1. Chapter 5 – Internal analysis.<br>2. Chapter 3 – Portfolio analysis. |
| **Session 5** | 1. Chapter 14 – Control page 273-279.<br>3. Chapter 7 – Internal analysis (including Appendix). |
| **Session 6** | 1. Chapter 2 – External analysis.<br>1. Chapter 4 – Segmentation.<br>2. Chapter 6 – Customer analysis. |
| **Session 7** | 1. Chapter 3 – Competitive intelligence.<br>2. Chapter 4 – Industry analysis.<br>2. Chapter 7 – Competitor analysis. |
| **Session 8** | 1. Chapter 6 – Developing a future orientation.<br>2. Chapter 11 – Forecasting.<br>3. Chapter 6 – Dealing with strategic uncertainty. |
| **Session 9** | 1. Chapter 7 – Strategic intent.<br>3. Chapter 8 – Obtaining a sustainable competitive advantage. |
| **Session 10** | 1. Chapter 8 – Strategy formulation.<br>1. Chapter 11 – Alliances and relationships page 223-228.<br>2. Chapter 13 – Building and maintaining defensible positions.<br>2. Chapter 14 – Offensive and defensive competitive strategies.<br>2. Chapter 18 – Marketing strategies for the 21st century.<br>3. Chapter 13 – Strategies in declining and hostile markets. |

| Session 11 | 1. Chapter 4 – Segmentation.<br>1. Chapter 9 – Targeting, positioning and brand strategy.<br>2. Chapter 9 – Segmentation and positioning principles.<br>2. Chapter 10 – Segmentation and positioning research.<br>2. Chapter 12 – Selecting market targets. |
|---|---|
| Session 12 | 1. Chapter 10 – Product development and innovation.<br>1. Chapter 11 – Alliances and Relationships page 228-233.<br>2. Chapter 15 – Competing through superior service and customer relationships.<br>2. Chapter 16 – Competing through innovation and new product development. |
| Session 13 | 1. Chapter 12 – The strategic marketing plan.<br>3. Chapter 16 – Formal planning systems. |
| Session 14 | 1. Chapter 13 – Strategic implementation.<br>2. Chapter 17 – Implementation through internal marketing.<br>3. Chapter 15 – Implementing the strategy. |
| Session 15 | 1. Chapter 14 – Control. |

# Table 3 – Marketing models

The text in the Companion Sessions refers to appropriate models but does not reproduce them as they can be seen at the references in the core textbooks shown in the table below. Please note that this does not necessarily represent the full range of models that you will need to study for your exam or assessment. Refer to the syllabus in Appendix 2 for further information.

| Session | Marketing Model | Reference |
|---|---|---|
| **Session 1** | ■ A model or market orientation.<br>■ Market orientation questionnaire. | ■ 2.  Page 9.<br><br>■ 2.  Page 11-13. |
| **Session 2** | ■ The basics of strategy.<br>■ Elements of strategic management.<br>■ The basics of marketing strategy.<br>■ Strategic marketing. | ■ 1.  Page 4.<br>■ 1.  Page 5.<br><br>■ 1.  Page 11.<br><br>■ 1.  Page 14. |
| **Session 3** | ■ Senior management cognitive composition.<br>■ Marketing assets. | ■ 1.  Page 95.<br><br>■ 2.  Page 116. |
| **Session 4** | ■ Innovation/value matrix.<br>■ BCG growth share matrix.<br>■ GE multi-factor matrix.<br><br>■ Shell directional policy matrix.<br>■ A framework for analysing corporate resources. | ■ 1.  Page 94.<br>■ 1.  Page 97.<br>■ 1.  Page 101/<br>  2.  Page 65-68.<br><br>■ 1.  Page 102.<br><br>■ 2. Page 106. |

| Session 5 | ■ Examples of profitability ratios. | ■ 1. Page 275. |
|---|---|---|
| | ■ Examples of liquidity ratios. | ■ 1. Page 275. |
| | ■ Examples of debt ratios. | ■ 1. Page 276. |
| | ■ Examples of activity ratios. | ■ 1. Page 276. |
| | ■ Shareholder value. | ■ 3. Page 115. |
| | ■ Economic value added. | ■ 3. Page 119. |
| | ■ Performance measures of long-term profitability. | ■ 3. Page 122. |
| Session 6 | ■ Influences on consumer behaviour. | ■ 1. Page 46. |
| | ■ The buying process. | ■ 1. Page 52. |
| | ■ JICNARS social grades. | ■ 1. Page 58. |
| | ■ New classes for 2001 UK Census. | ■ 1. Page 58. |
| | ■ ACORN consumer targeting classification. | ■ 1. Page 61. |
| | ■ VALS framework. | ■ 1. Page 67. |
| | ■ Monitor framework. | ■ 1. Page 68. |
| | ■ Webster-Wind framework. | ■ 1. Page 73. |
| | ■ Model of organisational buyer behaviour. | ■ 1. Page 75. |
| | ■ Organisational macro and micro segmentation. | ■ 1. Page 80. |
| | ■ Major factors for segmenting organisational markets. | ■ 1. Page 81. |
| Session 7 | ■ The 5 forces model. | ■ 1. Page 25. |
| | ■ Strategic groups in the airline industry. | ■ 1. Page 28. |
| | ■ Competitive intelligence cycle. | ■ 1. Page 38. |
| | ■ SPACE analysis map. | ■ 2. Page 94. |
| | ■ Competitors' capabilities. | ■ 2. Page 165. |

| Session 8 | ■ Time series analysis.<br>■ Trend analysis.<br>■ Cross impact analysis.<br>■ Forecasting methods, roles and ranges. | ■ 2. Page 270.<br>■ 2. Page 272.<br>■ 2. Page 289.<br>■ 2. Page 290. |
|---|---|---|
| Session 9 | ■ Influence on mission and objectives.<br>■ Examples of mission statements.<br>■ Level of adoption of a mission statement.<br>■ Hierarchy of objectives.<br>■ Balanced scorecard.<br>■ Gap analysis. | ■ 1. Page 128.<br><br>■ 1. Page 129-130.<br><br>■ 1. Page 134.<br><br>■ 1. Page 138.<br>■ 1. Page 141.<br>■ 1. Page 142. |
| Session 10 | ■ The formulation of strategy.<br>■ Competitive advantage.<br>■ Inconsistent strategy.<br>■ BCG strategic advantage matrix.<br>■ Sources of competitive advantage.<br>■ The value chain.<br>■ Attacking strategies.<br>■ Defensive strategies.<br>■ Product/market matrix.<br>■ Product life cycle.<br>■ Levels of product.<br><br>■ Traditional & VMS marketing channels. | ■ 1. Page 145.<br>■ 1. Page 145.<br>■ 1. Page 149.<br>■ 1. Page 151.<br><br>■ 1. Page 152.<br><br>■ 1. Page 154.<br>■ 1. Page 157/2. Page 339.<br>■ 1. Page 159/2. Page 343.<br>■ 1  Page 161.<br>■ 1. Page 165.<br>■ 2. Page 323 and Page 328.<br>■ 1. Page 228. |

| Session 11 | ■ Adapted Shell DP matrix for target market selection. | ■ 1. Page 179. |
| | ■ Perceptual map. | ■ 1. Page 185/2. Page 262. |
| | ■ Brand equity. | ■ 1. Page 189. |
| | ■ Alternative branding strategies. | ■ 1. Page 195. |
| | ■ Alternative options available for brand repositioning. | ■ 1. Page 202. |
| Session 12 | ■ Types of new product. | ■ 1. Page 210. |
| | ■ NPD process. | ■ 1. Page 211-212. |
| | ■ Mortality of new product ideas. | ■ 2. Page 375. |
| | ■ Strategic direction of NPD. | ■ 1. Page 214. |
| | ■ Generating innovation. | ■ 1. Page 217. |
| | ■ Marketing uncertainty map. | ■ 1. Page 219. |
| | ■ Six market model. | ■ 1. Page 229. |
| | ■ Relationship marketing ladder. | ■ 2. Page 355. |
| Session 13 | ■ Corporate and marketing planning hierarchy. | ■ 1. Page 235. |
| | ■ The strategic process. | ■ 1. Page 236. |
| | ■ A multi-dimensional model of marketing planning. | ■ 1. Page 241. |
| | ■ Example of strategic marketing plan. | ■ 1. Page 243. |
| | ■ Planning forms. | ■ 3. Page 307-320. |

# Session 1

# Adopting a market-led orientation

## Introduction

This first Session introduces the concept of marketing orientation and looks at the problems in achieving genuine market-led management. It also considers the fast pace of change within the external environment and the opportunities and threats that this presents to the strategic marketer.

---

**LEARNING OUTCOMES**

At the end of this Session you will be able to:

- Explain the concept of 'marketing orientation'.

- Define the role of marketing in market-led strategic management.

- Identify the main drivers of change in the business environment and explain their impact on organisations.

---

## Marketing orientation

The aim of marketing orientation is for the organisation to focus on identifying and satisfying customers' needs. Piercy (2000) has coined the term 'market-led strategic change' to illustrate the importance of the fact that the market should lead the organisation. The issue is that the marketing specialists develop the plan. Once these needs have been identified, all the activities and business processes in the organisation are aligned and geared to satisfying customers. The main characteristics of a marketing orientation are:

- A focus on the customer.

- Competitor orientation.

- Co-operation between all the functions of the business.

- Responsiveness to change in the environment and customers' needs.

- An emphasis on profit, not sales revenues.

This concept is simple and straightforward but difficult to achieve. The customer is just one stakeholder and one voice in the organisation. A market-led orientation is just one of the orientations found in organisations. Other business orientations with a more internal focus include:

- Production orientation – with the emphasis on operational schedules and achieving economies of scale.

- Product orientation – where the product itself provides some competitive advantage. The challenge here is for technology-led companies to understand customers' future needs well in advance. This is a key issue for companies who are working on products for launch several years away. In certain sectors, such as engineering and computers, this manifests itself as a technology orientation.

- Sales orientation – with its emphasis on delivering success by selling. It tends to be transaction-based and short-term, whereas marketing orientation is more relationship-oriented and longer-term.

The adoption of a particular orientation in an organisation is heavily influenced by the balance of supply and demand in the sector in which the organisation is operating. In past times and in sectors where demand exceeds supply, organisations tend to be product-oriented. Only when supply exceeds demand, as it does in many of today's markets, will organisations in a sector adopt the concept of marketing and develop a market-led orientation. The ability to switch from an internal to an external focus is cultural and may take the organisation time to achieve, particularly if it has been more internally driven with a production-led approach or a strong financial drive.

Marketing strategy is a set of tools for the Manager to analyse and make decisions about market opportunities and resources. It is about matching the capabilities of the organisation with opportunities available in the environment. The organisation has to take into account the competitive situation in the industry. It has to generate a profit. It has to respond to the many and varied challenges and the constant state of change. These are all features of a marketing orientation.

There is a range of models describing the main stages of strategy making which we will explore in the next Session. But strategy making is just one aspect of the activities of a truly market-led organisation. Once it has decided on its strategy, the organisation needs to implement this strategy, monitor its activities and make any changes needed, either because the environment has changed or because the strategy has not worked quite as intended.

Market-led orientation is often closely aligned with strategic management. In other words, it is about directing and managing the organisation based on a clear picture of the opportunities in its environment. Strategic management has therefore become synonymous with a structured, rational approach to planning and a logical framework for the basis of marketing decisions. As the rate of change increases, the ability of the organisation to respond therefore has to increase. A strategy has not only to be clear but flexible, so that the organisation can adapt as it encounters the unforeseen. This is a tricky balancing act.

The success of strategic management lies in the organisation's ability to implement the strategy and deliver results at the bottom line. This requires careful co-ordination to ensure that each function and activity in the organisation plays its part. The customer will experience the actions or tactics of the organisation and will judge it on this basis, not the quality of the original plan. A strong customer orientation, customer service and speed of response will all contribute to the success of the organisation.

In a market-led orientation, someone has to perform the functions of scanning the environment, monitoring customers' needs and directing the activities of the organisation that will ultimately satisfy customers. The challenges facing the marketing team in this kind of organisation are therefore complex and demanding. We explore these in the next section.

---

**Activity 1.1**

Explain the term 'market orientation'.

---

## The role of marketing

It is important to realise that the marketing function plays a different role in organisations that have one of the different orientations. For example, in an organisation with a strong sales orientation, marketing is likely to be about communications in support of sales. In an organisation with a product-led orientation, marketing may have the role of finding markets for products developed by specialists, very much a product-push approach.

The market-led philosophy and marketing orientation have developed the external focus of the organisation. Piercy (2000) has drawn a clear distinction between the **market-led** approach, where the focus should be on the market, and the **marketing-led** approach, where the leadership comes from the Marketing Department.

The ability to adopt an external perspective lies at the heart of marketing within a rationally planned approach. However, there are a variety of factors that make the process more complex:

- If one customer or competitor is seen as the focus of the organisation's actions, the danger is that another competitor may appear, taking the organisation by surprise. It is therefore vital to stress the broader focus on the market to ensure that the whole picture is clear.

- Resources available for the various tasks that marketing in these organisations has to perform.

- Organisational culture, whether internally or externally focused, and whether hostile or friendly to the concept of marketing.

- The skills and technology existing in the organisation and the organisation's ability to match these to the needs of customers.

- The time demanded by managing existing business and the challenges of satisfying the competing needs of stakeholders.

- The ability to challenge the existing marketing plan to take into consideration more indirect competitors and begin to build the barriers to entry to protect market share.

As an example, consider the changes in the airline industry with the growth of the budget airlines taking market share from established companies or the use of technology to access customers from a lower cost base. Smaller organisations are able to compete and enter perhaps profitable niche markets. Returns in the short-term have to be balanced with long-term investment. There are many routes organisations can take. The rational planning model offers a clear structure, but the choices within the framework call upon the expertise of the Marketing Manager to make decisions based on knowledge and understanding of the external environment as well as the capabilities of the organisation.

So what does marketing do? In a market-led organisation, there are various marketing functions to be performed:

- Scanning and monitoring the environment.

- Interpreting the signals coming in to identify significant opportunities and threats.

- Planning the organisation's response.

- Managing the implementation of the marketing activities decided upon as part of the response in areas such as products, pricing, promotions and channels to market.

- Measuring and evaluating the organisation's performance in the market so that the need for any adjustments can be identified and made.

In organisations with other orientations, these functions will not all be present or will be given a lower priority or carried out by other departments.

---

**Activity 1.2**

What are the main activities that the Marketing Department performs in your organisation?

How strategic are those activities?

How is marketing regarded in the organisation?

What do these answers tell you about the dominant orientation in your organisation?

---

## Drivers of change

We are constantly told that change is a fact of life for most organisations today. Their environments are turbulent and uncertain. The rate of change is increasing. Change can take one of two forms:

- **Evolutionary change** – is relatively gradual and predictable. Firms therefore have time to detect change, experiment with and plan an appropriate response and take action. Supermarkets, for example, are generally good at detecting shifts in consumer behaviours and plan the products and stores to meet these needs.

- **Revolutionary change** – is unpredictable, often sudden and represents a discontinuity in patterns established over time. It has the power to change the whole game, redefining the way in which business is undertaken. For example, the Internet has provided a new model for accessing customers and conducting business.

There are a number of general changes in the business world that are affecting most organisations and their Marketing Departments:

- Globalisation and deregulation are increasing competition. Even if an organisation does not export or operate in another country, firms from other countries are likely to be operating in their local markets. Lower entry barriers are attracting new players into markets, further increasing competition.

- Customers are becoming more sophisticated. As supply exceeds demand in many markets, so customer choice increases and the customer gains in power. Customers' expectations are therefore increasing.

- Governments and people in the developed world in particular are becoming increasingly aware and concerned over the impact of our actions on the environment. They are bringing pressure and legislation to bear on organisations that are forcing them to redefine their products, services and activities.

- People are becoming increasingly concerned with social and ethical issues. Marketing tobacco and alcohol to the young, selling powdered milk in the less developed world and charging unaffordable prices for drugs are all examples from recent years of high profile ethical concerns.

- Demographics are changing. People are living in smaller units, living longer and living in mixed-race societies and cultures. There are new opportunities for organisations but, at the same time, certain activities that are no longer required or socially acceptable.

- New technology has changed our lives. The aeroplane is about 100 years old, the computer just over 50 years old, the PC 20 years old, the mobile phone and the Internet about 10 years old. This pace of change is exciting for some, bewildering for others. Organisations have to decide what they want to adopt, make the investment and execute their plans, all before the next generation of technology wipes out their investment.

- Shareholders' expectations for steadily increasing returns on their investment, coupled with changes in corporate governance, are leading to increased emphasis on measuring organisations' performance in the market across a range of criteria, not just financial. Increasingly, marketing assets such as brands are coming under scrutiny and marketers have to measure and justify expenditure on marketing activities.

We will explore in later Sessions the use of SLEPT (and similar models) for analysing the macro environment of an organisation.

These changes, coupled with the shift towards a market-led orientation in many organisations, are creating a whole range of challenges to the marketer for the 21st century. Marketing and marketers need to develop a strong external focus, a deep understanding of human behaviours and customers' needs, and tools and techniques of marketing based on customer 'pull' rather than product 'push'. Marketers have to become multi-disciplinary so that they can relate to fellow professionals in other functions in the organisation. An understanding of strategic marketing management provides the essential underpinning knowledge to equip the marketer for these challenges.

---

**Activity 1.3**

Examine the impact of globalisation on an organisation of your choice.

---

# Case Study – Where did it all go wrong?

Most dotcom failures can be blamed on a deviation from basic marketing principles, says John Nicola.

A **brand** is not just a company name and logo; it encompasses the customer's entire experience with your organisation. Defined simply, the brand is the immediate image, emotion, or message that is experienced when a person thinks of your organisation.

An effective brand is key to gaining market share and creating customer loyalty. This is particularly important on the Internet where timescales are short, competition intense and mistakes can be costly. With the introduction of the web came the hype. We all heard: "the Internet will re-write the rule book", and "you need to build the brand quickly". Some Internet marketers fell under the spell, spending vast sums on brand building campaigns, many of which were not successful. Marketers felt they had escaped from the restrictions of the off-line companies and wanted to do things differently. Creativity, freedom and urgency overtook sound business practices.

Can a virtual brand be built quickly and compete with established physical brands? Should building a virtual brand be any different to building a traditional brand? According to Jez Frampton, Managing Director of Interbrand Interactive: "Brands really exist in people's minds. The difference between online and off-line branding is therefore not the brand, but the way in which it is created. Too many online experiences lack the distinctiveness required to create powerful brands."

Can a virtual brand successfully change behaviour? There are some brands that have effectively achieved this, such as Amazon.com. It not only had first-mover advantage, but also applied to the web traditional marketing principles of satisfying customer needs in areas such as convenience, range, price and customer service. Although online brands have to work harder, essentially the brand building process is the same. Even so-called 'new' methods like viral marketing and CRM have their foundations in the traditional principles of loyalty programmes and direct mail. In light of all this, how do you build a successful online brand? Consider the following process when developing and building an online brand.

# Know your customer

Be clear about the needs, characteristics and expectations of customers as every activity and process should flow from this. In this sense the virtual company is no different from a physical one. How will you enhance your customer's life? Which needs do you wish to fulfil? What problems will you overcome? Unless you have concrete answers, you may need to go back to the drawing board.

# Know the competition

Analyse the competition and its positioning – a unique brand cannot be built without awareness of the marketplace. In my company's experience of rolling out US Internet companies into Europe, there are varying degrees of market knowledge, irrespective of the size of the company. A case in point is Netscape's European launch of its Netcenter portal. Initially intending to launch one portal for all countries, Netscape finally decided to launch eight different localised Netcenter portals, whilst maintaining the brand's core values.

# Know yourself

Establish your intended position, competitive advantage and core competence as well as your vision and mission. Why should a customer choose you rather than the competition? Be objective – put yourself in the position of the customer. We have all thought at some point, mistakenly, that because we are passionate about our products and services our customers must also feel the same way.

# Decide brand's core values

Use the results of the previous steps, in particular the needs and characteristics of your customers, to completely describe the personality of the brand – not just a list of words. If it helps, put a face or personality to it.

# Meet consumer needs

Determine the product and services on offer that will satisfy the needs of your customers and differentiate you from your competitors. Make sure they can be delivered effectively over the Internet. Also consider customer service and logistics.

## Your Internet site

A well-designed site is crucial: it should reinforce the brand, and be easy to use and navigate. It should enable your customers to access your products and services easily and quickly. Remember the brand encompasses the entire customer experience. (Take the unfortunate example of Boo.com; one factor contributing to its failure was its extremely slow web site download time.)

## The marketing campaign

Tell your customers who you are, what you offer, the needs you satisfy, and your differentiator. Do not communicate too many messages in one campaign, as it will cause confusion.

Think about your customer's behaviour and develop your media plan to maximise exposure whilst limiting costs. Be creative and innovative using relatively low-cost methods such as PR and viral marketing. Using highly targeted publications can be more effective than costly TV advertising. Develop integrated campaigns incorporating both off-line branding (creative, content, graphics, etc.) and online branding, so that there is continuity and consistency. Always remember to communicate in the same language as your customers.

Finally, never become complacent as it will be necessary to continually refresh and re-energise the brand in line with the company. It must remain dynamic over time.

**Source:** *Marketing Business,* March 2001.

---

### Questions

1.  The Case Study refers to 'basic marketing principles'. Explain what basic marketing principles are.

2.  Why are these basic marketing principles difficult to achieve in practice?

3.  Devise a list of ten rules to assist an organisation in ensuring that they do not deviate from these basic principles and so are able to develop a market-led approach.

## SUMMARY OF KEY POINTS

In this Session, we have introduced the concept of marketing orientation, and covered the following key points:

- The principle of a market-led orientation is simple, but achieving it is more complex.

- Marketing orientation is an externally focused orientation, well suited to the needs of an organisation competing in a market where supply exceeds demand. It is just one of the types of orientation found in organisations.

- Strategic management and strategic marketing are rational, market-led approaches to directing and managing activities required to satisfy customers.

- The role of marketing will depend on the type of organisation and the dominant orientation. This can range from the tactical in a product-led organisation to the strategic in a market-led organisation.

- There are a number of challenges facing marketing and organisations for the 21st century.

## Improving and developing own learning

The following projects are designed to help you develop your knowledge and skills further by carrying out some research yourself. Feedback is not provided for this type of learning because there are no 'answers' to be found, but you may wish to discuss your findings with colleagues and fellow students.

### Project A

Talk to colleagues in your Marketing Department and identify two or three changes that have taken place in your external environment in the last 12 months.

Examine how your marketing has been adapted to accommodate these changes.

---

**Project B**

Describe and evaluate the underlying culture in your organisation.

How marketing orientated is it?

How does this affect the expectations the organisation has about the role of marketing?

---

**Project C**

Examine the perspective of your organisation. How externally driven is it?

---

# Feedback to activities

### Activity 1.1

Marketing orientation is the orientation within an organisation that embraces customer orientation, a focus on the integration of activities in the organisation and an emphasis on profit rather than sales volumes. A marketing, or market, orientation usually requires a strategic approach to marketing.

### Activity 1.2

The type of marketing in your organisation may be one of:

- Supporting sales activities.
- Primarily marketing communications.
- 'Operational' marketing including communications, research and CRM.
- A full spectrum of marketing activities with a strong strategic influence.

The activities that the Marketing Department performs will be indicative of the 'marketing model' used in the organisation and will determine how it is viewed by other departments.

If the dominant orientation is not an external marketing orientation, then your organisation will be more internally focused and is likely to have a sales (orders), product (technology) or production (efficiency) orientation which rank customers as less important than internal factors.

**Activity 1.3**

Globalisation may be:

- Increasing competition in the organisation's markets.

- Providing new opportunities for the organisation.

- Making its customers' needs more homogeneous.

- Enabling the organisation to manufacture more efficiently and profitably.

- Exposing the organisation to greater risk.

This is covered in more detail in the International Marketing Strategy module.

# Session 2

# Strategic marketing – an overview

## Introduction

In the last Session, we described how a market-led orientation underpins strategic management and strategic marketing. In this Session, we examine the strategic marketing process and how it relates to corporate strategy. We look at the role of senior management in bringing all aspects of strategy together into a coherent whole, and the process and cycle of planning and control.

---

### LEARNING OUTCOMES

At the end of this Session you will be able to:

- Describe the strategic marketing process.

- Explain the interface between corporate strategy and marketing.

- Explain key theoretical concepts that underpin the marketing planning process.

- Distinguish between, and explain the nature of, strategic, tactical and contingency planning.

---

## The strategic marketing process

The role of strategy is to match opportunities in the environment with capabilities of the organisation. This gives us two start points and two approaches to making strategy:

- **Market-led approach** – this starts by looking at the environment to identify opportunities. It then develops and refines the capabilities needed to exploit these opportunities profitably. This approach assumes that the organisation has the skills and finance to develop the capabilities needed, clearly a constraint in some organisations.

- **Asset-led approach** – this approach recognises that an organisation's capabilities are unique and cannot be developed as quickly and easily as we might like. It therefore starts by understanding the capabilities, assets and competencies of the organisation. It then looks out into its environment to find opportunities that it can use its capabilities to exploit.

In the Planning & Control module, we explore the application of strategic marketing. It is important that you remember this distinction between the market-led approach and asset-led approach to strategy making.

We can now move on to identify the main stages in the strategic marketing process. There is a wide range of models describing this process – you may already know SOSTAC, the Johnson & Scholes model and Drummond & Ensor's approach, to name three. But they have some common features:

- Identifying opportunities and threats in the external environment.

- Understanding the capabilities of the organisation.

- Selecting and matching opportunities and capabilities.

- Defining the scope and boundaries of the business, including the markets it is going to operate in.

- Deciding how the organisation is going to compete and the 'marketing tools' (the 4Ps or 7Ps) it is going to use to do this.

- Co-ordinating activities and measuring and evaluating performance to ensure objectives are met.

This rational model suggests a neat sequence of steps that begin with an analysis of the environment and then develop into corporate objectives, corporate strategy, then marketing objectives, marketing strategy and tactics, and concluding with evaluation. You might envisage this as an inverted triangle, becoming more specific as the progression from corporate to marketing tactics becomes more short term and precise.

The ethos of marketing strategy for Drummond & Ensor (2001) is to think about strategy as developing a long-term view with action and reaction. Some have likened it to sport: attack, defend and respond. The concept is that the organisation will deliver a future for the stakeholders using a variety of planning tools. These include the marketing models such as Shell, BCG, and PIMS. This presents a neatly structured process with each component playing a role in developing and shaping the future of the organisation.

However, this process is not always that neat: the stages tend to be iterative in nature. In reality an idea of direction will be developed, and objectives set, but resources are not available, the competitors would react in a hostile manner and some competitors are also customers. The complexity of this is further highlighted by the business not being able to access sufficient capital. The analysis is continuous and, as a plan is set, the competitors produce a new product or service and change the rules of the game.

This creates a dilemma for organisations:

- Do they maintain such a degree of flexibility that, if necessary, they have to leave the overall direction loosely defined and resources allocated only for the short term, with all the attendant uncertainty that can bring?

- Or do they define the direction tightly and plan in detail over a longer term, with the attendant lack of flexibility this can bring?

In practice, they have to find the somewhat precarious balance between the two approaches. The stages of the process must exist but must offer flexibility to respond. This can be achieved by a plan that is fed regularly with new information from the external environment and uses contingency plans to offer alternative views of possible events. The development of scenarios, as we will see in a later Session, is a useful approach and one that offers the opportunity to build a variety of possibilities into the strategy.

The success of the strategic process lies as much in its implementation, which is via the employees, and the tactics of, for example, customer service. The customer experiences the implementation and, as such, the whole of the strategy must be integrated or there will be poor delivery, quality and unmet customer expectations. Success also depends on the creativity and leadership of the organisation. Bringing all aspects together into a coherent whole is down to the skills of senior management.

Finally, it is worth noting that a formal and structured approach to strategic planning can yield a number of benefits for organisations. These include:

- The identification of risks affecting the organisation and any particular set of activities.

- Better control – measurable activities are defined and monitored.

- Consistency of actions across the organisation with corporate objectives.

- Objectives are clarified and made explicit as part of the process.

- Allocation of responsibilities is unambiguous and related to specific outcomes and activities.

---

**Activity 2.1**

Examine the strategic process and the ability to develop contingency plans in an organisation of your choice. Make notes of your findings.

---

## Where corporate strategy and marketing meet

Within the rational planning model of corporate and marketing strategy there are a number of key relationships. Essentially the corporate strategy is the overall strategy for the business and, as such, is longer term and broader than the marketing strategy.

1.  The first relationship is vertical and top down. Here, the corporate centre sets the overall direction from which all other business units or functional strategies are devised. For example, this might be 'to be the global leader in the ABC market'. It would then determine the marketing objectives and status, for example 'to generate Y% market share and to offer the highest quality service built upon generic strategies'. The Ansoff (1957) growth model could be used to show penetration into markets DEF and then to extend into markets GHI, followed by new products in partnership. This relationship maintains the overall philosophy throughout the organisation and results in consistency and balance between direction and flexibility.

2.  The second relationship is horizontal across the various sections in the organisation. The precise structure will reflect the organisational structure but could be, for example, departmental such as marketing, production, finance and human resources. Using the same example of growing market share as above, HR would be to ensure that there is sufficient staff with the required skills, operations would have to ensure that there is sufficient capacity and the delivery dates can be met, and the financial department would ensure that adequate financial resources exist to fund the expansion. The co-ordination between these aspects must be established, otherwise the customer will experience poor delivery times, and inadequate customer service.

3.  The third relationship is bottom up. Here the marketing strategy has been broken down into tactics and the delivery of each aspect carefully co-ordinated to ensure a seamless offering. This will then need to be evaluated to ensure that the marketing objectives can be met. The level of feedback and evaluation happens at tactical, operational and strategic levels but perhaps the easiest way to think of it is from the specific tactical evaluation of, for

example, the number of special offers taken up, to the overall sales of the specific product, to the improvements in brand image. This will then be fed back from marketing to the overall corporate plan.

The relationship between the marketing corporate is then from the top down, becoming more specific as it reaches the tactical stages and then from the specific tactical points broadening back out to the marketing objectives and back to the corporate level. The horizontal cross-functional links integrate the process to ensure that the customer experience reflects the overall objectives.

This illustrates that there are several facets to the corporate/marketing relationship. The most significant aspect is that they move with the changes in the environment to avoid strategic drift.

## Marketing strategy

Marketing strategy is based upon a number of key concepts.

1.  The ability to develop strategic intent or vision is the over-arching statement that sets the direction for the organisation. It is, for Johnson and Scholes (1999), the desired future state or aspiration of the organisation.

    However, vision has a broader role in terms of developing ownership throughout the organisation, which in turn leads to commitment and motivation of everyone in the organisation. It helps the organisation to move and develop, not just to do the same things a little better. It seeks new ideas and encourages creativity and innovation rather than only maintaining the status quo. It also enhances the consistency and co-ordination throughout the organisation. Success depends on communication and the ability to develop the organisational culture in line with the vision.

    Mission is, for Piercy (2000), to provide daily guidance. It should reflect the organisation's capabilities and is linked to the critical success factors. The concept of deciding what business to be in lies at the heart of the process and sets the overriding direction. It is also there for an organisation to define its current and future actions. The statement needs to be clear and unique, maybe based around being the best; the question is at what? The idea is that the statement conveys to the stakeholders a clear idea of the ethos of the organisation.

2. The internal capabilities of the organisation must be evaluated and matched to the external environment. These need to be considered in terms of transferable skills. Examine the capabilities or core competencies of the organisation and avoid dwelling on products. The differentiator is what the consumer experiences, so consider service, flexibility, creativity and relationships. These features are harder to replicate than a product and, with products becoming commodities, the internal capabilities become critical in developing sustainable competitive advantage. This can be developed to encompass branding, alliances, knowledge technology and operational efficiencies. The combination of these factors will deliver a range of capabilities that the organisation can develop so that they become instinctively XYZ organisation.

3. The overall ethos of the organisation, its culture and values, will also influence strategic decisions. For example, the Co-operative Bank has adopted the most ethical stance in the industry, which has used ethics to deliver competitive advantage. Strategy and culture are interdependent: ideally they should be mutually supporting. However, particularly in times of crisis, they can be out of step and the culture may dictate certain strategic decisions or prevent them from being implemented effectively.

The combination of all of these factors offers a solid base from which to establish the marketing plan.

---

**Activity 2.2**

What are the characteristics of strategic decisions at the corporate and marketing level?

---

## Strategy, tactics and contingency planning

Within the planning process there are various stages, each with its own role and position. It is important to clarify the role and contribution of these components.

Strategy is longer term overall direction, objectives and means. For example, an intended direction to be number one in the market can be achieved through an objective to achieve x% growth plus strategies of increased penetration and new product development with partnerships and joint ventures. A marketing strategy should specify the particular market segments in which the organisation is going to compete.

Strategy is a continuous process: it evolves and is fine-tuned with the needs of the external environment. Strategic plans are not documents necessarily to be updated every year.

Strategy is distinct from the tactics that deliver strategy and it is more than just a set of tactics bundled together. This must be stressed to meet the exam requirements. Tactics are more specific, usually short-term and can be bounded to take place at specific periods, for example a sales promotion to increase awareness of a new product.

The nature of the problems and the level of challenge posed by setting strategy and tactics also differs. The problem at strategic level is likely to be complex and uncertain, with a higher degree of risk. Tactics are more bounded and are solutions to specific problems within a defined framework, for example to illustrate a new price policy.

The decision making process for each task requires a different type of information. For strategy, information is likely to be incomplete and ambiguous, as is the case in high technology industries looking forward for several years. Tactical information is based mainly on information that is available or can be obtained using marketing research.

Strategy is painting the big picture whereas tactics are the detail. Evaluation of the tactics is usually easier as each action is specific and has a clear outcome. Strategy will take a much longer time to generate results and its outcomes are more difficult to measure. In an effective strategy, it is the series of shorter-term tactics that incrementally combine to create the success of the strategy.

Contingency planning is the opportunity to recognise different scenarios or series of events and to develop plans that involve different activities being taken at different times. For example, the launch of a new product may depend on the readiness of the market to accept the product, competitors' actions etc. A contingency plan may specify a different launch event and communications campaign at a different date from the base plan.

The differences between the various components of the planning process need to be appreciated. Tactics are the daily experience for the customer and the strategy is the longer-term plan that underpins their operation.

# Case Study – easyJet

easyJet is a low fare airline that operates a number of routes within the European market. Stelios Haji-Ioannou, the owner of easyJet, founded the airline based on the belief that reduced prices would lead to more people flying. easyJet's prices are low; for instance a return flight from Luton to Amsterdam costs between £70 to £130. Flights, with an airline offering a full customer service package, could cost around £315 upwards.

The organisation's main base is at Luton airport from where flights to European destinations such as Amsterdam, Geneva, Nice, Barcelona, Palma and Athens are available. The airline also flies UK domestic routes from Luton to Edinburgh, Glasgow, Belfast and Liverpool. Liverpool allows the company to gain access into the lucrative North of England market and is becoming a growing centre of activity for easyJet. Flights can now be taken from Liverpool to Nice, Amsterdam and Belfast.

Luton airport is around 30 minutes by road from north London and only 15 minutes from London's main orbital motorway, the M25. The airport is ten minutes away from Luton railway station from where a 27-minute rail connection to London is available. A shuttle bus to the station is available every 10 minutes. A return rail journey for easyJet passengers is available at around £8 sterling. Liverpool airport also has good motorway connections.

Connecting flights are not part of easyJet's product offering. The airline merely carries passengers to and from single destinations. This allows the airline to eliminate costly ticketing processes as well as intermediaries, such as travel agents. The company operates a paperless office policy and non-ticket flights. Simply by ringing the company's telephone number or using the company's Internet site, customers can book a seat immediately by credit card. In autumn 1998, 40% of bookings for a major promotion in the *Times* newspaper were via the Internet. Although a confirmation of the booking will be sent if requested, customers only have to produce identification at the airport and quote the booking reference number to be given a boarding pass for their flight.

easyJet flights are 'free seating'. Passengers are not allocated a specific seat when they check in, instead they are given a boarding card that carries a priority number. The first person to check in gets boarding card No. 1, the next passenger boarding card No. 2, and so on. Customers are then asked to board according to the order in which they checked in, occupying whichever seat they wish. The result is that passengers board the plane faster and tend to sit down faster than is the case when they have to search for an allocated seat, as is the situation in the more traditional airline operations. The faster passengers board an aircraft the quicker the plane can take off and the less time it spends on the tarmac. This results in reduced airport fees.

The fact that easyJet is not hindered by connections to other flights allows it to operate out of cheaper secondary airports such as Luton and Liverpool, rather than larger airports like Heathrow or Manchester. easyJet also exploits the lack of competition for time slots at Luton and Liverpool to keep the length of time its aircraft are on the tarmac to a minimum. easyJet's aircraft are therefore airborne longer, creating more hours of revenue earning per aircraft, than companies operating out of larger and busier airports.

Premium priced airlines offer business class seats, which take up more room on an aircraft, and will normally operate with 109 seats on a Boeing 737-300. These airlines also require additional cabin crew in order to provide the level of service business class passengers demand. easyJet operates without offering business class seats, which allows it to create 148 passenger places on a Boeing 737-300. Catering consists of a trolley from which cabin staff will sell drinks and a limited range of snacks to passengers. The only 'freebie' on the flight is a copy of the airlines in-flight magazine called 'Easy Rider', which is printed on recycled paper. Cabin staff look more casual in orange polo shirts and black jeans than traditional airlines and have a more relaxed attitude. However, they are equally safety conscious as staff on other airlines.

easyJet's telephone number is promoted widely. The company's telephone number, in bright orange, dominates the sides of the aircraft, where it has almost become part of the easyJet corporate image. The organisation's approach to advertising has been described as "a guerrilla promotional approach", distinguished by attacks on the airline establishment and a series of PR stunts. Press and magazine advertising is widespread. Sales promotional activity has included joint promotions in national UK newspapers such as the *Times* and the *Independent.* The airline has also been the focus of a documentary series on UK television. The owner, Stelios Haji-Ioannou, has been featured in many business articles in the press, particularly for his high profile campaign against British Airways launch of its own low-cost airline operation called 'go'.

easyJet has also started targeting companies that wish to keep travel budgets under control. easyJet emphasises that they do not offer a loyalty scheme where business customers can build up loyalty points and gain free flights. The suggestion is that although executives may like this perk, the executive's company could be saving hundreds of pounds per trip by sending their staff on easyJet flights.

The organisation's latest plan is to develop a family of companies with a common theme, beginning with the launch of a chain of cybercafés. Although the branding for this venture has yet to be decided, the working title is 'easyCafé'. The company still has to make decisions, such as whether easyJet's trademark bright orange colour is made a prominent feature of the cafés. Tony Anderson, who will oversee this new development, is quoted as saying that with these cafés, 'we are targeting Joe Public, not the middle classes.'

**Source:** SMM Planning & Control Examination Paper, December 1999.

## Questions

1.  Identify the core capabilities of easyJet that can be used to grow the family of companies envisaged.

2.  Which approach to marketing planning – the market-led or asset-led approach is most suitable for easyJet and why?

## SUMMARY OF KEY POINTS

In this Session, we have introduced the strategic marketing process, and covered the following key points:

- Marketing planning supports the achievement of the corporate plan and, in turn, specifies more detailed tactics.

- Planning defines the what, how, when and who of future activity.

- Strategic choices include how to compete, direction of growth and method of growth.

- Advantages of strategic planning include identification of risk, better control, consistency, clarification of objectives, and allocation of responsibilities.

## Improving and developing own learning

The following projects are designed to help you develop your knowledge and skills further by carrying out some research yourself. Feedback is not provided for this type of learning because there are no 'answers' to be found, but you may wish to discuss your findings with colleagues and fellow students.

### Project A

Talk to colleagues within the Marketing Department to establish how well the aspects of strategic planning are integrated within your own organisation. Identify ways in which the process could be improved.

### Project B

Establish how your organisation sets and evaluates its plans. How frequently does it set and review its strategic plans? Over what time horizon are its plans made?

### Project C

How well are corporate and marketing objectives communicated within your organisation?

# Feedback to activities

## Activity 2.1

The strategic process in the organisation is likely to consist of:

- Analysis and evaluation.
- Strategy formulation and planning.
- Implementation.
- Measurement, monitoring and control.

Few organisations have no strategic process. It may just be conducted informally by a few Senior Managers.

## Activity 2.2

Strategic decisions are characterised by:

- Long term outlook.
- Greater uncertainty and ambiguity.
- Broad focus.
- High level – about defining markets and competitive position.
- Use of less structured and exploratory approaches.

# Session 3

# The firm's capabilities and assets

## Introduction

Having established the foundations of strategic marketing, this Session moves on to consider the role of the marketing audit in assessing an organisation's capabilities. It introduces the concept of the firm as a portfolio of assets and capabilities. It then goes on to examine the resource and asset based views of the firm and how they can be used to achieve competitive advantage. Finally it looks at the various tools and techniques that can be used within the audit process.

---

### LEARNING OUTCOMES

At the end of this Session you will be able to:

- Explain the concept of the firm as a portfolio.

- Explain the 'resource-based' and 'asset-based' views of the firm as a basis for differentiation and competitive positioning.

- Describe the process for conducting and evaluating a detailed audit of the organisation's internal capabilities.

---

## The firm as a portfolio

The firm, or organisation, can be seen as a collection, or portfolio, of assets and capabilities. Each asset or capability has a specific set of resource and investment requirements, and will yield different outcomes. Investors and market traders talk about a portfolio of shares or stocks in companies: the assets and capabilities we are talking about here are in many respects similar to shares.

The concept of a portfolio encourages us to see the organisation from a holistic perspective. Analysis tends to lead us to examine assets and capabilities in a piecemeal fashion but portfolio analysis equips us to see the individual parts but manage them as a whole.

An organisation has many assets and capabilities that all need to be managed. It may be operating in a number of different markets or segments; it will have a number of products or services; it may have a number of channels to market; it will be using different media to communicate with the market. We can therefore think of the Manager who is trying to make decisions and control these different activities as a juggler trying to keep all the balls in the air. Let's look at a number of situations where portfolio management is used.

1.  **Investment and cash management** – at the strategic level, the Manager needs to consider the business units and the overall business that is at stake, and each unit (which could be geographical or by industry of market based) needs to be given attention. That attention includes time, skills and finance. If business unit A is performing well, then the cash it is generating could be used either to reinvest more in A to enhance its performance or to assist business unit B which might be under-performing. Portfolio analysis and management helps the Manager to understand the situation, identify options available and make a balanced decision.

2.  **Business development** – the ability to diversify using an overall brand strategy can be risky and affect the existing portfolio. The implications for the existing business must be considered when developing new ideas. Similarly with new products the balance across the portfolio in terms of the span of control and resource utilisation will affect the ability to manage the portfolio. Economies of scale can be gained from umbrella branding and also from using the same marketing tools wherever appropriate such as the channel of distributions to minimise the additional demands. Managers are faced with demands, constraints and choices and make those decisions depending on objectives to be met, sources of competitive advantage and the overall strategy.

3.  **Multiple markets** – consider an organisation that has a range of business units operating globally with several different products. Faced with an opportunity to enter a new market, the role of the management team is to assess the potential and the impact on the portfolio and to make a decision about resource allocations such that the overall performance of the portfolio meets corporate objectives, usually over the long term.

4.  **Risk** – think of firms such as insurance companies, telecommunications companies and pharmaceutical companies. Each type of company faces many exciting opportunities, all of which require substantial financial investment with no guaranteed outcome. In these cases, you can view the firms as a portfolio of risks that have to be managed such that the mix of risks will generate favourable outcomes whatever set of circumstances prevails at some point in the future.

The challenge therefore is to manage a portfolio in a holistic manner and appreciate the risks, rewards and implication of choices. Portfolio management and portfolio analysis are techniques and tools to help to deal with complexity and uncertainty. It is no accident that the portfolio tools, such as the General Electric (GE) multi-factor matrix and Shell directional policy matrix, were developed by large firms to help them manage large and complex portfolios.

The portfolio concept leads us to consider the firm as a collection of:

- Capabilities and competencies, which Drummond & Ensor refer to as 'resources'.

- Assets, which may have a more specific value or and more tangible.

To see the distinction between capabilities and assets, think of an asset as something the organisation owns and a capability or competence as how it uses an asset.

This gives us a framework for analysing and managing resources and assets within an organisation. We explore the resource-based and asset-based approaches in the next two sections as the basis for conducting an internal analysis.

## Resource-based approach

The resource-based approach identifies the need for the organisation to develop capabilities that are unique to it. Resources are the organisational capabilities and competencies that will lead to the development of competitive advantage if they match opportunities available in the external environment. These resources include:

- **Technical resources** – these include the technology development and product development functions, as well as the technical staff involved in delivery in service firms. The term encompasses access to research, information systems and processes as well as personal skills.

- **Financial standing** – this covers the ability of the firm to attract capital and invest to exploit opportunities. Firms are funded by a mix of debt (borrowings) and equity (money from investors) and the balance of these and investment yields are critical to the long-term well-being of the organisation.

- **Managerial skills** – firms have to have the strategic management skills to succeed in their chosen environment. One reason that firms sometimes suffer when a 'shock' occurs in their environment is that the management skills required to assess the event, consider the options and take action are not up to the challenge.

- **Organisation** – the organisation has a range of organisational resources such as processes, systems, collective skills and a culture that can provide a strong basis for competitive advantage.

- **Information systems** – information about the state of the environment and of the organisation are crucial for making appropriate decisions. If an organisation is scanning its environment for opportunities and knows the availability and costs of specific resources, it will be in a stronger position to exploit this information over a competitor that does not have this information readily available.

An alternative view of competencies is to link them to the specific processes of the organisation. These might include: strategic, operations and departmental or functional competencies.

For a 'resource' such as these to be considered a valuable capability or core competency, it needs to pass two tests:

- It should meet the needs of the environment.
- It should be difficult for the competitors to reproduce.

In markets where products have become commodities, the skill in developing competitive advantage is derived from the organisation's ability to combine a series of capabilities such as operational efficiency and speed of delivery. For example, financial service organisations attempt to differentiate based on customer service, offering a tailored solution and speed of response using technology to understand the customer. This enhances the service and helps to build the relationship with the customer.

> **Activity 3.1**
>
> Examine the resource capabilities and competencies in an organisation of your choice. Make notes of your findings.

## Asset-based approach

The asset-based approach emphasises the exploitation of the assets of the organisation. Assets are the financial and non-financial 'capital' that the organisation has accumulated over time. Accounting methods teach us that assets can be fixed, or tangible and intangible. As with the resource-based approach, these assets can be used as the basis for developing competitive advantage if they match opportunities available in the external environment. These assets fall under four headings:

- **Customer-based assets** – this group of assets are those that customers consider important. They include the tangible assets such as products, the image and brand, as well as the less tangible ones such as market position built up over the years.

- **Distribution-based assets** – channels to market provide companies with the means to reach customers in different markets. These assets are the physical distribution resources, such as warehouses and transport, and the relationships the firm has with members of the distribution chain. Control over the distribution chain is a potential source of competitive advantage.

- **Alliance-based assets** – this group of assets covers relationships with external parties whom the organisation uses for technology development, supply or reaching markets.

- **Internal assets** – the final group embraces the assets of the organisation itself. This group includes many of the capabilities and competencies listed above as well as any tangible assets that may yield competitive advantage.

There is considerable debate over the definition of an asset. Under accounting convention, tangible assets are included on the balance sheet. However, organisations have other assets that are more intangible such as brands. There is change in the wind in the accounting profession with moves to value and include intangible assets in annual reports. This will have a marked impact on the marketing profession.

**Activity 3.2**

Examine the assets of an organisation of your choice.

How could these help them achieve competitive advantage?

Compare these with the resources you identified in Activity 3.1 and comment on how they different or similar they are.

## Internal analysis

As discussed in the previous Session, there are two approaches to making strategy: market-led and asset-led. The order in which Managers conduct the internal analysis and external analysis should be determined by the approach being used. This and the next Sessions deal with the internal audit, or analysis, process.

The purpose of the internal analysis is for an organisation to examine how its assets and capabilities can be combined to match opportunities available in the external environment. When it understands this match, it can use it to develop a competitive advantage. Due to the ability of competitors to replicate products, the key to competitive advantage lies in combining the skills within the organisation's control to offer a distinctive advantage for long-term success.

Internal analysis involves an examination of the resources and assets of the organisation using the frameworks discussed above. It also includes the marketing activities audit, which Kotler divides into distinct sections:

- **Marketing strategy audit** – this examines if the marketing strategy is realistic, consistent, cohesive and achievable. It will include an assessment of the audit, objectives, strategy tactics and evaluation tools. This ensures that the process is continual and is keeping abreast of the changing times. The resource usage is a key issue. The outcomes from the actions so far need to be evaluated to discover if any changes need to be made.

- **Marketing structures audit** – this examines the structure of the Marketing Department and how it operates. This reflects the ties of management, the speed of response, the type of communication, and the ability of the organisation to respond given the way in which it undertakes business. It also reflects the links throughout the organisation from top down to vertical where the functions co-ordinate the complete offering, ensuring consistency and cohesion in its operation, and the levels of marketing orientation and customer focus.

- **Marketing systems audit** – this focuses specifically on the efficiency of the planning and control system. It examines the information system in terms of current information quality on customers and the ability of the database to offer relevant information on the possibility of enhancing the customer experience by offering new solutions. It also covers control systems, not only from a financial perspective but also the performance of the employees in delivering the strategy.

- **The productivity audit** – this examines the operational efficiency and profitability of individual products, and the overall process in terms of smoothness and speed. This also needs to be applied to market sectors and geographical areas. The precise content will reflect the structure of the organisation. The concept is to discover where the profits are being generated or absorbed. Each component needs to be considered as adding value and this is the role of the audit.

- **The marketing function audit** – this examines the detail of the marketing tools in terms of cohesion and consistency but also to evaluate each component. It includes the products in terms of current and future management through the life cycle, the ability to offer a structured and equitable pricing policy and to ensure clarity in terms of flexibility for the sales force in view of discounting policies, the effectiveness of the communications process in terms of meeting objectives and delivering the brand values. At this level each component is evaluated on a short-term basis to link back into the overall plan.

This process of internal analysis should yield a complete picture of where the organisation performs efficiently and effectively. It makes use of a range of auditing tools that are introduced in the next Session.

---

**Activity 3.3**

The majority of marketing audits are criticised as being too bland and of little real value.

Explain how a rigorous audit should be undertaken.

---

# Case Study – Making waves

During the 2000 Olympics in Sydney, the traffic authorities used satellite communications to manage traffic flows to prevent gridlock. Satellite phones also come into play whenever there is a natural disaster or war erupts to make sure the story reaches a global audience. And thanks to the wonders of this technology, climbers can now make phone calls from the top of Mount Everest.

Indeed, that's how satellite communications are usually perceived: for those exceptional circumstances where traditional techniques simply won't work, for whatever reason. This is what Stephen Rogers, Director of Marketing communications at Inmarsat, is wrestling with. He wants to convince companies that using the Inmarsat network for their global communications is as feasible for them as it is for ships at sea.

That's why he has spent a good part of this year on a major repositioning programme to create greater awareness of the brand and its relevance to the global business community.

To understand just how seminal this new direction has been for Inmarsat, it's important to understand its history and the competitive landscape in which it operates. Inmarsat was first set up as an Intergovernmental Organisation (IGO) over 20 years ago by a group with representatives in about 87 countries, under the auspices of the International Maritime Organisation. The aim was to use satellite communication for maritime safety as the size of ships and numbers of people travelling on them grew. The first operational service went live in 1983.

During the 1990s, however, the fact that many of its 'owners', the national telecoms carriers, were being privatised meant it was inevitable that Inmarsat would eventually follow suit. As Rogers explains, "There was a recognition that the marketplace in the intervening years was a very different one from when Inmarsat had first been set up. So we needed to have a more structured, more fiduciary basis and increased commercial awareness."

So in April 1999 Inmarsat was the first IGO to become a limited company. Over the years it has expanded beyond maritime communications, with customers now in the aeronautical, broadcasting, energy, emergency and aid relief sectors. It is currently owned by a consortium, which includes formerly public companies such as BT and Telenor, the Norwegian group. However, it is heading for the stock market next year.

That means it has to be reinvented as a marketing-led, entrepreneurial company, rather than one where engineering has dominated. This is happening in an increasingly complex and competitive market.

For example, there are what Rogers calls the terrestrial players, which include both fixed-line businesses like BT and the mobile phone networks like Vodafone. These companies are working hard to be seen as global through a combination of organic growth, acquisitions and, in the case of mobile phone companies, roaming agreements which let users travelling to other countries link up to the indigenous network. But, as Rogers points out, there are still large swathes of the world which are black holes for these networks.

Contrast that with Inmarsat, whose nine satellites positioned 36,000 kilometres above the earth's surface gives coverage everywhere except the North and South Poles. But Inmarsat has not got the satellite field to itself. At one end of the spectrum are the heavy-duty competitors like Intelsat and Eutelsat. These are also formerly public institutions that are either privatised or on the way to being so and offer very high bandwidth to customers such as international telecom carriers, Internet service providers and broadcasters, and corporate networks.

The other end of the spectrum was, until recently, inhabited by a number of enterprising companies like Iridium which tried to set themselves up as satellite-based mobile phone companies at the end of the 1990s. The idea was to offer business travellers mobile phones that would have almost universal coverage. But most have fallen by the wayside, falling victim to what turned out to be a long and expensive business planning cycle: from the design of satellites to launch can take up to five or six years.

What Inmarsat wants to do is position itself in the middle of that spectrum by convincing companies that are growing globally that satellite communications is neither too rarefied nor too expensive. Rogers says: "Our focus is very much on delivering high-speed global mobile data communications solutions in the business-to-business environment. This means being seen not just as a communications conduit but providing end-to-end services. This could be anything from wireless videoconferencing, to high-speed Internet connectivity, to a range of specialist applications."

"The new campaign was preceded by research into the perception of global mobile communications generally. There wasn't a lot of clear differentiation that either our existing or target markets could see between the companies. So we had to begin to create our own succinct positioning to be identified within what was a quite congested market," says Rogers.

Branding would be key to changing assumptions: "We found that when people think about satellite communications they have the idea it means remote communications, where you have to be wearing a safari suit or full snow gear. This isn't surprising but it's only part of the picture," maintains Rogers. "We needed to show companies what we could do, the benefits of the solutions we offered and the relevance to their businesses. We had to do that in the context of what they were already using for global mobile communications because this isn't about chucking everything away and saying all you need is Inmarsat. It's about positioning the brand to show where they should use it compared to other options."

There was another important qualification. While trying to convince companies that sending their highly critical corporate data whizzing around the world by satellite made economic sense, Inmarsat didn't want to alienate its current customer base, of which about three-quarters is in the maritime sector. "We wanted to make sure the message could work with the existing customer base while at the same time removing this perceived glass ceiling which has kept new customers away," he says.

He reckons that what they have come up with hits the mark. It uses the analogy of a 4x4 utility vehicle to sum up everything the company wants to say about the brand: driving it 'off road' is comparable to the tough conditions its traditional users face. But these vehicles are just as prevalent in cities as the countryside, so the campaign can also encompass those companies who are looking for better answers to the restrictions of current networks for global, high-speed communications.

And it fits in with the brand values Inmarsat wants to project. "These vehicles are seen as powerful, aspirational, high quality and world-class," he explains. "These are all attributes we want associated with what our brand offers."

The campaign, which was launched last May, will run through November, with the ads purposely designed to look like a car poster for maximum effect. Developed by Publicis, it is running in daily broadsheets and international business titles in Europe, the US, the Middle East and Asia. The image is also being used in its public relations, direct marketing and channel marketing.

And it's the channel where Inmarsat really has to focus a good proportion of its marketing energy, because it works through a range of distributors and service providers. "We are a wholesaler," agrees Rogers, "but really we are more than that because we provide added value down the way. We put solutions together, and support them and have a very active role in marketing. It could be easy as a wholesaler to be slightly divorced from the channel but we can't afford to do that. Nothing can be out of touch with the brand." This is why Inmarsat helps fund the marketing done by the distributors.

Getting employees on board has also been essential. So Rogers has developed a range of initiatives to help employees grasp the essence of the brand repositioning, including briefings, a video and competitions. He wants to make sure the new brand orientation doesn't stop at the door of the Marketing Department. "There has been a big exercise around this," he says. "For some it's a light bulb. For others there is a more gradual process. I am a fundamental believer that you have to get buy-in internally and then in the channel."

The campaign is already having an impact on the Inmarsat culture, he believes. "The sense of positioning and brand values, how we talk, the tone of voice we use and how we communicate the message – this has changed quite substantially over the last few months to show that we are far more 'real world' than many people expect."

A high brand profile will be important when Inmarsat heads next year for a public offering which could value the company at £2 billion. Rogers' brief is to make sure that marketing has done what it needs to do to boost brand recognition. "My challenge is to realise the genuine potential I believe this business has. From a marketing perspective we must position ourselves effectively to capitalise on that."

**Source:** *Marketing Business,* October 2001.

---

## Questions

1. How would a marketing audit have benefited Inmarsat before it started its major repositioning exercise?

2. Identify two strategic issues Inmarsat faced before the repositioning exercise.

## SUMMARY OF KEY POINTS

In this Session, we have introduced the marketing audit, and covered the following key points:

- Organisations can be seen as a portfolio of assets and capabilities, each with differing resource needs and yields.

- The resource-based and asset-based views of the firm's performance see the opportunity for competitive advantage as being dependent on historically developed resources.

- Organisations need to establish a 'start point' for planning, and the internal analysis and marketing audit can provide this.

- The marketing audit needs to be carried out rigorously to be of value.

## Improving and developing own learning

The following projects are designed to help you develop your knowledge and skills further by carrying out some research yourself. Feedback is not provided for this type of learning because there are no 'answers' to be found, but you may wish to discuss your findings with colleagues and fellow students.

### Project A

Talk to colleagues in your Marketing Department. When was the last full marketing audit carried out (if at all)?

### Project B

What changes were made as a direct result of the audit carried out above?

### Project C

What would you recommend the organisation to do now?

# Feedback to activities

### Activity 3.1

You should have considered the various categories of resource capabilities and competencies in your organisation including financial, technical, managerial and organisational. Ideally you should have identified any which your organisation is already using, or could use, to develop competitive advantage.

### Activity 3.2

You should have identified assets in categories such as customer-based, distribution-based, alliance-based or internal. They might help the organisation to achieve competitive advantage by being more efficient or more effective than those of the competition. The assets are likely to be more *tangible* than capabilities and competencies.

### Activity 3.3

A marketing audit is a tool used during the analysis stage, which assists an organisation to develop an understanding of its current situation, opportunities available and sources of competitive advantage.

- It should encompass the overall marketing capability and resources of the organisation (finance, production and people as well as marketing) focussing on its strategic capabilities.

- It should be supported by quantitative as well as qualitative data drawn from both external and internal sources.

- It should not just identify key issues facing the organisation but explore and resolve them.

- The output should be structured and provide a firm basis for objectives and strategies that develop the organisation's competitive advantage.

# Session 4

# Techniques for internal analysis

## Introduction

This Session builds on the process for internal analysis developed in the previous Session by exploring the uses, benefits and drawbacks of the various tools and models available. In particular, it discusses the portfolio models and their usefulness both in analysis and in the strategy formulation process.

---

**LEARNING OUTCOMES**

At the end of this Session you will be able to:

- Critically appraise a range of auditing tools.

- Apply auditing tools during an internal analysis and draw appropriate conclusions.

- Recognise the role of portfolio models in planning as well as analysis.

---

## Using auditing tools

A range of auditing tools and techniques are available to support the internal analysis and marketing audit, and so contribute to an understanding of the organisation's resources and assets. The purpose in this Session is to identify the main techniques and explain how they are used. The examiner expects you to be able to explain these techniques, how to use them and their advantages and drawbacks. You can find more details on each of these by following the references shown in Table 3 in the Study Guide at the start of this Companion.

## Portfolio models

The main group of models available for internal analysis and evaluation of the organisation's portfolio of businesses, markets and products consists of the portfolio models. These are described at greater length later in this Session.

## Value chain

The value chain (Porter, 1980) is used to identify areas of potential competitive advantage by examining the primary and secondary activities. The primary activities examine the logistical and operations processes and stress the competencies and efficiencies that can be gained. In addition, marketing and sales is a primary activity. Primary activities are supported by secondary activities such as human resources, technology, infrastructure and procurement. It is the combination of the activities that lead to advantage rather than each component in isolation. Originally applied to manufacturing, it is also applicable to the service industry, though the order of primary activities may be different.

The value chain is internally focused and must be related to the needs of the external environment. It should be remembered that the organisation may not control the whole of the chain and may have outsourced some activities. Therefore the total process, the 'value system' as Porter calls it, needs to be evaluated.

## Financial analysis

Financial analysis is an essential technique during internal analysis. Many of the other techniques for internal analysis provide qualitative outcomes, for example identifying resources and assets that are, or can become, sources of competitive advantage. Financial analysis provides quantitative outcomes that tell you how effective and efficient specific activities have been or might be.

The examiner is unlikely to require you to conduct a detailed financial analysis in the exam. However, he will expect you to be able to explain the different aspects of financial analysis and what they contribute to an understanding of the organisation's capabilities and assets.

Financial analysis is covered in more detail in the next Session.

## Experience curves

The concept underpinning experience curves is that experience, gained by frequent high volumes of production, decreases costs and increases profits. This is due to learning and economies of scale. Technology can lead to improvements in operational efficiency.

However, Aaker (1998) points out that multiple products dilute the effect, experience curves are not universally applicable, technology may make the curve redundant and low costs do not always lead to low prices. The preoccupation with scale, where size is seen to be the key to success, is due to the ability to bargain with suppliers and the advantages of being leader. However, gaining share requires investment and market conditions such as maturity affect the ability to grow share, which means sales will need to be taken from competitors and that could prove to be too costly.

## PIMS

A series of studies into the Profit Impact of Market Share (PIMS) have shown a positive relationship between share and Return on Investment (ROI). For example, where organisations gained market share of 40%, ROI was 30%, three times more than organisations with 10% share. However, PIMS does have drawbacks: it is not always easy to define the boundaries and scope of the market in which the organisation is competing and niche strategies have been successful. The key is to relate the PIMS findings to external environmental conditions such as maturity and competitor reactions.

## SWOT analysis

The gap between current and future helps to determine the future direction for building competitive position. Used to summarise the analysis, a SWOT analysis can be valuable in illustrating how the internal strengths can be used to exploit specific opportunities and handle threats in the environment as part of strategy. If used superficially and in isolation, the results this tool yields can be subjective and trite.

## Summary

These techniques are all part of the Manager's toolbox. It is a question of appreciating their relative merits and role in helping to build competitive advantage.

---

**Activity 4.1**

Evaluate the usefulness of the value chain in analysing an organisation's capabilities.

---

## The innovation audit

Another important part of the internal analysis is the innovation audit. Innovation is a key business activity and is seen to be the future of the organisation. Innovation needs to be thought of in broad terms. Innovation is not just the latest gadget but also the way in which business is undertaken. Innovation in the process is just as important as innovation in the output – the product.

The innovation audit examines the organisation's processes, assets and competencies to assess the strength of its ethos of innovation and to identify areas for improvement. The audit examines:

1.  Current approaches to innovation. This will cover the current support and climate for innovation and creativity, e.g. teamwork, resources, challenge, freedom, supervision, creativity infrastructure, recognition and co-operation. It will highlight the culture and support for innovation, and the ideas of openness to new ideas. The ability to work as a team to develop new products more quickly than in the parallel approach is seen as important in delivering improved time to market. It should also recognise that ideas and their development into products serve to motivate staff to solve problems by innovation.

    Restraining factors will include time, unwillingness to change, internal politics and pressure to be successful each time. This offers a firm structure for evaluation but for Morgan (1993) more understanding could be gained from using metaphors – where the organisation is described, for example, as 'sprinting through treacle – we don't seem to go far' or being 'like a Ferrari – fast and furious'.

2.  Quantitative measures of innovation performance. Here Davidson's framework of analysing number of innovations, success rate, sales from innovations, payback period, and customer satisfaction with the way in which business is conducted.

    Organisations can be classified according to the extent and rate at which they innovate.

    ■ Pioneering organisations launch the latest idea, such as Sony, 3M etc.

    ■ Migrators improve more than competitors.

    ■ Settlers offer the industry standard.

    Criteria for assessing which category an organisation falls into are: resources, attitude to risk and return, and the expertise and skills to innovate.

3.  Policies to support innovation. This might include resources being made available, cash rewards to staff for innovation and the ability to support.

4. The cognitive styles of management. This examines the preferred style of the management team. The four styles are: intuition, feeling, thinking and sensation (Hurst et al, 1989). It is thought that 'intuitors' and some 'feelers' offer the most forward-looking approach while others may place a premium on preserving the past. Balance is key: if the future is the only focus then current business may be adversely affected. Innovation is inherently risky and the ability to see the organisation as a whole is important to ensuring its present and future success.

---

**Activity 4.2**

Conduct an innovation audit for an organisation of your choice. What are your findings and recommendations?

---

## Portfolio models

The previous Session introduced the concept of the firm as a portfolio of assets and capabilities, each with its own resource demands and yield. We now explore some of the portfolio models in existence. They are used to identify and analyse the current position of the organisation, highlighting the current resources, capabilities and performance. We will also see how they can be used at the planning stage to screen options and select the most appropriate course of action.

## The BCG matrix

The Boston Consulting Group (BCG) matrix focuses on growth of the market and relative market share of the organisation. It can be used for either individual products or business units. The assertion on which it is based is that larger market share will be more efficient in terms of usage of the brand and because of economies of scale. If the market is growing rapidly this suggests that the organisation will need to invest to maintain its relative position.

The value of the BCG matrix is to examine the use of cash and its generation in the business. The model divides into four sections and the classifications are known as Rising Stars, Question Marks, Cash Cows and Dogs. There is a relationship between the BCG matrix and the product life cycle and, importantly, the quadrants indicate whether the product or business is generating or absorbing cash.

- Question marks are at the introductory stage, with high market growth and low market share. They are absorbing cash to fund development and marketing.

- The Stars are the future of the organisation with high market share and high market growth. They are at the stage of growth and early maturity, are balanced but are still absorbing cash to sustain and develop market share.

- Cash cows are at the maturity stage. By now, they have high market share but market growth is slowing. The firm can afford to reduce marketing expenditure so cash cows generate cash.

- Dogs are at the decline stage of the life cycle, having both a low share and low growth in the market. However, they are capable of generating cash in the short term.

The matrix highlights the need for succession planning and the issue of over-dependence on the current cash cows. In practice, there are many different patterns as products enter the market and fail, or their host organisations reinvest in them to prevent them becoming dogs. Some products, such as successful chocolate bars, have a long life in the star and cash cow stages.

While it is simple to use and communicate through, the BCG matrix has some significant drawbacks. For example:

- Its reliance on just two dimensions, market growth and relative market share, is overly simplistic.

- Definition of the market and hence the ability accurately to measure growth and share are not always possible. It is essential that the market can be measured to offer the ability to plot the relative position.

- It ignores factors such as competition and developing sustainable competitive advantage.

- Markets may grow slowly and still be attractive; indeed if a market is growing very quickly the cost of growing to keep pace with the market may not be cost-effective.

- It treats cash flow as the sole criterion for investment decisions. In practice, a range of other factors, such as ROI, market size, competitive position, costs etc. is used.

## GE multi-factor matrix

The disadvantages of the BCG growth-share matrix can be overcome to an extent by the family of multi-factor matrices. The GE matrix is one of a number of 3x3 matrices that are similar. It was developed by McKinsey for the General Electric Company. Products or businesses are plotted against two dimensions: business strengths and the attractiveness of the industry. The matrix is represented diagrammatically to show size and share that each product/business has of the market.

The GE matrix uses Return on Investment (ROI) as the criterion for assessing an investment opportunity. Investment opportunities are grouped in three categories graduated diagonally across the matrix from 'Invest for growth', through 'Manage selectively for earnings' to 'Harvest/withdraw'.

The matrix is extremely versatile since the user can define various criteria for each dimension, allowing the matrix to be used to good effect in a variety of contexts. Industry attractiveness may be based on factors such as: market growth, profitability and the nature of competition. Business strengths might include market share, partnerships, relationships and differentiated products. The process is to weigh the factors to show their relative importance. Again this can be completed for individual products or for business units.

Importantly, numerical values can be used to score and give appropriate weightings to each factor. Although subjective, this does provide a more robust form of assessing and comparing the elements of the portfolio. Hooley et al illustrate how the factors can be scored and weighted (see Table 3 in the Study Guide for the reference).

The GE matrix therefore offers a number of advantages over the BCG growth-share matrix.

## Shell directional policy matrix

The Shell Directional Policy matrix, developed by Shell in the 1970s, is similar in appearance and use to the GE matrix. Its two dimensions are prospects for sector profitability (in place of industry attractiveness) and the enterprise's competitive capabilities (in place of business strengths).

Investment opportunities, assessed like the GE matrix on ROI, are defined for each of the nine positions available on the matrix.

## Abell & Hammond investment opportunity matrix

The Abell & Hammond investment opportunity matrix again is similar to the GE matrix. Its two dimensions are market attractiveness (in place of industry attractiveness) and competitive position (in place of business strengths).

Investment opportunities are, like the GE matrix, grouped in three categories graduated diagonally across the matrix from 'High overall attractiveness', through 'Medium overall attractiveness' to 'Low overall attractiveness'.

## AD Little strategic condition matrix

The AD Little strategic condition matrix is a 5x4 matrix based on two dimensions of 4 stages of industry maturity and 5 types of competitive position. The twenty possible positions in the matrix have indicators of suitable strategies. These are based on a number of guiding principles, key amongst which is that strategy selection should be driven by the condition of the business.

## Summary of portfolio analysis models

Portfolio models have a useful contribution to make to marketing planning process but this must be viewed in perspective. Their relative value and disadvantages also need to be considered when using the concepts to appreciate the limitations. It is essential in the examination to show your awareness of their value and not simply to describe their features.

Portfolio models have to be used with caution:

- They are not as well known or widely used in marketing as they might be. This may be because they are time-consuming, even cumbersome, to use or that companies do not allocate significant resources to analysis.

- Even the more complex matrices are simplistic and easy to misuse. Successful use of them depends on identifying the range of factors relevant to the firm's specific markets, in itself no easy task.

- The overall tendency for portfolio models, to focus on scale as being the key to success, is debatable.

- There is an argument that the factors used to assess the current position of the portfolio do not necessarily reflect the future condition of the business and market.

Overall, the contribution of the portfolio models is to examine the current situation facing the organisation and analyse the relationship between the organisation's capabilities and the attractiveness of the marketplace. In this, they integrate the analysis of the internal and external audit. Like all tools, they have their strong and weak points but, in general, they assist us to develop a substantial understanding of the organisation's capabilities and so provide a foundation for developing strategy.

---

**Activity 4.3**

Compare and contrast the effectiveness of the BCG matrix and the Shell Directional Policy matrix in portfolio analysis to a chemical company organised into several operational divisions.

---

## Signposting strategic direction

Portfolio models also have a value in highlighting future strategic direction. It suggests that the models have a broader utility than purely that of analysis. They offer continuity within the planning process.

BCG highlights future direction in the management of products or business units in each stage.

- Stars – developing share to establish market leadership.

- Cash cows – holding strategic position to maintain share.

- Dogs – harvesting it if it generates cash; removing it from the portfolio if it does not. This is managing products in decline as many marketers face this challenge on a daily basis.

It can help in resolving options, such as taking the product into new markets perhaps geographically, managing its effect on other products in terms of component replacement.

The PLC, independently of BCG, can be used to show how the marketing tools can be manipulated throughout the life cycle. For example, extending the maturity stage by using short-term tactics of sales promotions such as special offers to generate more cash.

The GE matrix, and the other multi-factor matrices, can be used to illustrate future options. The visual presentation of the matrix will clearly show both current position and the options for development.

- Where the closest match exists between the organisation and its environment, the concept is to hold that position.

- The organisation can improve its own strengths, which in GE means moving across the axis from right to left. Making the environment more attractive is another matter, but can be achieved for example by reducing the pressure from competitors by working together and sharing expertise.

- In the middle ground, decisions on managing selectively to offer the greatest impact will need to be taken.

- For products in the weak, unattractive bottom right triangle the option is to harvest or withdraw from the market.

Each of these options requires a careful evaluation using set criteria and examining each option against those same criteria for consistency and objectivity. We will be looking at this again when we come on to targeting and evaluating strategic options.

The overall value of using the models is to provide the opportunity to analyse, reflect and think strategically about the organisation in a holistic way. This will enable the organisation to plan over the long term to close the gap between current and future performance.

All these models are provided in the models table at the beginning of this Companion.

# Case Study – Marks & Spencer

Over the last three decades Marks & Spencer (M&S) has been seen as the leading clothing retailer in the UK, operating around 300 stores. The quality and range of its functional and fashionable clothes combined with good customer service had proved to be unbeatable in the past. The retailer's position was so strong in the UK market that it could even refuse to take payments by credit cards from customers. The company also did not see the need to undertake any advertising.

## Marks & Spencer's recent performance

M&S's fortunes however, have recently been in decline. This started initially with a poor year in the South East Asian market, which by itself should not have been too damaging. However, in the last few years there has been increasing competition in UK clothing from more aggressive middle market High Street retailers such as Next and Gap, as well as revitalised department stores such as Debenhams and discount outlets such as Matalan. The result has been a sharp decline in annual profitability for M&S since 1998 with a consequent fall in the company's share price, dropping 70% from its peak in 1997 (see Table 1). In fact the share price fell as low as £1.70 at one point in the year 2000, sending M&S's market capitalisation to under £5 billion from its 1998 value of £17 billion.

| Year | Profit (£m) | Share Price £ (High) |
|------|-------------|----------------------|
| 1996 | 996 | 5.31 |
| 1997 | 1,102 | 6.65 |
| 1998 | 1,115 | 6.20 |
| 1999 | 546 | 4.61 |
| 2000 | 418 | 3.32 |

**Table 1: Marks & Spencer's profits and share price 1996-2000**

## Competition

Gap – this middle market company has taken market share by creating a high profile lifestyle brand, based on attitude and meaning.

Next – in May 2000, another middle market competitor, Next, demonstrated its increasing ability to attract consumers by reporting a 19% increase in sales. Next bases its business on giving 25-45 year old customers fashionable clothing at a reasonable price.

Matalan – is a discount clothing and homeware retailer operating 111 stores, mostly out of town. Garment sales make up 82% of group profits. Matalan forecasts that it can continue to grow at 30% a year compound for the next three years. Matalan's plans include entering the financial services market with its own credit card and personal loans and potentially, insurance products.

Debenhams – has also been attempting to take market share away from mid-market retailers such as Marks & Spencer by focusing on the needs of working women. In the financial year 1999-2000 Debenhams increased its share of the UK lingerie market, previously an M&S staple, from 3.75 to 4.8%.

## Marks & Spencer's responses

M&S has taken a number of measures in the last two years to regain its market position, in particular introducing more fashionable lines of clothing. These, however, have not been an overwhelming success. They were widely seen as alienating the company's traditional customers, mainly ABC1 housewives. At the same time younger, more fashion-oriented customers did not associate fashion with the M&S brand.

M&S has also been undertaking a severe round of cost cutting measures. As part of this process the company has started to shift production of its clothing from the UK to cheaper factories internationally. This has led to large-scale redundancies in the UK clothing industry. The move to international production has also meant that M&S is no longer as able as it was to place late orders for particular items or colours that are proving popular.

October 2000 saw a new management team announce a range of new initiatives. To accompany the women's designer collection, which features clothes designed by Betty Jackson, Julien Macdonald and Katherine Hamnett, M&S then also launched its first ever designer menswear collection in five stores in the UK.

Marks & Spencer Financial Services are to open in around 30 of the company's stores, offering customers confidential consultations on their personal finances. M&S's financial services are also planning to launch a range of new products. Both these moves are likely to lead to greater competition with the traditional banks. The company aims to launch a poster advertising campaign involving placing advertisements in areas near traditional banks stating 'Unhappy with your bank? Come to M&S'.

The company has taken a stake in the Confetti Network, a web site business specialising in products bought for weddings. The aim is that M&S will become the leading retailer in the online retail site developed by Confetti.

M&S has also unveiled plans to open a chain of new lingerie boutiques in continental Europe, starting in Paris, Hamburg and Dusseldorf. The stores will operate under the brand name of 'msl'. Twenty five per cent of the lingerie range will be exclusively designed for the new stores; the rest will come from M&S's current range. There are no plans to open msl boutiques in the UK.

Finally M&S has also launched a £20 million advertising campaign, emphasising quality and wide range of products, under the slogan 'Exclusively for everyone'.

**Source:** SMM Planning & Control Examination Paper, June 2001.

---

**Questions**

1. Using the GE matrix, analyse the current strategic position of Marks & Spencer in the UK clothing market.

2. Discuss the relative merits of other portfolio matrices in assessing the position of Marks & Spencer.

---

# SUMMARY OF KEY POINTS

In this Session, we have introduced portfolio analysis, and covered the following key points:

- There are various models available to assess the nature, effectiveness and efficiency of the organisation's resources and assets as part of the internal analysis.

- Most of these techniques provide qualitative outcomes but financial analysis develops quantitative outcomes that can be used specifically to assess the efficiency and effectiveness of the organisation's resources and assets.

- An innovation audit plays an important role in establishing the effectiveness of the organisation's innovation processes. As such, it is a complement to the marketing activities audit.

- Portfolio models are a valuable part of the internal analysis. The advantages and disadvantages of each make it more or less useful in a variety of situations.

# Improving and developing own learning

The following projects are designed to help you develop your knowledge and skills further by carrying out some research yourself. Feedback is not provided for this type of learning because there are no 'answers' to be found, but you may wish to discuss your findings with colleagues and fellow students.

**Project A**

Talk to colleagues in your Marketing Department about ways in which portfolio models are used in your organisation.

Identify any changes that have been made as a direct result of such analysis.

**Project B**

Use the BCG matrix and any one of the 3x3 matrices (GE, Shell, etc.) to analyse your product portfolio.

How are the results different?

Which gives the best results?

What lessons can be learned from the exercise?

**Project C**

Carry out an innovation audit on your own organisation.

Suggest two improvements as a result of your findings.

# Feedback to activities

### Activity 4.1

This activity is typical of an exam question asking candidates to evaluate a tool. The approach to answering this kind of question can be fairly standard. In this case, your answer might consist of the following elements:

- Introduction briefly describing the value chain, its context in a wider value system, its author and the basic structure (primary activities, secondary activities and margin).

- Organisational capabilities – made up of *assets* (marketing assets are: customer-based, distribution-based, alliance-based and internal) and *competencies* (marketing, selling, operations and finance).

- Application – you should now debate the usefulness of the value chain in identifying areas of unique capabilities. Such an evaluation will usually point out the strengths or benefits (e.g. it does help to identify specific capabilities and linkages on which competitive advantage may be based) and balance these with the drawbacks (e.g. not easy to use, particularly for service organisations).

- Conclusion – you can then make a short concluding statement on how useful you see the value chain as being in analysing an organisation's capabilities. To overcome the drawbacks, you may recommend that it is used in conjunction with other tools.

### Activity 4.2

The purpose of an innovation audit is to identify the level of innovation needed in an organisation and to show how effectively it is meeting this need. In conducting an innovation audit in an organisation, you should have examined:

- The organisational climate and its attitudes towards innovation.

- Policies and practices that support innovation in the organisation.

- Measures of performance in innovation, such as the percentage of turnover generated by new products and the number of new products launched.

- The 'styles' of the management team and their attitudes towards innovation.

**Activity 4.3**

This is another typical exam question on the use of tools, in this case for analysis. You comparison should have covered:

- The basic structure and axes (market growth and relative market share) of the BCG matrix.

- Weaknesses of the BCG matrix.

- The basic structure, axes (prospects for sector profitability and competitive capabilities) and criteria of the Shell matrix.

- The strengths of the Shell matrix: takes a wider view of 'sector profitability' rather than just cash flow; it can be tailored by the criteria used to the circumstances of the organisation; it can be used to stimulate constructive debate between Managers.

You can see a full specimen answer to this question (Question 4 from the Planning and Control paper, December 2000) on the CIM student web site.

# Session 5

# Financial and ratio analysis

## Introduction

Session 4 looked at the tools and techniques available during the internal analysis and their contribution to the planning process. One of these tools, financial analysis, plays an essential role in assessing the effectiveness and efficiency of the organisation's portfolio using quantitative techniques. This tool is also used as part of the external analysis, which we will be covering in the next two Sessions. This Session looks at a range of quantitative analyses using financial and management accounting information and how they can contribute to marketing analysis. We also consider the shortcomings of using financial measurements in isolation.

## LEARNING OUTCOMES

At the end of this Session you will be able to:

- Explain the purpose and contribution of financial and ratio analysis to the marketing analysis process.

- Explain the limitations on the validity of ratio analysis and the constraints they may impose on the use of ratios in certain circumstances.

- Identify and apply a range of ratios and analyses that would contribute to a marketing analysis.

- Demonstrate an awareness of both the shortcomings of a purely financial measurement of a firm's value and performance and of current approaches based on a wider range of 'metrics'.

## What do you have to know?

It is worth noting at the outset that the inclusion of financial and ratio analysis in the syllabus is intended to develop your knowledge and understanding of the full range of tools and techniques available for strategic marketing management. The emphasis is on what tools are available, what they are used for and the kinds of conclusions they are likely to help you to reach. You are unlikely to have to calculate more than a few basic ratios, if at all, in the exam.

So, try not to be blinded by the figures and concentrate on what the tools do, rather than how to use them. If we were looking at the tools available to a carpenter, the aim of this part of the syllabus is for you to understand the tools available and what sort of result each can produce. It is not the aim that you should become a master carpenter.

## Using financial and ratio analysis

Financial ratios are used most effectively during the analysis stage as part of a comparison. For example, if you calculate that a firm has earned 14% return on investment for a period, you will know whether this is 'good' or 'bad' only by comparing it with the firm's performance in another period or with another firm for the same period. So, ratios tend to be used most effectively for:

- Comparing a firm's performance over time, or from period to period. This is done to identify trends.

- Comparing the performance of an organisation with that for the same period of one or more competitors who are operating the same type of business. Here, we are benchmarking the organisation against others in the industry. The comparison may also be done over time.

It is important that all available information is used, not just the financial information in isolation.

Financial ratios are used by Managers throughout the marketing planning process to evaluate the efficiency and effectiveness of the organisation's performance, its use of resources and productivity in relationship to its peers.

Let's consider the contribution and value of financial evaluation at each stage of the marketing planning process.

- **Analysis** – ratios are used to assess the current and recent past performance. They are used as part of the internal analysis to assess the organisation's performance and as part of the external analysis to assess the relative competitive position of the organisation. We can use profitability ratios to assess relative performance over time within the portfolio. We can also examine trends and the differences in performance between the organisations that have faced similar market conditions. Productivity or utilisation ratios can show how well the organisation and its competitors are using vital assets such as employees, production or retail space, customers or their products and services. Investment performance and assessment of opportunities will be of interest to external investors such as shareholders.

- **Objectives** – setting realistic objectives requires the development of quantitative measures based on an understanding of the current position. Objectives specifying growth and improved performance are usually based on quantitative or hard financial measures. This requires estimates of resources, the ability to improve or maintain performance and sets up the control and evaluation loop.

- **Strategy formulation** – the financial impact and resource implications of the various strategic options have to be assessed as part of the selection of the most appropriate option. This will examine the amount of investment required, cost benefit, viability and payback. It will assist in determining the strategy but is only one part of the equation, since other issues, for example market position and branding, need to be included to provide a balanced picture. The concept of long-term investment and short-term tactics will need to be planned within the financial restrictions and the opportunity to access additional funds. Cash flow and liquidity over the life of the strategy will need to be carefully managed to ensure that the business does not run short of cash.

- **Control and evaluation** – ratios can be used as measures to control the implementation of the plan and to measure success. This is becoming an increasingly important aspect of strategic marketing. Performance evaluation can be conducted 'bottom up', measuring the tactics to assess their relative success against the objectives. This illustrates the close links between the analysis, objectives and evaluation within the control loop. Evaluation can also take place 'top down', for example monitoring the effect of an integrated campaign and its impact over time on market share. This information is also important within some organisations as it may be used as the basis of rewards for employees in terms of bonuses and the security gained from the success of the organisation. It can also be used to give stakeholders, such as customers and suppliers, a sense of continuity from a successful organisation.

Financial ratios are also used to make investment decisions. One of the roles of strategic marketing is to identify opportunities for developing the capabilities and offerings of the organisation – and these require investment. This requires careful consideration and ideally should not be abrogated to the Finance Department, although their help can be invaluable.

Marketers therefore need to see investment decisions as part of the planning process. For example, increasing sales revenue from entry to a new market or launch of a new product might generally be welcomed. However, the costs of gaining the increased sales need to be examined. If the costs of marketing in terms of sales promotions and price discounting are too high, then the increase in sales will result in lower profits. This would clearly not be acceptable so the investment needs to be reconsidered.

---

**Activity 5.1**

Examine the how financial information is used in an organisation of your choice.

---

## The limitations of ratio analysis

We have seen that you can use financial analysis to examine the performance of an organisation over time or compare the performance of a number of organisations. Typically this information will come from the published accounts of a company consisting of its balance sheet, profit and loss account and cash flow statement. (Note: It is more difficult to obtain financial information about partnerships, sole traders and some foreign companies.) In the case of your own organisation, you may also have access to management accounts. It is important to appreciate the factors that affect the composition and interpretation of this information.

A golden rule of financial analysis is to compare like with like. There are many ways in which accounts differ, because of different accounting policies and circumstances, from period to period, from company to company and from country to country. The notes to published accounts provide valuable information to help in understanding how the accounts have been compiled and what they cover. It is important to take this information into account in comparing and assessing results. They will explain and provide information such as:

- The accounting policies and conventions that have been used. This particularly affects stock values and the depreciation of fixed assets.

- How long the accounts are for – sometimes accounts are for 53 weeks, not the usual 52.

- The scope of the business during the period. For example, it is difficult to compare Tesco directly with Marks & Spencer because their businesses are very different. It may be possible to compare the performance of the food businesses of the two companies if that information is provided.

- Overseas operations and any major foreign currency transactions, for example when a multinational is repatriating profits from an overseas subsidiary.

- Any exceptional financial transactions included in the accounts, such as sale or purchase of a business, restructuring or costs associated with a major new development.

Figures should not be viewed in isolation. For example profits may show a decline in the short term but if there is investment in new products it illustrates that the organisation is planning for the long term. Remember that the balance sheet is a snapshot at a 'point in time' at the end of the period; the profit and loss account is for the whole period, usually one year. The ability to balance short and long term is a challenge especially to ensure that all stakeholders are satisfied.

Remember that revenues last year are not worth the same as revenues this year. This is the effect of inflation. Some adjustment of the figures may be needed to bring figures onto a 'like for like' basis. This is less of a problem when inflation is low and you are comparing adjacent years for say 1 to 3 years. However, when inflation is high or you are considering long term trends, your adjustment will have to express all values in 'real terms' at today's values.

Setting objectives requires an estimate of future sales. We explore methods for forecasting in Session 8 but a common way of estimating future sales is to extrapolate from current sales. This makes the assumption that the future will be the same as the past – an assumption that some companies have found to their cost to be flimsy. It is well worth remembering that the past is no guarantee of the future.

In short, financial analysis can be valuable in evaluating performance but, like any tool, it has to be used with care. In this case, it means conducting the evaluation in context.

### Activity 5.2

Explain the challenges that exist in analysing the performance of your organisation, or one you know well.

## Which ratio should I use?

There are a wide variety of financial ratios that can be used to examine the health of the organisation. Each focuses on a specific aspect and will need to be complemented by a range of other ratios. This is where many candidates become confused. Which ratio shall I use? Now I have calculated it, what is it telling me?

The key to financial analysis, like any other form of analysis, is to decide before you start what you are trying to establish or get out from the analysis. Remember that you are working from a strategic marketing perspective, not from an accountant's perspective. You are interested in the relative competitive performance of the organisation and those elements of the portfolio that marketing has some control over, such as products and the main groups of customers. Although the solvency and liquidity of the organisation are important, it is reasonable to assume that the Finance Department is monitoring these areas and will take the necessary action. However, you should be aware of any constraints there may be on the organisation's ability to fund future marketing activities so that your objectives are realistic.

Below, we highlight some the key ratios. They are divided into broad groups to reflect the different types of information that is required.

## Profitability ratios

Profitability ratios are used to assess the effectiveness of the organisation's use of available resources. They include:

- Gross profit margin.
- Net profit margin.
- Return on Sales (ROS). Note: This may be used for gross margin.
- Profit Before Interest and Tax (PBIT).
- Return on Capital Employed (ROCE). This is a useful overall indicator of business performance, using PBIT. It can be used between sectors.
- Return on Investment (ROI).
- Return on Equity (ROE).

These ratios offer the ability to compare performance over time and also, in comparison, the key competitors.

# Efficiency or utilisation ratios

These are strictly profitability ratios; however, they are identified separately here because they may require management accounting information rather than just information included in published accounts. These ratios equip you to explore the level of efficiency with which an organisation utilises its assets. Commonly used ratios include:

- **Asset utilisation ratio** – examines the efficiency of the organisation's use of fixed and current assets, for example its buildings, systems and stocks. A firm can try to reduce its assets, for example by holding less stock or leasing rather than owning fixed assets, to show that it is being efficient.

- **Profit per unit of asset** – examines the use of key assets such as retail or production space (per square metre), products, channel, segment or key customer accounts. They enable you to examine the main drivers of profitability for the type of business. The key is to identify which are the critical assets for the industry. For example, retail space is critical for supermarkets and passenger kilometres in the airline industry.

- **Contribution** – is calculated by sales – cost of sales – sales and marketing costs. This is arguably one of the most powerful ratios in the armoury of the marketer who is trying to establish where the profitable parts of the business lie. Contribution can also be used as an alternative to profit per unit of asset, since it will tell you about the efficiency of the marketing mix which is controllable.

- **Value added ratios** – measure the amount of value added to inputs during the firm's transformation process. They are often expressed per unit of input (per employee, per £ of pay, per square metre, per £ of materials, etc.). They are used to compare the efficiency performance of different portfolio elements or investment opportunities.

# Investment ratios

Investors and financial stakeholders use investment ratios to examine the performance of their existing investments and assess investment opportunities. Companies have to monitor these ratios to ensure that they have a steady supply of investment for capital. The ratios include:

- **Earnings per Share (EPS)** – shown in the accounts as the allocation of profit before exceptional items to each share issued.

- **Dividend** – what the company actually pays out per share to investors and, depending on the company's dividend policy, not necessarily the same as EPS.

- **Share price** – the price quoted on a stock exchange for a share at a specific point in time.

- **Price to Earnings Ratio (P/E)** – the ratio of share price to EPS, one of the main ratios that investors use to assess the performance of a share on the stock market.

## Liquidity ratios

Liquidity ratios measure the capacity of a company to pay its short-term debts. As mentioned above, the marketer will not usually have to be concerned with liquidity, except in so far as it acts as a constraint on future investment.

- **Stock turnover** – the number of times stock is turned over in a year. The alternative to this is the stock holding period, the average length of time a stock item is held.

- **Debtor/creditor payment period** – the length of time it takes to pay or be paid. Credit control is tasked with ensuring that balance is achieved between paying and being paid.

- **Current ratio** – current assets/current liabilities. This is used to examine whether the organisation can meet its current liabilities without having to raise finance. It is expressed as 2:1 – this means the organisation can cover its liabilities (1) with the first figure showing the amount of cover in this example, twice or even three times. If the ratio is lower than 1:1, the organisation is technically insolvent.

- **Quick ratio or acid test** – a more stringent test looking at the ability of the organisation to meet its liabilities immediately from its liquid or current assets.

- **Net working capital per £ of sales** – for a marketer involved in product development and launch, it is helpful to know how much working capital (stock + trade debtors - trade creditors) is required for each £ of new business brought in. While a new product may increase sales revenues and profits, it may be thirsty for cash that may be in short supply.

## Solvency ratios

Finally, solvency ratios measure the ability of the organisation to meet its long-term financial commitments such as long-term loans and corporate bonds. They are used to assess the risk of investments to long-term cash flows.

Like the liquidity ratios, they are not the prime concern of the marketer who needs only to recognise any constraint they may impose on investment. The ability of an organisation to manage debt can be a key challenge, especially where the market is expanding rapidly and funding is required with no immediate return to pay back the investment. This is currently a major issue in the telecommunications industry, which requires support from the financial stakeholders.

The two main solvency ratios are:

- **Gearing** – highlights the ratio of debt (borrowings) to equity (investment) and hence the requirement of the organisation to pay interest.

- **Times interest covered** – measures the ability of the organisation to meet its interest commitments.

---

**Activity 5.3**

Now let's put this into practice. Use appropriate ratios from the above to assess the efficiency and financial health of an organisation of your choice.

---

## Analysing from financial, marketing and employee perspectives

Evaluating the performance of any organisation is essential. It has two purposes:

- To examine past performance.

- To allocate resources for future activities.

It can be seen as the last stage of the marketing plan but also the first stage of the next plan. Indeed the planning and control cycle should be a continuous process with evaluation feeding into the audit.

Financial performance is the result of a combination of factors. One of these is successful marketing – the ability to understand and meet the needs of the customer in a competitive environment is a key challenge. The organisation needs to evaluate its performance from its customers' perspective and from that of the employees who deliver customer service. The evaluation from financial, customer and the employee perspectives provides the basis of holistic performance evaluation of the organisation.

## The customer perspective

One of the key roles of marketing is to satisfy the customer. As such the evaluation of the customer experience needs to be examined. This should begin with an examination of the total process, from understanding and analysing buying motives, through understanding changing needs for new products, to evaluating the impact of a new communications campaign.

The examination could include the impact of the current marketing strategy. This will establish whether the customer and the organisation view the plan and process in the same way. For example, if the organisation claims superior customer service but customers do not recognise it or believe that a competitor has better customer service, then the issue needs to be addressed.

The aim then is to set standards for current and future performance to examine the impact on profitability. This can be achieved by pre- and post- testing using marketing research, by quantitative analysis of, for example, customer complaints and return products.

## Employee perspective

Recruitment, selection and turnover of staff are key issues in developing the organisation's capabilities to implement the overall strategy. The ability of the organisation to engage employees in continuous improvement, to attract and retain employees, so maintaining a low staff turnover, and to increase motivation, is key.

## Taking a broader perspective

One of the main criticisms of financial analysis and reporting is that it gives a narrow, incomplete and short-term view of the organisation. Given that one of the main functions of the annual report and accounts is to give shareholders and prospective shareholders information about the company, the document contains little of substance about the future prospects of the company. It gives us little on, say, the value of products in the development pipeline, or brands.

The balanced scorecard (Kaplan and Norton, 1992) was developed to redress these shortcomings by encouraging Managers to consider the wider strategic drivers of value. The addition of customer, internal and innovation perspectives to the traditional financial perspective provides a wider framework for matching the analysis of the current situation into a logical structure from which to develop a strategy. It also helps by taking each strategic objective and relating it to a specific strategic measure. The balanced scorecard is a valuable addition to the marketer's armoury of tools for evaluating the performance of the organisation.

# Case Study – Marketing drives the bottom line

Marketers have long had a poor image for numbers: yes they have a passion for customers, a zest for creativity, a focus on delivery… but an aversion to finance. No wonder marketers struggle to find a voice in the boardroom, that budgets are under threat when the case to retain or grow them is weakly made, and that effectiveness and accountability are regularly identified as the key issues for marketers today.

At the same time, Marketing Directors are increasingly concerned at the amount of time spent on data analysis, and the value it creates. The mountains of customer data provided by one to one relationship programmes, the precision of sophisticated research and database capabilities, and the numerous metrics introduced to improve marketing effectiveness, have introduced a level of science to marketing, but also created a fear of "analysis paralysis".

One Marketing Director recently described her frustrations in seeking to recruit good marketers. "There are a lot of well disciplined, analytically strong marketers out there. But I really struggle to find ones who also have a creative edge these days". London Business School's Tim Ambler also expresses concern that the focus on numbers is in danger of killing marketing's passion and creativity. He even argues "marketers do not need to understand and use finance-speak, but only as an addition to their more important value-generating skills."

The answer is to use finance wisely. Marketers must think harder about which are the right numbers to use, and how they can be used to open up new marketing opportunities, to strengthen the case for investment and support, to demonstrate the impact on the business short- and long-term, and to remind the CEO that marketing is actually the best thing he or she could do. Indeed, PA's new research shows that marketing is the biggest driver of value creation in a business, yet few companies and their marketers have made the connections to make the most of it.

Market leaders such as Nike and Orange are examples of outstanding shareholder value creation, in large part due to excellent marketing. In the case of Nike, CEO Phil Knight has driven a culture of constant market and product innovation, with a keen focus on the bottom line, showing that even long-haired revolutionaries can embrace financial discipline. Similarly mobile phone brand Orange has created a bright future for its shareholders, and is estimated to have delivered around £27 billion to its various owners, as measured by its cumulative acquisition values.

## First, find the bottom line

The bottom line for marketers is the same as in every other part of the business. It is the commercial and legal requirement of the company to deliver a return to shareholders. Marketing's focus tends to be closer to the top line – the revenue and sales contribution – which is seen as more relevant to their actions, yet can often conceal a whole set of factors which determine the real performance of the business, and can therefore blinker marketers from making the right decisions.

"Shareholder value" is a much-quoted and often-challenged phrase. It inevitably invites questions about other stakeholders, whether a focus on shareholders detracts from a customer orientation, and whether it encourages a short-term focus rather than longer-term investment. These are actually red herrings, and shouldn't distract us from pursuing the benefits of a value-based approach.

So what does shareholder value actually mean?

- Shareholder value is measured by the total return to investors over time.

- We call this the Total Shareholder Return (TSR).

- It incorporates the long-term growth in the value of shares, and dividends that investors might receive along the way.

- Internally it is best reflected by "Economic Profit" (EP) which is sometimes known as economic value added.

- EP measures the future cash that is likely to flow to the business based on its existing and future products and services.

## And what's so different about that?

- Shareholder value is a long-term measure, not to be confused with short-term rise and falls in share price.

- It is therefore a lead indicator, creating a better view of the future, enabling better decision making at both strategic and operational levels.

- EP differs from operating profit, in that it subtracts a charge ("the cost of equity") for the return shareholders would expect on their investment.

- EP therefore focuses each area of the business – including every product and activity – on exceeding the expected returns of shareholders.

Marketers who measure results by volumes, market shares, revenues, sales contributions, and even operating profits are not necessarily focused on the bottom line. Whilst these are worthy metrics, and all have the potential to support better marketing, there is no guarantee that they actually do contribute to the bottom line or that they actually do create additional value for shareholders.

Typically a product may look operationally profitable; however, when one takes into account the amount of capital involved, it is actually economically unprofitable (because the high cost of equity eats up the operating margin). Trying to sell more of such a product would be the worst thing you could do.

An example of this thinking in action is at Diageo, where virtually all marketing effort is on the eight brands which generate the vast majority of economic profit. Diageo realise that most of the other brands are actually destroying value, and therefore have their support restricted unless they can be re-engineered to create value.

## Second, make the connections

The real test, and the real trick, is to make the hard connections between these economic measures that drive the bottom line financially, and the practical marketing activities that are driven by the decisions and performance of marketing people. For example, a real understanding of what drives the best TSR has helped marketers at Coca-Cola know whether brand building, driving sales volume or tactical pricing has the biggest impact on their business performance. This knowledge influences the reward structures of marketers, and the decisions they make.

Indeed, whilst marketing objectives such as improving customer retention sound like worthy goals, they may not be the most important drivers of the bottom line in your business. The value drivers of each company will differ, partly influenced by the amount of capital employed in the business, and the dynamics of the market, although they will probably be similar across a sector.

The simplest way for marketers to think about what creates shareholder value is perhaps to focus on the concept of future cash, and imagine a pipe of cash stretching from today into the future. The marketer's challenge is to make this cash pipe as long, as fat, and as fast-flowing as possible. The bigger the size of the future cash pipe, the more shareholder value. Consider:

- How can you make the cash pipe fatter? Marketing should focus on competitive differentiation and improving pricing, improved communication effectiveness and cost of sale, and on driving sales of value-creating products.

- How can you make the cash pipe longer? Marketing should drive market and product innovation, developing positions in emerging markets, strengthening customer relationships and brands, and thereby reducing risk and future volatility.

- How can you make the cash flow faster? Marketing should accelerate new products to market, focusing on the time to penetrate markets rather than just to reach them, activating relationships and cross-selling, locking into existing market networks rather than seeking to create their own.

This is a simple model, but starts to demonstrate why the CEO must use marketing rather than anything to drive shareholder value. Process efficiency will never create a fatter, longer, faster pipe. In reality these connections must be defined through more rigorous "value driver analysis", maps which connect marketing decisions to marketing outcomes, marketing outcomes to financial impacts, and financial impacts to shareholder value.

The benefits can be huge, and quick. Microsoft found that such connections across their sales and marketing activity delivered over $1 billion benefit in the first year.

## Third, drive the bottom line

John Sunderland, CEO of Cadbury Schweppes, knew what he was talking about when he took up his position in 1997 and announced "Within four years I will double the value of this business… economic profit will be our key measure of success, and building strong brands will be at the heart of achieving this."

So if your CEO sets out an ambition like this, as a marketer what should you do differently?

1. Where and how to compete… a value-based market strategy will look very different from a conventional one, identifying which existing and emerging areas of the market offer the best long-term return on equity. Dixons, for

example, realise almost two-thirds of their group's value from emerging business areas which currently generate less than 10% of revenue.

2.  What to focus your effort on... a value-based portfolio analysis will identify which products are the value-creators, and which are the value-destroyers, and therefore where to focus effort. Taking into account the cost of equity creates a very different picture than a typical Boston Grid. A similar analysis will identify the best customers.

3.  How to capture the value you create... a value-based proposition rightly focuses on creating value for customers, addressing customers' real needs and outperforming the competition. It is equally about finding ways to capture as much of this value as possible for shareholders, by maximising the perceived value, and optimising pricing whilst still offering "value for money".

How to get a better return on spend... a value-based marketing programme identifies the marketing actions that will generate best returns, this year and longer term. It identifies which levers to pull (e.g. advertising, sales promotion, product development, relationship building) and how to most effectively leverage your marketing assets (such as brands, customer knowledge and distribution networks).

Value-based marketing is often dismissed as sophisticated analysis, or complex performance metrics. It is much more. It is fundamentally about decision making – choice of markets and positionings, choice of products and customers, choice of offering and price, choice of activities and investment.

Most conventional data analysis is driven by the need to create a broad range of proxy measures because there appears to be no best measure; or marketers are so unsure about their criteria for decision making that they take comfort from thick reports. So does a value-based approach to marketing create more analysis and inhibit creativity? Quite the opposite.

## Great news for marketers

The great thing about value-based marketing is that it focuses on the numbers that really matter, and the right basis for effective decision making. Invest once in the process to generate the right data, then you have less data, quicker to generate, with a much clearer focus... and therefore much clearer scope to focus innovation, and much more time to creatively do it. And the CEO will like it too. What board will argue with a new marketing proposal that creates significantly more value for shareholders?

At Cadbury-Schweppes, four years later, John Sunderland's value-based marketing approach focused on creating exceptional value for customers by investing in leading brands, and on market and product innovation. With stretching performance targets, clear marketing priorities, and billion-dollar acquisitions such as Snapple, he achieved his targets thanks to great marketing.

This is a message for every CEO as well as every marketer. PA's new research demonstrates how value-based marketing really can create much more shareholder value – on average 5 times more – than anything else a business can do.

This is great news for the marketer (ready to command a much stronger voice in the boardroom, and gain support for new initiatives and bigger budgets), great news for the customer (who will benefit from the increased investment in existing and new products and service), and great news for shareholders (who are likely to get a better return on their investments).

PA's checklist for getting to grips with value-based marketing:

1. Value base: Is your business likely to meet or exceed the expectations of investors? Are you delivering a positive economic profit? Does the sum of future cash flows match your market capitalisation?

2. Value drivers: Which marketing results will most effectively drive value creation in your business? How do sales revenue, brand awareness, or customer retention drive performance?

3. Value sources: Where are the best sources of future cash in your markets? Are there any emerging rich niches to tap into? E.g. in the automotive market, financing and after-sales support offer the best returns.

4. Value assets: how can you most effectively leverage your marketing assets, such as brands and relationships, market networks and knowledge? Focus less on how valuable brands are, and more on the value it can drive.

5. Value creators: Which are the products and customers in your portfolio through which you can generate the best return on equity? Refocus your investment on these, and re-engineer those that are unprofitable.

6. Value propositions: How can you create more value for customers, and stronger differentiation from competitors? Focus on your distinctive benefits and quantify the value customers can derive from them.

7. Value levers: Which marketing actions should you spend your budget on for best short- and long-term return? Advertising to build brands, or sales promotion to drive sales? Relationship building or product development?

8. Value capture: How will you maximise the capturable value from your propositions? How can you improve the perceived value of an offer, and thereby increase the price whilst still offering value for money?

9. Value metrics: What are the measures by which you can tell whether your marketing is creating value? Which are the most important to achieve? How are they linked to marketing performance and rewards?

10. Value creation: How can you most effectively embed a value-thinking, value-creating mindset in your marketers? What difference does it make to your marketing, and how can you most useful introduce the disciplines?

**Source:** *What's new in marketing* e-newsletter.

---

## Questions

1. The author recommends that marketers should use finance wisely. How might they achieve this?

2. Write short notes, which you can use later to revise, on the ratios measures listed below. Explain why they are relevant to marketing.

 - Shareholder value.

 - Economic Profit (EP).

 - Economic Value Added (EVA).

 - Total Shareholder Return (TSR).

## SUMMARY OF KEY POINTS

In this Session, we have introduced the role of financial analysis, and covered the following key points:

- Financial ratios play a useful part in the marketing planning process, both for analysis and decision making they should not be used in isolation.

- Cost analysis and financial ratios can be combined with marketing analysis to obtain a full picture of where the organisation is now and where it might go in the future.

- Financial ratios can be used to assess profitability, efficiency, investment performance, liquidity and solvency.

- Comparing performance of your own organisation and that of competitors can help inform the decision making process.

- Remember that you must always compare like with like to draw valid conclusions.

## Improving and developing own learning

The following projects are designed to help you develop your knowledge and skills further by carrying out some research yourself. Feedback is not provided for this type of learning because there are no 'answers' to be found, but you may wish to discuss your findings with colleagues and fellow students.

### Project A

Talk to colleagues in your Marketing Department about how financial analysis is used to feed into your marketing information system and decision making.

### Project B

Carry out an analysis from a marketing perspective of the financial performance over the past three years of your own organisation or one you know well. (Financial reports and accounts can be obtained from the Internet).

What does your analysis tell you about the company?

**Project C**

Look at the annual reports you used in Project B and identify any non-financial information that would be useful if these were the accounts of a competitor.

# Feedback to activities

### Activity 5.1

Organisations typically use financial information to support decision making and activities in four areas:

- Analysis.
- Objective and target setting.
- Strategy formulation and planning.
- Monitoring and control.

You may have found evidence in the organisation of your choice of the use of financial information in some or all of these areas. If you could find little or no evidence for some areas, was that because it is not used? Or is the information not used explicitly? What does the level of use of financial information tell you about the organisation?

### Activity 5.2

The challenges facing someone wishing to analyse the financial performance of the organisation in which they work include:

- Gaining access to the relevant information. This kind of information is usually freely available.
- The information required may not be available as the basic data has not been analysed and computed to give the performance measures required. For example, what percentage of sales comes from customers who buy only once from the business?
- The data required may not have been collected. For example, the average number of sales visits to clients before they place their first order.

These problems are even more difficult for someone wishing to analyse the performance of another organisation.

## Activity 5.3

Assuming you have been able to obtain the relevant information about the organisation, you should have used examples of the following types of ratios:

- Profitability ratios.

- Efficiency or utilisation ratios.

- Investment ratios.

- Liquidity ratios.

- Solvency ratios.

As marketers, we are interested mainly in the first three groups of ratios, although you should be aware of what liquidity and solvency ratios tell us and how they are calculated.

# Session 6

# The external environment

## Introduction

Having examined the internal environment, we turn in this Session to look at the organisation's external environment and why an understanding of it is important. We examine techniques and models that can be used to analyse the external macro environment and to monitor changes within it. It also considers part of the microenvironment, customer behaviour. The final part of the microenvironment, the competitive environment, is covered in Session 7.

---

**LEARNING OUTCOMES**

At the end of this Session you will be able to:

- Explain why a regular and detailed analysis of the organisation's environment and markets is important.

- Explain how environments are changing.

- Identify the key elements of a firm's environment.

- Apply appropriate techniques for analysing a firm's environment, markets and customers.

- Identify likely customer behaviours using appropriate models and concepts.

---

## The external environment

The audit of the external environment forms the second main part of analysis during the marketing planning process. It helps in understanding the opportunities and threats facing the organisation and its overall competitive situation. As such, it sets the scene for the direction and strategy decided in later stages.

The external environment presents organisations with both opportunities and threats. These originate from a variety of sources such as the changing needs of customers, competitors and government policy. Each of the key sources will be explored later. The external environment is often divided into two main parts:

- The macro environment – the wider environment that affects the organisation by providing opportunities to exploit and threats to, or constraints on, the organisation's activities. We look at this further in this Session.

- The microenvironment – the stakeholders with whom the organisation is in contact: customers, competitors and channels to market. In some industries where it is strategically important, this may also include the supply chain. We look at customers in this Session and competitors in the next Session.

It is essential for the organisation to be able to detect and respond quickly to any changes in its environment. This is the function of environmental scanning, which we consider in more detail later in this Session. Changes in the environment can be:

- Continuous – whether fast or slow. These are often detected as 'trends'.

- Discontinuous – one-off events, often major, such as an environmental 'shock'.

Let's briefly consider the current environment within which the airlines in Europe are operating. In the macro environment, deregulation in the 1990s has allowed low-cost carriers to enter the market and gradually encroach onto routes that were historically the domain of the national flag carriers, so increasing competition and reducing profits. However, remaining regulation of the industry by governments has precluded international mergers of the larger airlines, particularly with US airlines, to achieve economies of scale and so help their profits. Some governments within Europe have also maintained subsidies to their national flag carriers with the result that there is overcapacity. There was also the shock of 11th September; its impact was to reduce catastrophically demand for flights for the airlines, especially on the profitable transatlantic routes.

This illustration shows how a series of continuous, therefore predictable, changes brought about by changes in government policy have resulted in increased competition in the airlines' microenvironment. It also shows how an environmental 'shock', unpredictable change, has further hit passenger numbers and affected sales revenues and profits.

Organisations use the understanding of their environments to detect changes and determine how to respond and how to allocate its resources. For example if the organisation detects a developing customer need it will be able to decide if it wants to enter the market and then what impact this will have on current resource allocation. It may decide that the customers require a higher level of service.

---

**Activity 6.1**

For an organisation of your choice, examine the relevance and importance of the changes in the external environment.

---

## Trends in the environment

The importance of understanding the pressures in the external environment has been established. We will now look briefly at some of the ways in which the external environments of many organisations are changing.

- Customers are becoming more knowledgeable. The Internet is a huge source of information and offers the opportunity for consumers to compare prices, research products, and understand, for example, a whole range of mortgages helped by the built-in calculators in the web site.

- The customers are becoming more demanding and markets are becoming more fragmented as organisations offer wider product ranges to meet the expanding needs. The result is customisation of the product/service, fragmentation of the market and then reduction in some product ranges as the markets have become not viable.

- In turn, organisations are attempting to satisfy and exceed expectations, so building their competitive advantage on service. As products have become commoditised (i.e. they are really quite similar and the opportunity to develop competitive advantage is limited), organisations are having to find other ways to differentiate themselves though customer service to enhance the offering. For example, this is very evident with retailers who sell electrical white goods such as kettles, fridges etc.

- Globalisation, resulting from development of the Internet, communications and logistics infrastructure, means that companies can reach markets anywhere in the world. It may open up markets but it also means wider competition.

- There is a discernible trend to greater litigation with the media playing a more visible role. Organisations have to be able to protect themselves and ensure that their product/service meets the specification.

- As the technology has developed, the need for a high street presence has declined, for example in the insurance sector. The advent of call centres offers the opportunity to enter new markets at lower cost. This opens up new opportunities for companies to enter new markets and compete with much larger players.

- Using technology, organisations can respond more quickly. It has become a part of customer service standards, for example, for organisations to answer enquiries in so many days and to then complete the transaction very quickly. Advertising agencies used to take several weeks to set up and print literature but, with technology, this has been reduced to days and even hours.

- Customer lifetime loyalty is a key aim for organisations as it is much more cost-effective. However, given the greater knowledge of consumers, they are more able to compare and evaluate a range of options and do not necessarily wish to be loyal to just one organisation.

---

**Activity 6.2**

Having undertaken a market analysis, a company that designs female clothing in Hong Kong is considering launching a new range of garments. What environmental criteria would you advise them to use in evaluating which potential target market or markets to enter?

---

## Elements of the macro environment

The macro environment is composed of a number of key elements. The importance of each of these elements will vary from sector to sector, so each organisation will have to decide which it will monitor. Daft (1989) lists the following elements of a firm's macro environment:

- Economic conditions – rate of inflation, interest rates, availability of capital and incentives.

- Technology – available to the organisation to incorporate into its products or use in its processes for satisfying customers.

- Government – laws, regulations, taxes and actions.

- International – foreign markets, foreign competition, customers, regulations and currency exchange.

- Financial resources – availability of debt and equity finance.

- Socio-cultural – society at large including demographics, attitudes and work ethic.

- Human resources – the supply of skilled and educated labour.

- Raw materials – availability of the raw materials, supplies and real estate needed by the organisation.

These elements are usually grouped into four or five headings, referred to by the acronyms SLEPT or PEST. You may see ecological issues added to these acronyms with another E, as PESTLE. These acronyms offer a structure for systematically examining the macro environment.

- **Social** – encompassing the socio-cultural and human resources elements and factors such as demographic changes, age of the population, lifestyles and family structures.

- **Technological** – changes in technology that affect the way in which we do business, including everything from communication with customers to internal efficiencies.

- **Economic** – encompassing the economic and financial resources elements and factors such as interest rates, inflation, money supply, business cycles and employment levels.

- **Political** – encompassing government, and international elements and such factors as employment laws, consumer protection, regulations such as the National Health Service management, international trade, environmental controls and monopoly controls.

Let us look at application of the PEST framework using the example of the supermarket industry.

- **Social** factors would include the age profile of the population, working habits and the increase in single households.

- **Technology** factors would include development of the Internet for home shopping and stock management.

- **Economic** factors would include disposable income and levels of need plus the regulations on company law and taxation, not forgetting the staff and employment law.

- **Political** factors would include planning regulations, food hygiene, labelling of food.

The PEST and other acronyms are used to identify the key trends and events in the environment that can be resolved by the organisation into opportunities to be exploited and threats to be handled. The impact of these trends must be followed through into the organisation's microenvironment where the firm is directly affected by decisions made by and about customers, competitors and channels to market.

---

**Activity 6.3**

For your organisation, develop the PEST framework to examine key factors and their impact.

---

## Techniques for obtaining information

Organisations seek a range of information about their environments. The main categories of information can be summarised as:

- Market and competitor intelligence.

- Technical intelligence.

- Acquisition leads – possibilities for JVs, mergers and acquisitions.

- Broad issues – general conditions and actions and policies by governments.

- Other intelligence – suppliers, raw materials, human resources and any other information specific to the organisation and its environment.

To obtain these types of information about the macro environment there are three main techniques that organisations have available to them.

### Environmental scanning

Environmental scanning is a continuous process of monitoring. The concept is to establish a method of routinely collecting and analysing. The key to success lies in identifying the most important elements or sectors of the environment and to monitor those. It is impossible to obtain or develop perfect knowledge about the environment, so the 80/20 principle should be used. In other words, obtain 80% of the information needed with the 20% of resources.

For example, a consumer organisation can use published sources of information such as social trends surveys and economic indicators to detect and monitor long term trends and changes in the demographic structures of the population.

Scanning can take three forms and the organisation should probably consider a mix of these.

- **Continuous** – its main stakeholders such as customers and competitors should be continuously monitored to identify any changes in patterns of behaviours or other trends.

- **Periodic** – periodic scanning may be conducted each year at the start of the organisation's annual planning cycle.

- **Irregular** – this kind of scanning might be undertaken for a specific project or review of strategy, when it may concentrate on specific issues in the environment.

Environmental scanning is a sound business discipline and has a number of benefits for organisations that use it:

- It enables opportunities to be identified early and capitalised on.

- It provides objective information for decision making.

- It ensures sensitivity to changing needs in the environment.

- It can improve public image of the organisation.

- It provides a continuing broad-based education for executives and intellectual stimulation for strategic marketers and planners.

Scanning will both monitor trends and detect sudden events or changes, such as a competitor introducing a new product. Marketing has the role not just of detecting these events but also assessing the impact for the organisation and recommending one or more courses of action. Little effort is needed to detect environmental crises of the magnitude of September 11th, but marketing's role in assessing the consequences for the organisation and recommending a course of action is more challenging.

## Secondary research

Secondary research, the use of information that has been published, may form a significant part of the organisation's environmental scanning system. Sources of secondary information should include not just external information but internal information as well. Examples of internal information include contact reports, reports from the sales team, monthly sales and contribution figures and market reports produced by members of the Marketing Team. These are an invaluable source of information if collated in a structured format and on a regular basis.

A review of 'what you know' will identify any gaps in the organisation's knowledge of its environment which it can then fill with further secondary or even primary research.

## Primary research

Primary research is the process of obtaining specific information directly from a source. It involves choices in approach and the methods to be used. There is a selection of quantitative and qualitative methods available, including one to one interviews, telephone surveys, observation, focus groups, and accompanied shopping to name but a few. Primary research may also have to be conducted inside the organisation, for example to evaluate the success of a communications campaign in generating leads for a new product.

As research was covered in the Management Information for Marketing Decisions module at Advanced Certificate level, it is not covered in any more detail here.

# Summary

The organisation's ability to understand its external environment, the dynamics and changing structure, is essential to inform its decisions. Environmental scanning builds a picture and provides a flow of information into the marketing information system. The more specific tools of research are also available to support the organisation's information gathering activities.

This concludes our review of the macro environment.

---

**Activity 6.4**

From the activity in the previous section, where you examined the nature of the external environment, examine how you will be able to gather the information needed to make decisions.

---

## Customers and customer needs

We now move on to the microenvironment, which consists of three main elements: customers, channels to market and competitors. We cover the first two of these in the remainder of this Session and look at competitors in the next Session.

Identification and satisfaction of customer needs is key to developing competitive advantage. This is one of the fundamental tenets of strategic marketing and organisations that miss or ignore changes in customers' needs do so at their peril. At this stage of the analysis, we are concentrating on identifying customers, their needs and key behaviours. This information will be used later to identify and target specific segments.

## Customers

Analysis of markets needs to start with some basic questions about customers.

- Who is the customer?
- What is the extent of their power with regard to the organisation?
- What do they buy?
- Why do they buy?
- When do they buy?
- Where do they buy?
- How do they buy?

Answers to these questions will begin to yield an understanding of the structure of the market, possible segments and, most importantly, customer behaviours. An understanding of the benefits that customers are seeking should also start to emerge, that can be used later in identifying and defining segments. You should also start to develop estimates of the size of the actual and potential markets to enable you to set realistic marketing objectives.

# Buying behaviour

Customer behaviour is complex and is affected by factors such as culture, pressure from peers and reference groups, personal situation and outlook, psychological factors (where Maslow's and Freud's theories of motivation play a part) and status. These combine to shape behaviour of buyers. The mix of factors will be different for consumers and organisational buyers and frameworks by Webster & Wind and by Sheth can assist the marketer in identifying variables relevant to a specific context or situation.

We have then a vastly complex and largely unpredictable set of behaviours. Incidentally, this is one area where marketing really does need more powerful tools. The profession is reliant on behavioural and psychological research to provide more sophisticated tools but, until then, we have to work with the crude tools at our disposal.

Let us look at a simple and generic model of the buying process that can be used in both consumer and business markets. It consists of the following stages:

- Recognition of the problem.
- Search for information.
- Evaluation of options.
- The purchase decision.
- Post-purchase behaviour.

The role of marketing is to understand how customers in its target markets make their buying decisions and then to try to influence those decisions using the range of techniques available in the brand proposition and marketing mix.

# The decision making unit

The marketer has also to take into account the make-up and role of the Decision Making Unit (DMU). DMUs are used formally in the business-to-business sector where they will usually involve:

- An initiator.
- A user.
- A buyer.
- An influencer.
- A decision maker.
- A gatekeeper.

The DMU is used informally in consumer markets, particularly in major purchases involving the family such as cars and holidays. Again, the role of the marketer is to understand the structure and behaviour of the DMU.

## Towards segmentation

Outcomes from this analysis of customers and their needs and behaviours will lead to the identification of bases for segments and, with other factors from the internal and external analyses, feed into the decisions on which segments to target. We will pick this up in Session 11.

## Channels to market

The second element of the microenvironment is channels to market. Analysis at this stage should identify the existing and potential channels to reach the customers we have identified. It helps to identify the main channels used by competitors or existing players in the industry. These channels should cover both communications and physical distribution.

The channels to a particular market may include the following:

- Retail outlets.
- Catalogues/Internet.
- Direct sales force.
- Distributors and agents.
- Wholesalers or other intermediaries.

It is also worth looking at the ownership structure of these channels. For example, are they owned by the players in the industry? Are they independent? Are they franchises? Are they licensed? Are they joint ventures? Answers to these questions will help to assess the options for positioning and the resources required to use these channels.

A good tool for summarising the structure of the market and showing the channels available is the 'market map', adapted from Porter's value system. A simple version of a market map for shoe manufacturers is illustrated below. The firm is using a combination of a national retail chain, which it supplies direct from the factory with shoes under the chain's own brand, and a wholesaler supplying independents with the firm's brand to reach its 3 target segments. Competitor A uses the wholesaler and independents to reach the same 3 segments. Competitor B uses a focus strategy, targeting only Segment III which it serves through its own exclusive outlets.

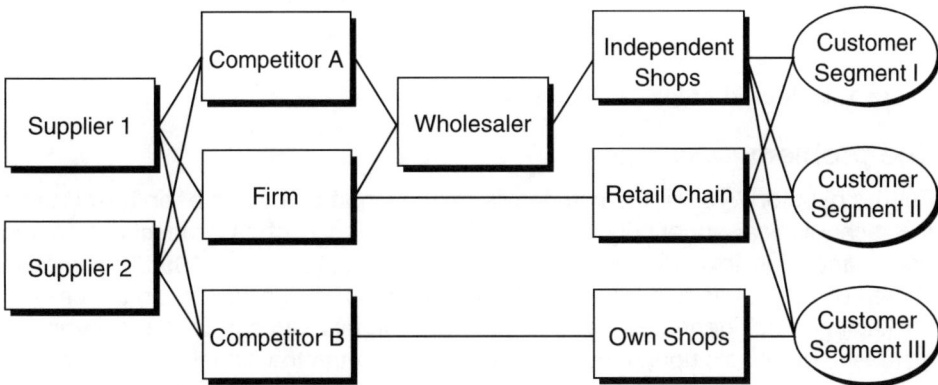

# Case Study – TMM industries

## The Company

TMM Industries is a German packaging company which markets its products across Northern Europe through independent distributors. These distributors have typically been given the exclusive sales rights to a geographic area for a given period and are able to call upon TMM for specialist sales and technical support. Promotional material is supplied by TMM which also provides firm guidelines on prices and discount structures. Sales targets are agreed annually between TMM and the distributor.

The company's operations are divided between three Strategic Business Units (SBUs): packaging machinery, packaging materials, and specialist consultancy services which are offered to organisations with complex packaging problems. Selected sales and financial data appear in Table 1.

| | TMM Sales (1997) £m | Number of Perceived Direct Competitors | TMM's Perception of its Position in the Market | | Forecast Annual Market Growth Rate (1998-2001) |
| --- | --- | --- | --- | --- | --- |
| | | | 1995 | 1997 | |
| Packaging Machinery | 140 | 9 | 3 | 5 | 6 |
| Packaging Materials | 86 | 34 | 9 | 12 | 11 |
| Consultancy Services | 35 | 5 | 2 | 1 | 8 |

**Table 1: Selected sales and financial data**

# The problem

For the past forty years, the company's marketing strategy has been based upon the technological superiority and technical excellence of its products, premium prices and high levels of after-sales service. However, since 1995, the market shares of each of its two biggest SBUs have dropped significantly. In the case of packaging machinery, the principal causes of this appear to have been an increased emphasis upon innovation on the part of the traditional competitors, the entry to the market of an aggressively price-based and technically sophisticated company from South-east Asia which is targeting TMM's customers, and a general shortening of delivery times which TMM has not yet been able to match. The effects of this have been seen not just in an erosion of market share, but also in four of the company's largest distributors having taken the decision at the beginning of 1998 to drop their TMM franchise.

# The solution?

Following a crisis meeting of the firm's main board at the end of the first quarter of 1998, the decision was taken to appoint the company's first Marketing Director; prior to this, the responsibility for marketing within what is undoubtedly a product-led organisation had been unclear. The new Marketing Director has begun by reviewing the entire sales strategy. His initial conclusions are that:

1. The company has too little formal market information and no clear idea of how its markets are likely to develop over the next few years.

2. The competitive stance is generally unfocused and appears to be based upon assumptions that are no longer necessarily valid.

3. The product range and approach to selling/distribution are both in need of review.

**Source:** SMM Planning & Control Examination Paper, June 1998.

---

**Questions**

1. Explain the benefits TMM would gain from the development of an effective environmental monitoring system.

2. Explain how a monitoring system should be structured, including the expected inputs and outputs.

---

## SUMMARY OF KEY POINTS

In this Session, we have introduced the external environment, and covered the following key points:

- The external environment is divided into the macro environment and the microenvironment.

- PEST, SLEPT or PESTLE frameworks can be used for analysing the macro environment.

- The microenvironment consists of customers, channels to market and competitors.

- The environment is constantly changing and so needs monitoring on a continuous basis.

## Improving and developing own learning

The following projects are designed to help you develop your knowledge and skills further by carrying out some research yourself. Feedback is not provided for this type of learning because there are no 'answers' to be found, but you may wish to discuss your findings with colleagues and fellow students.

---

**Project A**

Carry out a SLEPT analysis on your own organisation or one you know well.

What are the key opportunities and threats identified from the analysis for the next 12 months?

---

**Project B**

Talk to your Marketing Manager or colleagues in your Marketing Department, about major ways your organisation's environment has changed in the last 2 years.

What changes has the organisation made as a direct result of these changes?

---

**Project C**

What changes are envisaged in the next 12 months?

---

## Feedback to activities

### Activity 6.1

The first task is to identify changes that have or are taking place. These may be continuous trends or sudden one-off events. Tools like SLEPT can be helpful as a 'checklist' of areas to cover. The impact on the organisation has to be assessed. Only then can you determine which of these are important for the organisation.

## Activity 6.2

Having completed an analysis, the company now has to select one or more markets that it is going to launch its female clothing range. We will be looking at selection of target markets in more detail in Session 11 but here we are concerned mainly with the environmental criteria. SLEPT provides us with some useful headings:

- Social – demographics, social attitudes to dress codes, style preferences.

- Legal – specific laws that facilitate or constrain choices of market and entry method.

- Economic – economic performance, size and growth of market, availability of funding for business growth.

- Political – trade barriers, domestic industry that local government may wish to protect.

- Technological – design and manufacturing skills in market.

## Activity 6.3

The driving forces will vary across industries and the ability to examine trends, such as the ageing population, can offer opportunities. Were you aware of the key issues and how closely does your current marketing strategy match the opportunities and constraints of the external environment?

## Activity 6.4

Consider both the one-off analysis and long-term environmental scanning. Look at how each can be established and resourced, then the choices of primary and secondary, internal and external sources that can be most effectively used.

Remember that it is not just the Marketing Department that is monitoring the external environment. For example, the Legal Department will be monitoring legislation. Marketing has to take an overall view as the foundation for marketing strategy and it can be extremely valuable to obtain information about changes in the external environment from these people.

# Session 7

# The competitive environment

## Introduction

In this Session we explore the final part of an organisation's microenvironment – that of the competitive environment. We look at how the activities of competitors can impact on an organisation's performance. We also look at tools and techniques for analysing the competitive environment, and undertaking an industry analysis. Finally, we look at the concept of competitive intelligence and steps the organisation can take to collect and use it.

---

**LEARNING OUTCOMES**

At the end of this Session you will be able to:

- Explain how competition can determine a firm's performance in the market.

- Evaluate competitive relationships between companies in an industry using a variety of tools and techniques.

- Define competitive intelligence and explain how it can be obtained and used to benefit organisations.

---

## The impact of competition

Competitor analysis is the process of identifying competitors, determining their objectives and strategies, identifying their strengths and weaknesses, and establishing how they are likely to respond to actions that the organisation may take.

Davidson suggests that there are 7 specific steps in analysing competitors:

1. Who are the competitors? Now? 5 years from now?

2. What are the investment priorities, objectives and goals of the major competitors?

3. How important is the specific market to each competitor and what is the level of commitment?

4. What are the competitors' relative strengths and weaknesses?

5.   What weaknesses make the competitor vulnerable?

6.   What changes are competitors likely to make in the future strategies?

7.   What effects will all your competitors' strategies have on the industry, on the market and on your strategy?

The first step is to identify competitors. This is not quite as straightforward as it sounds because there are four types of competition in a market:

- Companies offering a similar product or service to same target market with same technology. Kellogg's and Nestlé compete against each other in the breakfast cereals market.

- Companies operating in same product/service category. Kellogg's is also competing indirectly with Quaker, which makes porridge oats.

- Companies supplying products/services that deliver the same service. If they consider themselves in the breakfast cereals market, Kellogg's is also competing against providers of other forms of breakfast including the ingredients for cooked breakfasts or coffee and croissants from the café on the way to work.

- Companies competing for same spending power. Kellogg's is ultimately competing against all the potential alternative claims on the money the consumer would spend on a box of cereals. This might include the early morning gym, lunch or even just the paper on the way to work.

In these examples it is relatively clear-cut where Kellogg's should focus its attention, namely on its direct competitors. But when you start considering high value consumer goods manufacturers, they may find that their major competition comes from holidays, household furnishings and other alternatives to that new washing machine.

When analysing the competitors, ensure that you think widely. The smallest competitor can surprise you and take market share. For example, direct operations in the financial services market brought in a whole new range of competitors.

When you have identified the competitors, use Davidson's next steps to work through the information gathering and evaluation. This is the process of building what Davidson calls a competitor's response profile.

- Think about their objectives using published company reports that usually cover mission and broad aims.

- Consider how important the market is to your competitors. Where else are they competing? Again, use the company's accounts to tell you where the majority of their sales revenues are coming from and where the profits are coming from.

- Examine the relative strengths and weaknesses of your organisation compared to competitors as seen from your customers' perspective. Avoid using the company view as the only view, as opinions may differ. Consider their capabilities in areas such as management, marketing, innovation and production or operations.

- Ask yourself which of your competitors' weaknesses make them vulnerable to actions you can take. For example, can you exploit their lack of an effective web site for taking orders directly from customers?

- What are your competitors likely to do next? What if they launch new products or an aggressive communications campaign, how will this impact on competition in the market? Use the press, annual reports and monitoring of their web site as part of your intelligence gathering to find out what they are up to.

- How is what your competitors might do likely to affect you? How aggressive are the competitors and will they respond to your actions? Use scenario planning to identify the major possibilities and consider contingency plans.

The key to competitor analysis is to understand the indirect as well as direct competitors. This will help to develop an understanding of the competitive environment and contribute to the development of competitive advantage, at the same time being ready for responses from other competitors and even from the unexpected new entrant.

---

**Activity 7.1**

Consider the competitors for Marks & Spencer – who are they and how have they changed over the last 5 years?

---

## Industry dynamics

The ability to understand the dynamics in an industry to assess the competition, its level of attractiveness and opportunities for competitive advantage can be undertaken using tow models from Michael Porter. These are Porter's 5 forces model and the strategic groups model. We look at both below.

### Porter's 5 forces model

The aim is to establish the scope and intensity of competitive forces in the industry.

1. **Buyers' power** – the starting point is the power buyers have due to their size and number. A key account will have greater power than a lone consumer. For example if a major supermarket decides not to buy from one of the main chocolate manufacturers this would have a major impact on the company; but an individual consumer deciding not to buy a chocolate bar would be very limited. Clearly the supermarket has considerably greater power.

2. **Supplier power** – if it is easy to switch from one supplier to another then power of the supplier is decreased. Financial services providers have attempted to diminish power over rivals by undertaking to manage any account changes for the customer. Supermarkets are launching more and more own brands to reduce the power of the established brands – even the mighty Kellogg's has recently succumbed and has been manufacturing own brand corn flakes for a supermarket.

3. **Threats of new entrants** – the ability of new competitors to enter the market depends on size of barriers to entry. Sometimes existing players can erect these barriers, like P&G and Unilever using massive advertising budgets to defend their position in the soap powder market; sometimes these barriers are regulatory. Setting up call centres is an example of entry with lower costs than a high street presence. The ability to restrict access to market is often used. For example, a new idea has to get to market but if access is denied the alternative is direct to customers or joint venture. Simply being seen as the best in the business can deter prospective entrants, so building competitive advantage is essential.

4. **Threats of substitutes** – the ability to substitute products is closely linked to the ability to differentiate the product and the level of competition from direct to indirect. Often the threat comes from new technology or a new player outside the industry, for example mobile phone networks have been developed mainly by companies that do not have large fixed networks.

5. **Rivalry between competitors** – rivalry between competitors is affected for example by low growth in the market and high exit barriers, so escape is too costly. Industries that face such issues are the car manufacturers. If there is plenty of growth then the market is likely to be more attractive as there is room for company expansion without being forced to take share from competitors.

## Strategic groups model

The second model for analysing competition in an industry is the strategic groups model. A strategic group is a set of organisations in an industry that have adopted and are following similar strategies.

Consider the airline industry, for example. The competitors divide into strategic groups such as low cost, charter and full service. These can be represented on a 'graph' with two axes defined by strategically important factors in the industry. In the airline industry, these axes may be scope of operations (from local to regional to global) and price.

The difficult part of using the strategic groups model is to identify relevant and meaningful axes. Porter suggests a long list of attributes that can be used to plot the companies and groups within an industry. Analysis of the macro environment and the 5 forces model can be used to suggest candidates for the axes; however, a certain amount of trial and error is involved.

The goal in using the strategic groups model is twofold:

- To identify competitors in the same group and identify their skills, such as marketing and innovation skills, and their responses, such as low-level retaliation or aggressive reaction.

- To identify positions on the graph which are vacant or offer a potential position to develop competitive advantage.

---

### Activity 7.2

The Marketing Director of a cosmetics company has asked you to undertake a competitor analysis. Outline the content and structure of such an analysis.

---

### Competitive intelligence

Competitive intelligence is information about a competitor that allows a company to undertake specific actions to forestall or counter the activities of the competitor. This is a new part of the syllabus.

Competitive intelligence involves:

- Planning and allocation of resources.

- Information gathering activities, including storage.

- Analysis and evaluation.

- Dissemination to decision makers.

It may be seen either as part of, or an extension to, the marketing information system, or as completely separate. Its close relative, military intelligence, should not conjure up images of espionage or other subterfuge. Far from it – much information about competitors is available in the public domain and simply needs to be collated. So called 'synthesis reports' containing underlying trends and key issues can then be generated and circulated to key decision makers.

Competitive intelligence activities can be used not only for their primary purpose of anticipating competitors' activities, but also to develop a deeper understanding of the nature of competition in the industry which the organisation can convert into competitive advantage. By giving the organisation an external focus, competitive intelligence can also stimulate learning and innovation within the organisation.

---

**Activity 7.3**

What sources of competitive intelligence might you use in the professional services industry (architect, accountant, consultancy, engineer, lawyers, etc.) and how might you disseminate within the firm?

---

## Case Study – TMM industries

You are already familiar with this case from the previous Session, which we use to explore issues in the company's macro environment. We are using it again here, this time to explore responses to events in its microenvironment.

# The company

TMM Industries is a German packaging company which markets its products across Northern Europe through independent distributors. These distributors have typically been given the exclusive sales rights to a geographic area for a given period and are able to call upon TMM for specialist sales and technical support. Promotional material is supplied by TMM which also provides firm guidelines on prices and discount structures. Sales targets are agreed annually between TMM and the distributor.

The company's operations are divided between three Strategic Business Units (SBUs): packaging machinery, packaging materials, and specialist consultancy services which are offered to organisations with complex packaging problems. Selected sales and financial data appear in Table 1.

|  | TMM Sales (1997) £m | Number of Perceived Direct Competitors | TMM's Perception of its Position in the Market | | Forecast Annual Market Growth Rate (1998-2001) |
|  |  |  | 1995 | 1997 |  |
|---|---|---|---|---|---|
| Packaging Machinery | 140 | 9 | 3 | 5 | 6 |
| Packaging Materials | 86 | 34 | 9 | 12 | 11 |
| Consultancy Services | 35 | 5 | 2 | 1 | 8 |

**Table 1: Selected sales and financial data**

# The problem

For the past forty years, the company's marketing strategy has been based upon the technological superiority and technical excellence of its products, premium prices and high levels of after-sales service. However, since 1995, the market shares of each of its two biggest SBUs have dropped significantly. In the case of packaging machinery, the principal causes of this appear to have been an increased emphasis upon innovation on the part of the traditional competitors, the entry to the market of an aggressively price-based and technically sophisticated company from South-east Asia which is targeting TMM's customers, and a general shortening of delivery times which TMM has not yet been able to match. The effects of this have been seen not just in an erosion of market share, but also in four of the company's largest distributors having taken the decision at the beginning of 1998 to drop their TMM franchise.

## The solution?

Following a crisis meeting of the firm's main board at the end of the first quarter of 1998, the decision was taken to appoint the company's first Marketing Director; prior to this, the responsibility for marketing within what is undoubtedly a product-led organisation had been unclear. The new Marketing Director has begun by reviewing the entire sales strategy. His initial conclusions are that:

1.  The company has too little formal market information and no clear idea of how its markets are likely to develop over the next few years.

2.  The competitive stance is generally unfocused and appears to be based upon assumptions that are no longer necessarily valid.

3.  The product range and approach to selling/distribution are both in need of review.

**Source:** SMM Planning & Control Examination Paper, June 1998.

---

### Questions

1.  Identify the criteria which should be used in deciding whether and how to respond to the price-based attack from the South-east Asian competitors.

2.  Outline the information that you would collect about competitors to feed into a Marketing Information System.

## SUMMARY OF KEY POINTS

In this Session, we have introduced the competitive environment, and covered the following key points:

- It is important to understand the competitive nature of an industry and how it can impact on an organisation's performance.

- Organisations need to consider how competitors are likely to respond to their marketing activities, and also understand their strategies as closely as possible.

- Porter's 5 forces and strategic groups models are valuable tools in understanding the scope and intensity of competition in an industry.

- Competitive intelligence forms an important part of the organisation's marketing information activites.

## Improving and developing own learning

The following projects are designed to help you develop your knowledge and skills further by carrying out some research yourself. Feedback is not provided for this type of learning because there are no 'answers' to be found, but you may wish to discuss your findings with colleagues and fellow students.

### Project A

Identify your main competitors and carry out an assessment of them.

Talk to colleagues in your Marketing Department about the responses your organisation has made to actions by each in the last 12 months.

### Project B

Carry out an industry analysis on your own industry using Porter's 5 forces model.

---

**Project C**

Your organisation is planning a 5% reduction in prices.

Explain how you would assess the impact of this on competitors.

Identify the likely responses of each of your key competitors to the price decrease.

---

# Feedback to activities

### Activity 7.1

Marks & Spencer has experienced considerable change in its competitive environment in the last 10 years. Traditional competitors like C&A and Littlewoods have left the high street. New competitors, such as Matalan and Primark at the low cost end, have entered the market so M&S are now facing a mix of competitors, such as Gap, BHS and Debenhams. You should think about the impact these high street stores have made as they have improved quality and repositioned.

### Activity 7.2

A competitor analysis should cover:

- Strategic groups.
- Competitors' objectives.
- Competitors' current and past strategies.
- Competitors' capabilities.
- Competitors' future strategies and reactions.

Your answer should briefly identify some of the problems an organisation faces in conducting a competitor analysis.

This was Question 3 in the Planning & Control exam paper in December 2000. You can see a specimen answer on the CIM student web site.

## Activity 7.3

Sources of intelligence might include:

- Secondary sources, such as commercial sector or market reports, government statistics, reports by professional bodies, competitors' web sites and publicity material. Note, as many firms are partnerships, financial reports will be difficult to obtain.

- Primary sources, such as customers, other professional firms, 'mystery customer' research into prices and products.

Partners and other professionals within the firm will not thank you for lists of data. So you will have to do some analysis and pull it together into a one-off report on competitors which you might then be able to update through a simple database (which the firm's staff can query) or a short regular competitor profile update.

# Session 8

# Forecasting – developing a future orientation

## Introduction

In this Session we look at the important role of forecasting and the way in which it can be used to provide a sound foundation for the marketing plan. It considers various techniques for forecasting including scenario planning, modelling and market sensing, highlighting their main strengths and limitations. The Session ends by emphasising the important role that forecasting plays in shifting the planner's thinking out of the past and present, represented in analysis of the current situation, and towards decisions about the future.

---

### LEARNING OUTCOMES

At the end of this Session you will be able to:

- Explain how a range of forecasting techniques can be used.
- Critically appraise a range of forecasting techniques.
- Develop a sound foundation for realistic marketing planning.
- Move conceptually from an understanding of current situation (analysis) to making decisions about the future (planning).

---

## Forecasting

In the previous five Sessions, we have looked at the process of analysis: understanding the current situation in which the organisation finds itself. If the organisation is to plan effectively, it has now to develop a view of the future. This is where forecasting comes in.

Forecasting is the process of using available information to project one or more views of the future. It consists of a number of techniques that can be used independently of each other or in combination, depending on the situation. Forecasting is used to provide quantified estimates on which marketing objectives and plans can be based. Forecasts used in marketing planning usually cover such variables as the size of the market, levels of demand for a particular product or service, competitors' likely shares of the market and rates of adoption or market growth.

There are essentially two views of the future:

- The first says that the future will be incrementally the same as the past. This might be a workable assumption for an established business operating in a mature market, selling to customers who are quite conservative in their approach to life. It would lead them to use forecasting techniques that extrapolate the future from the past.

- The second says that the future will be radically different. This would clearly be a better assumption for a new business working in the high technology sector with products that have short life cycles and customers who are innovators and early adopters. It would lead them to use forecasting techniques that take little account of the past, relying instead on envisaging conditions at some point in the future.

So forecasting has to satisfy these conflicting views of the future and provide techniques to support both. In the next section we explore the range of forecasting techniques available.

## Forecasting techniques

Forecasting is not the same as marketing research. Research is valuable in attempting to understand past and current events and to gather information about customers' perceptions of the future. For longer-term, more strategic issues, where information is less readily available or reliable, marketing research is of less value. Forecasting is therefore different to marketing research, although research can be used to provide some of the data on which forecasts are based.

The forecasting techniques available are as follows:

- **Trend extrapolation** – also known as time series analysis. This uses statistical techniques to examine past trends in the market and extrapolate that trend into the future. It works well when the trend is established and follows a pattern. This is clearly a technique that is based on the view of the future as incrementally the same as the past. It is therefore unsuited to situations where the future is radically different.

- **Modelling** – a model is a representation of a situation in which a number of variables are present and whose outcome is determined by the values and interaction of those variables. It will usually allow various different assumptions and scenarios to be modelled and tested ('what if') by specifying different values for certain variables. Models that are easy to build and understand may be too simplistic; on the other hand, accurate simulation requires extremely complex models, which take time to research and build. The UK Government, no doubt like other governments, uses complex economic models to predict future trends by examining a range of economic variables such as disposable income, demographics etc. If a model is built that predicts the impact on the demand for a product given price changes, sales and profits can then be deduced.

- **Individual forecasting** – an individual, often someone considered an 'expert' or 'genius', predicts events. This can be a high-risk approach: while the individual may well come up with an accurate forecast, it is ultimately a personal judgement and a biased view of the world. This weakness can be overcome to some extent by consensus forecasting.

- **Consensus forecasting** – it uses a panel of experts who produce a judgement. In the case of Jury forecasting, they work together to produce a forecast on which they agree. The danger of this approach is 'groupthink', namely the members of the jury influence each other more strongly than the outside world with the result that the forecast may not be realistic. The Delphi forecast attempts to overcome this weakness by using similar experts working independently of each other. It may employ a series of rounds in which each expert gives a view which is then fed back to other experts to be refined. It does not attempt to arrive at a single view and consensus is not required. Indeed difference can stimulate fresh ideas.

- **Scenario planning** – this is the process of identifying a number of possible futures, rather than a single view. It is usually used by a group of Managers who define the scenarios they consider possible and proceed through set stages to identify relevant variables and critical issues. A model may be built to evaluate the scenarios and ask 'what if?'. This allows the team to produce a plan, which may have several alternatives varying from the safe to the more imaginative, with appropriate contingency plans. This technique is valuable in situations where there is high uncertainty and complexity with only limited linkage to the past. Its use by a team allows a range of viewpoints to be considered.

- **Market sensing** – this is an approach rather than a technique. It about is the way in which information is interpreted and understood, not the way in which it is gathered. It is similar to scenario planning, with the emphasis on Managers developing a detailed understanding to be able to implement plans. The role of the marketing planner is to facilitate the process by which Managers achieve this deeper understanding. It has been the subject of an examination question.

- **War gaming** – this is not strictly a forecasting technique but can be used in this way. A team of Managers takes on the role of a competitor and is provided with actual information. The team is asked to identify the decisions and course of action that one or more competitors would take. This simple technique, borrowed from the military who have used it extensively for developing tactics and new weapon systems, can yield surprisingly effective results. The main reason for its success lies in the adoption by the team of the competitors' perspective from which decisions are made.

These tools assist the business in a number of ways. Hindsight may be a most precise science but what matters to planning is an accurate view of the future.

Building competitive advantage, by identifying a new market or customer need, is a key aspect of long-term planning. Pharmaceutical companies, for example, take several years to develop and test new drugs. The choice of which products to develop is decided by the long-term view of the industry and health issues in 20 years' time. This cannot be undertaken by marketing research. Similarly, the electronic industry faces pressures to decide which new technologies to bring to consumers, which research into consumers' needs can do little to support. Forecasting techniques therefore help organisations to identify patterns and estimates of demand from afar as the foundation for planning and developing marketing actions that will bring benefits to customers and profits to the organisation many years ahead.

---

**Activity 8.1**

Your Marketing Director has asked you to write a briefing paper outlining and evaluating the techniques available to help the organisation form a view of the future.

In particular, she has asked you to explain the difference between the concept of market sensing and marketing research.

---

## Difficulties in using forecasting techniques

There is little argument that an organisation needs to understand the future it faces in terms of the pressures and changes in the external environment. The issue for organisations is how they can use these techniques to assist in developing that understanding. It is important to take into account the limitations and problems of the forecasting techniques.

The difficulties can be grouped into two main issues.

- Firstly, predicting changes in external environments that are complex and unstable is a huge challenge, even with the most sophisticated tools available.

- Secondly, selecting and applying the appropriate techniques, taking into account their characteristics and limitations.

## Forecasting and uncertainty

Human and consumer behaviour is, as we saw in Session 6, inherently unpredictable. Even with more and more information available, it remains difficult to build into a model. How different the shape of the telecommunications and dotcom industries might have been, had their forecasts been able to predict the tailing off of mobile phone sales or slow take-up of Internet shopping. Perhaps if the patterns of demand over time could have been predicted, the declines in these industries could have been managed and the impact would have been diminished.

The organisation needs to take into account the probability of discontinuous or sudden change such as a new entrant to the market, a competitor introducing a totally new product or an environmental 'shock', all of which may change the dynamics of the market. For example Hoover was affected when the Dyson cleaner was launched, bringing a new meaning to the vacuum cleaner and the products in the industry. While it is not possible to foresee specific events, it is possible to consider possible categories of events and ask 'what if' they occurred.

The variables currently used to predict the future may be suited to the world of today but not the future. The ability to 'think outside the box', and avoiding a single track thought process, is paramount. Conflict is an essential part of this process of challenging norms and rules. For example, a jury can fall victim to groupthink, as when its ideas become self-enforcing and any dissenters are pressured to conform. But someone challenging the group, playing 'devil's advocate', can prevent the group from falling into this trap. Not all groups and organisations value the dissention and conflict inherent in challenging norms, but the outcomes will be the more effective for it.

## Selecting and applying the techniques

Since each of the techniques we have described has its own strengths and limitations, we have to choose carefully the specific techniques we are going to use for a particular application. The choice may depend on factors such as:

- The nature of the forecast required.

- The time horizon it has to cover.

- The degree of stability or rate of change of the environment.

- The probability of significant events or 'shocks'.

- The degree of complexity of the environment and the factors to be considered in arriving at a forecast.

The accuracy of the forecast on which the plan is based can be evaluated at the end of the period. By comparing the actual market or sales against the forecast, you can assess its accuracy. If it was inaccurate, you can then examine the data, process or influence from Managers that may have caused this. You can then improve the process for the next forecast.

Finally, while recognising the value of these techniques in helping us to develop a view of the future, let us remind ourselves how difficult it is to predict the future. Even with all the techniques available, the future can remain largely uncertain. We have only to make a note of predictions for the stock markets or individual shares from a variety of analysts and then compare them with actual results at the end of the period. Predicting accurately the economic conditions around the world, recession or recovery, continues to challenge the best. These two examples illustrate the problems of the uncertain nature of the external environment and the weaknesses inherent in the models.

---

**Activity 8.2**

Outline and evaluate how scenario planning may assist a large regional electricity company to gain a better understanding of the future of its markets.

What advantages does scenario planning have over traditional econometric models?

---

## Using forecasts to inform planning

A forecast of demand, sales or market share over time will incorporate conclusions drawn from the analysis of the current situation and even views of experts about the future. Through a process of 'gap analysis' and discussion with Managers which we will explore further in the next Session, the forecast becomes the bedrock on which objectives for the plan are set. Since this is a political process involving negotiation and use of power in many organisations, the forecast of the future can provide a vital focal point and possibly even be accepted as a 'fact' about the future. Once objectives have been set and agreed, the organisation can develop appropriate strategies for meeting these objectives. This is how the plan is established on the foundation of a forecast. It is no wonder that Managers demand that forecasts should be accurate.

However, the main value of these forecasting techniques does not lie in the answers or predictions they generate. It lies in the way they engage planners and Managers in asking questions and thinking about the influences and events that will shape the future for a given organisation. There is no such thing as a perfect model or perfect view of the future. What matters therefore is an approach to planning that recognises and takes these uncertainties into account. The approach should develop an understanding of the variables at play and their dynamics in a particular context and result in a plan that is sufficiently flexible, with contingencies built in, to cope with changes as the future unrolls.

---

**Activity 8.3**

List the influences and variables that you would consider when building a model of the market for your organisation or one that you know well.

---

## Making the move from analysis to planning

Coming as it does in the planning process between analysis and decision making, forecasting provides a valuable bridge. Analysis is an activity located essentially in the past and present. It is often 'comfortable' since analyst is looking at the known information. Planning and decision making are located in the future which by its very nature is uncertain. Some people, particularly those with limited experience, can find this aspect less comfortable than analysis. The result is that they avoid making decisions, looking instead for more information from the analysis which may not be there. The term used to describe this condition is 'analysis paralysis'.

Forecasting, as a bridge, helps to turn the focus from the past and present to the future. The techniques of forecasting encourage planners and Managers to identify the variables relevant to the future and ask questions about how they will interact. This may not yield absolute certainty, but it does perform the valuable function of helping users to become better acquainted and more comfortable with the future and its uncertainties.

The step in the planning process at which the view of the future is formed is both vital to the plan and valuable to the planner. In the same way that an inaccurate forecast can prove fatal to the success of a plan, so a rushed or skimped forecast will omit the engagement the planner and Managers can develop with the future.

# Case Study – Weetabix

The breakfast cereal market in the UK is estimated to be worth around £1 billion a year and has been growing at around 2%-3% a year in terms of value. Consumers in the UK eat 171bs of breakfast cereal a year, more than in any other country in the world. The nearest rivals are consumers in the United States of America who eat 101bs a year. This sector of the UK market is highly competitive with both Kellogg's and Nestlé – two of the world's biggest food companies – being actively involved (Cereal Partners being Nestlé's joint venture with General Mills). The market share breakdown is shown in Table 1.

| Company | Market Share % |
|---|---|
| Kellogg's | 43.5 |
| Weetabix | 15.2 |
| Cereal Partners | 12.0 |
| Others | 29.3 |

**Table 1: Share of the UK breakfast cereal market by company**

As well as having major global players active in the market, retailer own label brands have been growing in strength. In the last three years alone, retailers' own label brands have increased their share of the market from 22% to 33%.

Weetabix is a medium-sized company employing 2,000 people in the UK. Yet, against this market background in the year ending February 1999, Weetabix's annual turnover had risen 12% from £274 million to £308 million. Pre-tax profits had grown 23% to £52 million from £42 million. In fact Weetabix has shown steady growth for a number of years. Back in 1982 Weetabix had a turnover of just £55 million with profits of just over £1 million.

Weetabix (the product) was developed in Australia around 1900. It is a sugarless flaked wheat biscuit with a consistency that turns into a soft pulp once milk is poured over it. When eaten this biscuit delivers nourishment in the form of a strong mix of complex carbohydrates. Due to its soft consistency it can be eaten by any age group. In particular, it is ideal for weaning babies. It is currently the number two brand in the UK breakfast cereal market (see Table 2). Unlike the other leading brands, no other retailer or manufacturer has managed to launch successfully a 'me-too' product. The majority of own label flaked wheat biscuits are actually manufactured by Weetabix.

Weetabix (the company) has six major products which are: Weetabix (plus a variation, Frutibix), Alpen, Crunchy Bran, Weetos, Ready Brek and Advantage. This gives the company some advantages in concentrating investment and management effort over a small range of products. Some observers see this situation arising because Weetabix is poor at innovation and see the company as having a conservative new product development policy. This is especially noticeable given that the other major players in this market have launched a number of minor variations on their basic breakfast cereal products in recent years.

| Position | Brand | 1998 Listing (£m) | % Change on Previous Year | Company |
|---|---|---|---|---|
| 1 | Kellogg's Corn Flakes | Over 90 | -7.8 | Kellogg's |
| 2 | Weetabix | 75-80 | 0.7 | Weetabix |
| 3 | Kellogg's Frosties | 60-65 | -5.9 | Kellogg's |
| 4 | Nestlé Shredded Wheat | 45-50 | 14.2 | Cereal Partners |
| 5 | Kellogg's Rice Krispies | 35-40 | -6.2 | Kellogg's |
| 6 | Kellogg's Crunchy Nut Corn Flakes | 35-40 | -3.7 | Kellogg's |
| 7 | Kellogg's Healthwise Bran Flakes | 30-35 | -5.2 | Kellogg's |
| 8 | Kellogg's Special K | 25-30 | 0.9 | Kellogg's |
| 9 | Quaker Sugar Puffs | 25-30 | 8.8 | Quaker |
| 10 | Kellogg's Optima Fruit 'n Fibre | 25-30 | -2.5 | Kellogg's |

**Table 2: The UK breakfast cereal market**

Weetabix does not compete in every segment of the market and does not have multiple products in each category. However, it does tend to dominate the categories where it chooses to compete. For instance, Alpen is the brand leader in muesli, Ready Brek created and still dominates the hot cereal sector and Weetabix leads the wholewheat biscuit category.

| Company | Advertising Spend in £m (April 1998-March 1999) |
|---|---|
| Kellogg's | 55 |
| Cereal Partners | 19 |
| Weetabix | 15 |
| Quaker Oats | 1.7 |
| Others | 2.2 |
| **Total** | **92.9** |

**Table 3: Advertising spend, cereals**

One of Weetabix's key strengths is its high level of service. The Federation of Wholesale Distributors awarded the company a gold medal for service levels in 1995. Weetabix has a reputation of having products in stock, delivering when they say they will deliver and of offering merchandising and marketing support. This is in an industry where wholesalers are used to being let down on as many as one in ten orders.

At the end of 1998 Kellogg's decided to increase its advertising expenditure by 40%. At the same time it cut its prices on six of its leading brands by 12%. This price war was started in retaliation to the growth of the own label brands; however, it has obvious implications for Weetabix. The Chairman of Weetabix said in February 1999 that he was 'concerned that the tactics of our major competitors may harm the whole breakfast cereal sector'.

Trends are also changing in the breakfast cereal market. Fewer consumers are having a sit down breakfast and are instead eating food such as croissants that can be eaten while travelling. A number of manufacturers have developed products to address this market (see Table 4). Kellogg's in particular has been active in this area of product development. Kellogg's Nutri-Grain is a bar high in fibre that the company is branding as a 'morning bar'. This product is now being extended with the addition of Nutri-Grain Twists containing separate sections of yoghurt and fruit purée that are twisted into the Nutri-Grain bar. Kellogg's is also extending three of its breakfast bar brands into cereal bars. The Kellogg's brands of Frosties, Coco Pops and Smacks are all being launched in a cereal and milk bar format. Cereal and milk bars are bound together with dried milk and are claimed to contain the equivalent amount of milk as in a traditional bowl of breakfast cereal.

|              | £m   | %    |
|--------------|------|------|
| Kellogg's    | 14.1 | 25   |
| Jordan       | 13.9 | 25   |
| Mars         | 11.4 | 20   |
| Quaker       | 6.2  | 11   |
| Other brands | 0.8  | 1.5  |
| Own label    | 9.8  | 17.5 |
| **Total**    | **56.2** | **100** |

**Table 4: Estimated manufacturers' shares in the UK cereal bar market in 1997**

**Source:** SMM Planning & Control Examination Paper, June 2000.

**Questions**

1. Explain how scenario planning might have helped Weetabix to avoid their current situation.

2. Summarise Weetabix's current situation in preparation for decisions on the strategic options open to them.

**SUMMARY OF KEY POINTS**

In this Session, we have introduced the importance of forecasting, and covered the following key points:

- We need to understand the past and present, in order to forecast the likely future, and plan for it accordingly.

- There are several techniques for forecasting, including trend extrapolation, market sensing, scenario planning, and modelling. Each has its strengths and limitations so needs to be selected carefully.

- Forecasting forms a sound foundation for the plan for the future. It also acts as a valuable bridge between the analysis, located in the past and present, and planning, located in the future.

## Improving and developing own learning

The following projects are designed to help you develop your knowledge and skills further by carrying out some research yourself. Feedback is not provided for this type of learning because there are no 'answers' to be found, but you may wish to discuss your findings with colleagues and fellow students.

**Project A**

Talk to colleagues in your Marketing Department about the forecasting techniques used in your organisation.

How have they influenced marketing strategy in the past year?

**Project B**

Has your organisation used trend extrapolation to set sales objectives?

If so, how successful was the approach?

Were objectives achieved?

What can you learn from this for the future?

---

**Project C**

Identify ways in which your organisation might use scenario planning. How would you organise a scenario planning activity involving a group of Senior Managers?

Devise two alternative scenarios for one of your products and markets.

What action might your organisation take as a result of these scenarios?

---

# Feedback to activities

## Activity 8.1

To plan effectively and make effective strategies, organisations need to form a view of the future. The main techniques available are:

- Trend extrapolation.
- Modelling.
- Individual forecasting.
- Consensus forecasting including Jury and Delphi forecasts.
- Scenario planning.

At a strategic level marketing research may not be wholly reliable, so it is important for Managers to understand the markets. This is the emphasis of market sensing, rather than simply relying on data contained in market research reports.

This was Question 5 in the Planning & Control exam paper in December 1999. You can see a full specimen answer on the CIM student web site.

## Activity 8.2

An electricity company will typically use a demand model to forecast demand at certain periods under certain conditions so that it can determine how much it needs to buy or generate. The disadvantage of this type of model is that it contains relatively few variables and does not take into account the more complex nature of the environment since privatisation. Scenario planning is less 'deterministic', more flexible and capable of dealing with a larger number of variables. Once the main scenarios have been identified, the demand model could be used to assess the impact on demand.

## Activity 8.3

The models for any two organisations will be different. However, they may include common influences and variables, perhaps grouped under headings of macro and micro, such as:

- Economic growth.
- Demographics.
- Nature of demand: *independent* (e.g. cars) or *dependent* (e.g. car gearboxes).
- Rate of new product development.
- Distribution chain capacity.
- Level and extent of competition.

# Session 9

# The strategic intent – vision, mission and objectives

## Introduction

The previous Sessions have covered how organisations answer the question 'where are we now?' through a process of analysis. Having looked in the last Session at forecasts and views of the future, this Session deals with 'where do we want to be?' and the decisions involved. It explores the various forms that statements of intent, such as mission and vision, can take, the hierarchy of objectives within the organisation and techniques for setting objectives.

---

**LEARNING OUTCOMES**

At the end of this Session you will be able to:

- Define the terms 'vision', 'mission statement' and 'strategic intent'.

- Explain the difference between corporate and marketing objectives.

- Identify factors that influence the selection of visions and mission statements and the setting of goals and objectives.

- Identify the dominant orientation in a firm as an influence on objectives.

- Explain the balanced scorecard and its purpose and scope within organisations.

---

## Vision, mission and strategic intent

There is a wide range of terms used in marketing for defining the future direction of the organisation. Before the organisation can determine its strategy, it needs to establish some boundaries round its areas of operation. Such definitions seek to answer the question 'what business are we in?'. This may seem a simple question, but is a ferry company in the business of (a) passenger and freight ferrying, (b) floating hotels or (c) holidays? The answer to this question is not straightforward, requiring considerable thought and discussion within the company. The outcome will determine what the company's strategy will be and how it will operate.

The terms used to define future direction are often used interchangeably in everyday use. Some companies therefore use a mission statement both to define the business it is in and its aspirations. Others see a distinction and may use a vision to define its aspirations.

- 'Vision' or 'strategic intent' is the '… desired future state or aspiration of the organisation' (Johnson and Scholes, 1999). It provides the opportunity for the organisation to develop a clear idea of its future, stressing the long-term competitive advantage that is critical to its success. An organisation that has a clear vision focusing on the future identifying core competencies and offering the opportunity to move forward and not simply fine tuning the existing situation will be more dynamic and proactive. It can offer ownership and motivation to the employees. It also offers a starting point for evaluation.

- The 'mission' is the unique purpose of the organisation and the scope within which it operates. It is written down in the mission statement. 'Purpose' is the reason that the organisation exists. Piercy (2000) sees mission as being more concerned with offering daily guidance and must show the maintenance of core competencies and critical success factors. The organisation should ensure that it is communicated to all employees to be able to deliver customer value.

- The 'business definition' is a simple factual statement of what business the organisation is in. It is rarely published or even written down. However, it is fundamental to determining a strategic intent and defining a strategy. It usually covers the customer groups, the benefits delivered or functions served, and the technology used. For example, XYZ Computers Ltd is in the business of providing graphics designers and gaming enthusiasts (*the customer groups*) with highest quality computer graphics (*function served*) using state-of-the-art hardware and software (*technology*).

The distinction is that the mission defines what the organisation does; the vision includes some degree of aspiration. Which of these an organisation chooses to use will usually depend on management culture.

For any mission or vision to be regarded by staff as of value it needs to:

- Be credible. Employees in particular have to believe it.
- Be unique. It has to be specific to its host organisation and its stakeholders, not applicable to just any organisation.
- Specify the core capabilities of the organisation.
- Motivate by providing a relevant and aspirational statement.

Some statements tend to be rather generic: phrases such as '… we will provide excellent quality and customer service…' are commonplace. The trend now is to make a mission more specific and offer greater meaning and ownership to the employees. It should also reflect the needs of the stakeholders.

The balance is to provide a mission that reflects the drivers in the external environment, the needs of the stakeholders and to define a future direction. This is difficult to achieve, as the direction needs to offer clarity and also flexibility given the changes in the environment. The difficulty in achieving this balance and to avoid frequent changes is probably the main reason that mission statements are similar.

---

**Activity 9.1**

Obtain a few mission statements and visions from different organisations. These may include your own organisation's, those from organisations you know or work with, or examples from a textbook (Drummond & Ensor provides a few of these).

Compare these statements. Why are they different?

What do they tell you about the organisations they come from?

Which stakeholder groups are they addressed at?

How effective are they in communicating what the organisation is about to each stakeholder group?

---

# The role of objectives

The role of marketing objectives is to contribute to the achievement of corporate or business objectives. We can think of this as a hierarchy of objectives.

- **Corporate objectives** specify the direction and targets of the whole organisation. They reflect stakeholders' expectations, are long-term and are often expressed in financial terms.

- **Business objectives** specify the direction and targets of a single company, business or strategic business unit. In a single company, corporate objectives and business objectives are the same thing.

- **Marketing objectives** specify the targets for the organisation and its marketing activities, reflecting the product/market match. In organisations with a strong marketing orientation, marketing objectives have a strategic role and therefore come before functional objectives.

- **Functional objectives** specify the detailed targets and activities of the departments or functions of the organisation. In organisations with a weak market orientation, marketing is likely to be just one of the functions in the business and so marketing objectives in this case would also be functional objectives. Functional objectives across the organisation have to be integrated and co-ordinated.

- **Communications objectives** are usually part of the marketing plan and therefore contribute to the achievement of marketing objectives.

Objectives must be SMART:

- Specific.
- Measurable.
- Aspirational.
- Realistic.
- Time-bounded.

## Factors influencing mission and objectives

When the organisation is deciding its future direction, its mission and objectives, it is influenced by a number of factors, which it needs to take into account. These can be summarised as (Johnson & Scholes, 1999):

- Corporate governance – whom the organisation should serve and how the organisation should regulate itself. The term of 'act global think local' illustrates the different regulations that can affect an organisation and the choices it can make.

- Stakeholders – the priorities amongst stakeholders, taking into account the varying relative levels of power they wield.

- Business ethics – the expectations of behaviours by the organisation in fulfilling its social and ethical responsibilities. This is becoming increasingly important. It differs between countries and globalisation has a major role to play.

- Cultural context – the influences on the organisation from its national environment, industry environment, professional environments and internal culture. Culture will affect strategic choices. For example a new entrant to the market may have a whole new approach to the market than established players.

These influences often conflict with one another. For example, pressures from consumers and environmentalists to adopt ethical policies and deliver environmentally friendly products can be costly to implement and in conflict with pressure from shareholders. Balancing the conflicting needs is a key issue for any organisation.

## The dominant orientation

A key influence on deciding mission and objectives is the internal culture of the organisation. In Session 1 of this Companion we explored the types of orientation within an organisation:

- Production orientation.

- Technology or product orientation.

- Sales orientation.

- Market orientation.

These were broad descriptions of the priorities an organisation places on the various activities it has to perform to survive: product development, production, obtaining sales and satisfying customers. The first two of these orientations are essentially focused inside the organisation. The sales orientation is a transaction focus, placing greater importance on the customer's order than on the customer relationship.

The market orientation is the only one with a truly external focus. However, although externally focused, it can manifest itself in one of two forms:

- Customer orientation – the organisation continuously monitors and anticipates customers' needs and designs its marketing programmes accordingly. Here the focus is on satisfying customers over the long term and the battleground is the customer's mind.

- Competitor orientation – this form exists in industries where firms' decisions, actions and marketing are determined with reference to their competitors, rather than to their customers.

Ideally, an organisation should have a balance of the two (along with the other 3 key aspects of the market orientation covered in Session 1). A dominant customer orientation may lead an organisation to overlook its competitors' activities; a dominant competitor orientation may lead an organisation to overlook the benefits its customers are seeking.

One of these orientations may be dominant within the organisation and particularly within the group of Managers that makes decisions about mission and objectives. It is therefore important to understand the impact that any dominant orientation can have on the choice of mission or objectives. It is often possible to identify the dominant culture or orientation from a mission statement or vision.

---

**Activity 9.2**

An expanding, family-owned food processing company and the largest employer in the rural area in which it is based is undertaking a strategic review. The Managing Director of the company has asked you for a briefing paper discussing the issues that the company should take into account when redeveloping its mission and objectives.

---

## The objective setting process

Objective setting should be conducted top down. It is a key part of the planning process. The lower levels of objectives cannot be set until the higher levels have been defined (or assumed). They then contribute to the achievement of higher level objectives. For example, consider a manufacturer of cosmetics. The mission might reflect its values of being the key provider of innovative skin care solutions. To achieve this, the corporate objectives will be market leadership and specified levels of sales revenues. Marketing objectives will be to offer new products and solutions to skin care problems to specific target segments.

A valuable technique for use in setting objectives is gap analysis. This simple technique identifies the gap between where the organisation is now and where it wants (or is told) to be. This is illustrated in the diagram overleaf.

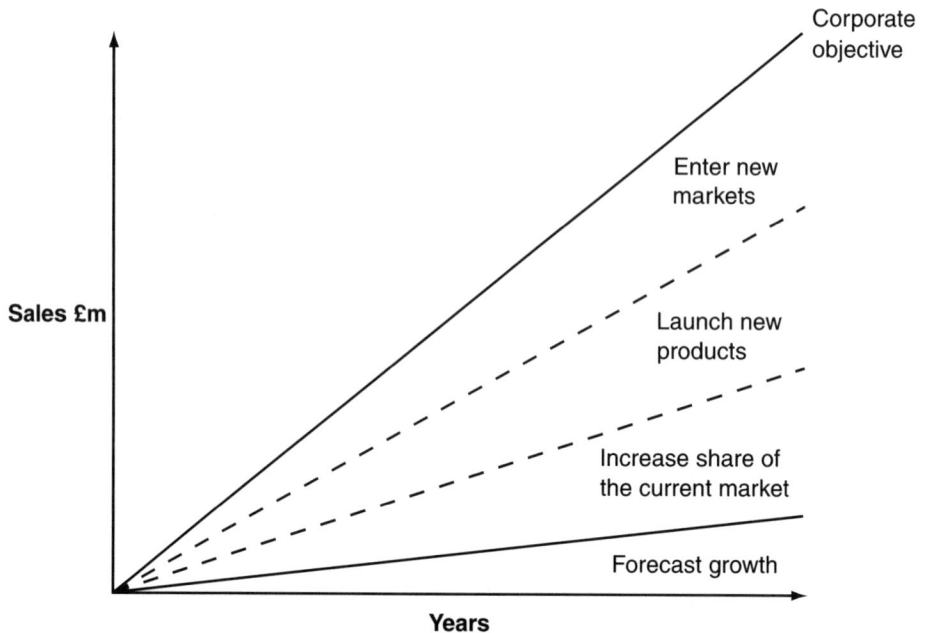

In this illustration a business has to fill the 'gap' between its current sales level, represented by the horizontal axis, and the corporate objective. Using forecasting techniques explained in the previous Session, it has developed a forecast showing how demand is growing. This shows that, by holding its current share of the market, the business can start closing the gap. However, it still has a significant gap to fill. In this case, it has identified three objectives that will help it to close the gap and meet the corporate objectives. These are:

- To increase share of the current market.
- To launch new products.
- To enter new markets or segments.

This technique can be used to identify and set quantified objectives. Once these objectives have been set, strategies can be identified for achieving them. We look at this in the next Session.

When setting objectives, try to think about how the objective will be measured. Consider the difference between quantitative and qualitative objectives and measures, sometimes referred to as 'hard' and 'soft'. Quantitative objectives, e.g. to maintain our 20% market share, are relatively easy to measure. Qualitative objectives, e.g. to improve customers' perception of product x, can be measured by marketing research both at the start and at the end of the period. The balanced scorecard, described in more detail later in this Session, is a useful technique for setting objectives and identifying measures that cover both financial and non-financial aspects of the organisation.

Setting objectives is an iterative process and often requires negotiation with Senior Managers and Managers of other units affected. The marketing planning process suggests that it is a straight linear development but it is rarely that simple. Objectives are set and plans proposed and evaluated to ensure that they are realistic. In cases where it may not be feasible to achieve a particular objective in the timescale or due to market conditions, Managers will fine tune objectives to ensure that the plan is cohesive and consistent.

This highlights the importance of cross-functional links. For example, if marketing suggests an objective of a 10% increase in sales, the impact on other parts of the business needs to be appreciated. What is the impact on production, employees and financial resources? If the objectives across the whole organisation are not fully integrated, the result will be disappointed customers.

## The balanced scorecard

The balanced scorecard was developed by Kaplan and Norton (1992) to assist in setting objectives for the organisation that bring together the perspectives of a variety of stakeholders and link objectives directly to performance evaluation.

The balanced scorecard is a concept which ensures that the organisation develops a holistic approach and sound cross-functional links to ensure seamless delivery of the customer experience. It is also a process that helps in co-ordinating activities throughout the organisation. It offers the ability to develop direction simultaneously and not in a linear fashion, for example with marketing deciding their objectives and then another function with the obvious problems of control and cohesion. In this, it has similarities with the team approach to product innovation.

The scorecard encourages Managers to cascade strategy through the whole of the organisation's processes and to rethink the way in which business is undertaken. It offers the opportunity to link strategy with the structure of the organisation.

The process requires objectives to be set under four key headings with matching methods of evaluation:

- **Financial** objectives and measures are those traditionally found in organisations, such as profitability, cash flow and return on capital employed. This provides the necessary quantitative measures for almost all organisations.

- **Customer** objectives and measures such as satisfaction and value. Here, measures would be evaluated using marketing research and relative rankings in comparison with competitors. These measures will highlight whether the customer sees the organisation in the same way as the organisation sees itself.

- **Internal** objectives and measures include evaluation of the activities and processes undertaken within the parts of the organisation, such as marketing, manufacturing, logistics and quality. Examples include developing new products, costs of manufacturing, speed of delivery and rate of rejects.

- **Innovation and learning** objectives and measures provide indicators of the organisation's capabilities for the future. They might include speed to market, employee empowerment, the proportion of sales coming from new products and the number of new products developed. Measuring learning is not easy but therein lies one of the benefits of the balanced scorecard approach in that it encourages teams within the organisation to become involved in exploring and defining these measures.

The view of the organisation as a whole is perhaps the greatest contribution of the balanced scorecard. Each function or group of processes has a key role to play in enhancing the organisation's performance. Objectives are closely related to the ability of the organisation to deliver its strategy which in turn depends on the employees, their knowledge and skills, and the culture of innovation and continuous improvement. It is these activities, carried out in the depths of the organisation on a day-to-day basis, that deliver the overall financial and corporate objectives.

---

**Activity 9.3**

Evaluate the usefulness to organisations of the balanced scorecard approach as advocated by Kaplan and Norton.

---

# Case Study – Freeplay Energy

In the early 1980s Trevor Bayliss, the British inventor, developed the concept of a self-powered radio. Electricity for the radio would be provided by an integral wind-up generator. Bayliss's idea was that this self-powered radio would allow people in remote villages across Africa to gain access to news and information from around the world. In 1994 the South African based BayGen Power company (later renamed Freeplay Energy) signed an exclusive agreement with Trevor Bayliss to develop and commercialise the product.

Although Trevor Bayliss no longer has an active involvement with Freeplay Energy, the partners who run the company are still driven by the desire to improve the lives of individuals in the less developed world. The company's Cape Town factories are co-owned by local charities that represent the disabled, single mothers and former offenders. Around one third of the company's employees are from these disadvantaged groups.

The first commercial version of the wind-up radio was the FPR1 and this was distributed to villages by aid agencies. Very early on, it became apparent that the radio was too heavy, too fragile and more crucially too expensive for its intended market. Villagers appeared to be more willing to spend £2 to £3 a month on batteries, than an initial £29 on a radio that did not require battery replacements. The product however, began to develop sales in more affluent markets. In the UK the Design Council awarded the wind-up radio 'Millennium Product' status. One national newspaper went as far as naming it the most significant invention of a generation.

Freeplay Energy began to realise that volume sales could be developed by concentrating on the European and North American markets. Sales growth in these markets has allowed Freeplay to invest further in the technology, and as a result develop products that are smaller, lighter, more durable and less expensive. The FPRI had to be wound for 20 seconds in order to produce 30 minutes of playing time. The FPR2, which Freeplay launched in 1997, weighs less, is more compact and supplies an hour of playing time after being wound for 20 seconds.

In 1999 the company added to the radio range with the launch of a new model, the Freeplay S360. The company also launched the 20/20 flashlight, which contains an integral energy storage unit to generate power for instantaneous or later use.

Currently Freeplay Energy has a £30m turnover and was forecast to produce 1.2 million units in the year 2000. Around 70% of its sales are in the United States of America and 25% in Europe, with Africa and the Middle East making up the balance. The company's promotional budget is around £3m.

Through market research the organisation has identified that the product is positioned differently in the various international markets. In Germany the product appeals to the consumer's strong environmental consciousness. In the USA and Japan, where there is a strong outdoor culture, the product is bought as a component of tornado or earthquake survival kits. In the UK, the company's biggest market per capita, the general public is proud of the fact that the product was invented there.

The company still has an aspiration to create products that will bring modern forms of communication to individuals in remote rural villages. However, they believe that entering into the European and North American markets has allowed them to develop much larger manufacturing volumes which in turn has enabled them to gradually lower prices.

Freeplay Energy has a number of new product ideas under investigation. One initiative is the concept of a satellite telephone that can be charged with energy provided by a 'self-powered' generator rather than costly disposable batteries. The company believes this product would overcome some of the problems faced by African economies. Some African states cannot afford to develop the landlines and other facilities needed for a modern telecommunications infrastructure. This approach would allow these states to make a technology leap and allow individuals access to the global communications network. Other product ideas include self-powered pull cord lights, water purification systems and even feotal heartbeat monitors.

The company's philosophy is to attempt to create a range of products that will help improve communication across the less developed world. This is reflected in its tagline, 'Powered by You'.

The company now has to consider how it plans to develop over the next five years. There are a number of strategic choices to be made. It could move away from making its own products or it could carry on some manufacturing but license out its technology to mobile phone manufacturers such as Nokia, Ericsson and Motorola.

**Source:** SMM Planning & Control Examination Paper, December 2000.

**Questions**

1.  Prepare a brief to Freeplay Energy advising them of the issues they need to consider in developing the organisation's mission, goals and objectives.

2.  Describe their current situation and stage of development.

## SUMMARY OF KEY POINTS

In this Session, we have introduced terms and techniques involved with determining the organisation's strategic intent. We have covered the following key points:

■ Strategic intent, vision and mission are terms used to describe the direction the organisation intends to take. Although used interchangeably, there is a distinction between mission and vision.

■ Marketing objectives are part of a hierarchy of objectives within the organisation. SMART marketing objectives can be set only when higher level objectives are known.

■ The choice of mission and objectives are affected by a range of factors that can be grouped under four headings: corporate governance, stakeholders, business ethics and cultural context.

■ The orientation of the organisation and particularly its Senior Managers can be a strong influence on mission and objectives.

■ Gap analysis is a valuable technique in identifying and filling the gap between where the organisation is now and its level of expectation.

■ The balanced scorecard provides an approach to objective setting and measurement that embraces the activities of the whole organisation and ensures that the activities are co-ordinated.

## Improving and developing own learning

The following projects are designed to help you develop your knowledge and skills further by carrying out some research yourself. Feedback is not provided for this type of learning because there are no 'answers' to be found, but you may wish to discuss your findings with colleagues and fellow students.

---

**Project A**

Obtain the mission statement or vision and the business objectives for the organisation for which you work or are studying.

Discuss with a colleague what these tell you about the dominant or prevailing orientation among Senior Managers and why have they adopted this orientation.

---

**Project B**

Find out what the corporate or business objectives are in your organisation. You may have to ask your Manager for these. Then try to find out what process the organisation uses to identify and set marketing and functional objectives that support the corporate objectives.

Identify the similarities with, and differences from, the process we have covered in this Session.

---

**Project C**

Organisational culture is clearly an important influence on the choice of mission and objectives. Why do you think this is?

Try exploring this link further by reading more about culture and its relationship with strategy in one of the additional texts listed in the syllabus, Johnson & Scholes or in works by Mintzberg.

---

# Feedback to activities

## Activity 9.1

The statements you have looked at have come from different organisations, so it is natural that they are different. If they were all the same, they would have limited value to the organisations that developed them or their stakeholders.

Looking at the statements you have found, you may be able to detect which stakeholder group is the most important to the organisation. Some may address all stakeholders; others may address just one or two groups. Shareholders are important to publicly quoted companies, but so are customers. How do the statements you have found strike the balance between these two groups?

## Activity 9.2

The main influences on missions and objectives are:

- Corporate governance.
- Stakeholders.
- Business ethics.
- Cultural context.

You should identify examples of specific internal and external influences. You should also identify the trade-offs that have to be made when setting objectives, such as:

- Short versus long term.
- Profit versus competitive position in the market.
- Risk avoidance versus risk taking.

This was Question 5 on the Planning & Control examination paper in June 2001. You can see a full specimen answer on the CIM student web site.

## Activity 9.3

The balanced scorecard links objective setting to performance measures. It was developed to give organisations a broader set of measures than the traditional financial (therefore purely historical) view. It provides three perspectives in addition to the traditional financial perspective:

- Customer perspective.

- Internal perspective.

- Innovation and learning perspective.

Its value is in broadening the view of Managers of the organisation's performance and focussing on the activities of today that are going to generate value in the future.

This was Question 4 on the Planning & Control examination paper in June 2000. You can see a full specimen answer on the CIM student web site.

# Session 10

# Approaches to creating strategic advantage

## Introduction

In this Session we explore various approaches to creating strategic advantage. We start by developing an understanding of sustainable competitive advantage and identifying the sources of advantage that organisations can exploit. We then describe a range of development strategies available: generic strategies, alternative directions and alternative methods. We then look at offensive and defensive strategies and their use to sustain specific market positions. We also look at strategies for specific situations such as hostile markets and wear-out. Finally, we explore how the organisation should choose a strategy from all the options discussed in the Session.

## LEARNING OUTCOMES

At the end of this Session you will be able to:

- Explain the concept of sustainable competitive advantage.

- Identify the sources, and explain the development, of sustainable competitive advantage.

- Explain how organisations can develop competitive advantage by undertaking generic strategies, alternative directions and alternative methods for development.

- Explain offensive and defensive strategies available to organisations.

- Explain the range of strategies available to firms for specific purposes.

- Apply the concept of strategic choice.

## Sustainable competitive advantage

The concept of sustainable competitive advantage is fundamental to an understanding of strategy and crucial to the success of the organisation.

Competitive advantage is a position that an organisation achieves relative to its competitors by using the resources and capabilities available to it. It may consist of a single large advantage or a number of smaller advantages. In simple terms, competitive advantage yields a superior return on investment for the organisation.

Porter emphasises that, to be significant, competitive advantage has to be sustainable. In other words, an organisation's competitive advantage should not be susceptible to being eroded by imitation by competitors or changes in the environment.

Building sustainable competitive advantage is made difficult by three groups of factors:

- Customers – they are becoming ever more demanding and less likely to remain loyal to any one supplier.

- Changes in the environment – globalisation and technology are just two factors causing markets to become more competitive, to fragment and to 'commoditise'. They are also contributing to faster rates of change.

- Competitive pressures – increasing levels of competition and imitation are eroding the ways in which any one organisation can make itself distinct. For example, many technological or product innovations may be easy for competitors to imitate and will yield only a short-lived advantage.

These factors highlight the importance of the assets and capabilities as that which makes an organisation unique. This is enshrined in the resource-based approach to strategy. By developing a unique bundle of assets and capabilities and reflecting these deep within its brand, an organisation can differentiate itself. For example, Sony and Nokia are seen as technologically innovative in their respective markets; Porsche as a producer of fast, quality sports cars; and Virgin as a strong brand with a dynamic leader. These are all difficult to imitate.

## Developing competitive advantage

A fundamental part of defining strategy is to develop one or more sources of competitive advantage. The concept of sustainable competitive advantage also means that, to avoid imitation or erosion of its position, organisations must continuously improve the way they conduct their business.

Davidson (1997) suggests that there are a variety of sources of competitive advantage. An organisation, he argues, can develop advantage based on just one large, or a number of smaller, advantages. Basically, for him it is simply being better in some way than the competitors. This is a practical approach and takes into account the realities of business. The sources he identifies are:

- **Superior product** – where the product is objectively and measurably better than competitors' offerings; the idea of the best in class. Rolls-Royce has entered the English language as a term for best in class. This is becoming more difficult to achieve in many industries as competitors can imitate quickly.

- **Perceived advantage** – where the position and image of the product result in the customer perceiving that the product is better than the competitors'. For example, there may not be much to separate a BMW from a Mercedes from an Audi from a Volvo. However, a sample of customers would probably reveal perceived differences and preferences.

- **Global skills** – encompass the R&D, production, distribution and marketing skills of an organisation. The car industry, for example, is now a global industry in which different models of cars within one firm are developed, produced and marketed in different countries.

- **Low cost operator** – sets out to achieve the lowest possible costs throughout the development, production, distribution and marketing process. As such, it forms the basis of Porter's strategy of cost leadership. easyJet and Ryanair are examples of low cost operators in the airline industry.

- **Superior competencies** – encompass the processes and capabilities of the organisation, as discussed in Session 3. 3M provides a good example of an organisation with a superior innovation process that yields advantages.

- **Superior assets** – are the physical and intangible resources of the organisation such as capital, equipment and brands. For example, high street banks like Lloyds TSB and HSBC have a network of branches that would be extremely costly for competitors to imitate, so yield competitive advantage.

- **Scale advantages** – allow organisations to amortise their fixed costs over a higher level of activity, yielding economies of scale. This is reflected in the comparative returns on investment discovered in the PIMS research. For example, Unilever and P&G have scale advantages in the soap and detergents markets that allow them to advertise more heavily than smaller competitors.

- **Attitude advantages** – attitudes reflect the culture and ability to act decisively in areas such as innovation, investment, response to competitive threats and long-term development of the market. Shell's attitude to markets is that it should always be number one or two.

- **Legal advantages** – gained by use of patents and protection of copyright. For example, the pharmaceutical industry makes heavy use of patents to protect their products and so recover development costs.

- **Superior relationships** – encompass all forms of relationships with customers, distributors, competitors and suppliers and allow organisations to achieve with others what they cannot do on their own. They are used to share expertise, knowledge and risk. For example, Disney and Coca-Cola have recently formed an alliance to market a new soft drink exploiting Coca-Cola's drinks expertise and Disney's marketing strength.

For Davidson, future competitive advantage lies in developing efficiencies in operations, superior competencies and relationships. This reflects the pressures on organisations today. The ability to consider the wider skills of the organisation as sources of competitive advantage is essential to its long-term future.

---

**Activity 10.1**

What is the nature and importance of competitive advantage for your organisation? In other words, why should a consumer buy from you?

What are the sources of its competitive advantage?

What other sources might it be able to develop or exploit?

---

## Achieving competitive advantage – generic strategies

In developing his theories on competitive advantages, Porter (1980) identified three primary sources of competitive advantage and generic strategies used to compete. These are:

- **Cost leadership** – competing from a low cost position on a broad front.

- **Differentiation** – competing on perceived uniqueness, again on a broad front.

- **Focus or niche** – competing on a narrow front in one or more specific segments on the basis of either low cost or perceived uniqueness.

The aim of **cost leadership** is to develop competitive advantage by being the lowest cost producer in the industry. This ensures a continual focus on cost reduction and efficient production methods. Usually only the largest companies in an industry can use this strategy since they have economies of scale. Other factors that can contribute to cost leaderships are:

- Global sourcing of raw materials and products – e.g. manufacture in a lower cost country. This is currently employed by Marks & Spencer and also by the UK High Street banks where back office work is conducted outside the UK.

- Use of technology and intensity of capital investment.

- Lean production methods.

The low cost producer does not necessarily set the lowest price in an industry. Its competitive advantage comes from being operationally more efficient so that its profits are higher. For example, British Airways in the 1990s had one of the lowest cost bases in the industry, yet commanded high prices with its strongly differentiated service ('The world's favourite airline').

**Differentiation** is where an organisation seeks to offer something that is perceived as unique or better than competitive offers. This can come in many forms, from service to quality, and relates to the sources of competitive advantage. If a product is seen to offer superior benefits, then premium price can be charged. An offer is differentiated when it delivers augmented benefits beyond the customers' core and expected benefits. For example the cosmetics industry has a wide range of prices of lipstick, but those that are seen to last longer and to be creamier are more expensive.

**Focus** is a more specific concentration on one or more small targets or 'niche' markets. Here the organisation seeks to specialise and concentrate specifically. The focus can be on the geographic area, a specific customer need or segment, or a specific technology. Organisations famous for their focus strategies include many of the luxury brands such as Rolex watches, Ferrari cars and Armani designer clothes.

Porter was extremely clear that a choice must be made between these strategies to avoid becoming 'stuck in the middle'. He was also clear that the resources and capabilities of an organisation needed to implement one of these strategies makes it difficult for an organisation to switch easily from one of these generic strategies to another.

This has been challenged because, such is the speed of change in many markets today and the ability of competitors to respond, it is very difficult for an organisation to be a 'pure' differentiator or cost leader. Many organisations today are equally concerned with cost reduction even if they are attempting to follow the differentiation strategy. This challenge does not reduce the validity of the strategies as viable options but serves to highlight the complexities of the competitive world in which organisations operate.

---

**Activity 10.2**

A venture capital company aims to turn around the fortunes of a car manufacturer in decline by following a focus or niche strategy and concentrating on the production of specialist sports cars.

What are the benefits of a niche strategy to this company and in which circumstances is it likely to be most effective?

---

## Achieving competitive advantage – alternative directions

Porter's generic strategies deal with the scope of an organisation's competitive activities, whether on a broad or narrow front, and the basis of competition, whether low cost or perceived uniqueness. Within this, there are alternative directions for growth that an organisation can take. These were broadly defined by Ansoff in his product market matrix.

The potential of the organisation to develop and grow is determined by its choice of markets or customers (existing or new) and of products (existing or new). This gives four quadrants and four possible directions for a business.

- **Market penetration** – this is where an organisation continues to offer its current products to existing markets with the aim of maintaining or increasing share. It may also include acquiring more customers like the ones it is already serving. In addition to developing its position it can also protect what it has achieved through consolidation, or withdraw, allowing it to concentrate on other markets elsewhere.

- **Market development** – this is where an organisation offers existing products to new markets with the aim of increasing a product's penetration of the market. This includes the exploitation of new channels to market.

- **Product development** – this is where an organisation develops new products or services for existing customers with the aim of obtaining a larger share of customers' expenditures.

- **Diversification** – this can take one of two forms. Related diversification is where a company develops a new product for a new market, but still within the confines of the industry or based on its existing resources or capabilities. Unrelated diversification is where it opts for a new product and new markets, outside the confines of the industry or based on new resources or capabilities.

Results are achieved most quickly by market penetration activities, most slowly through diversification. Risks increase as the organisation seeks growth and development through market development and product development, reaching a peak in diversification.

## Achieving competitive advantage – alternative methods

Not only does the organisation have choices on how to compete (its generic strategy) and which direction to take (Ansoff), it also has a choice of how to develop, referred to by Johnson & Scholes as 'methods of development'.

These are simply:

- **Internal development** – where the organisation chooses to implement its strategy by building up its own resources and capabilities. This is a first choice for many organisations but can take a long time to achieve.

- **Joint development** – where an organisation chooses to share resources with one or more other organisations to achieve specific goals. A range of informal and formal arrangements, such as partnerships and alliances, are used to share the costs and benefits of development, production, distribution, and marketing. This is a good way for an organisation to gain access to specific capabilities or resources at an affordable cost but success will be determined by the ability of the parties to co-operate.

- **Acquisition and merger** – where an organisation develops its resources and capabilities by acquiring or merging with another organisation that already possesses those resources or capabilities. This method has the advantage of providing faster access to the capabilities needed, but can be expensive and issues over post-contract integration make it risky.

Most organisations today are lean and do not carry resources and capabilities beyond those that they need from day-to-day. They are having to consider joint development as a method to achieve development, so alliances are becoming increasingly common.

**Activity 10.3**

A major bank is considering a strategic partnership with a mobile phone operator to provide customers with a package that offers home banking, bill paying and smart cards.

Discuss the bank's motivation for such a move and assess the issues that are likely to be critical to a successful alliance.

## Offensive and defensive strategies

The word 'strategy' comes from a Greek word meaning general. It is not surprising therefore that military analogies are used in the world of business and marketing. A number of strategies are derived from the military approaches developed over centuries. Simply put, an armed force can attack or it can defend. An organisation can attempt to increase market share (or attack) or to hold existing share (or defend).

## Strategies for attack

- **Frontal attack** – direct head-to-head competition. Since it can be expensive in resources and a long process, the attacker has to be certain that it can sustain losses and survive. The attacker must offer a clearly defined advantage to make the attack credible. Walmart's purchase of Asda could be seen as a frontal attack on the UK supermarket sector.

- **Flank attack** – attack on a competitor's weakest spot, such as an undefended segment or an aging product. Airbus has used this strategy effectively to attack Boeing's dominance of the large airliner segment (747 jumbo jet) with its new A380 aircraft.

- **Encirclement** – surrounding an opponent with attacking its main position. The idea is to compete on a number of different aspects, such as cost and distribution channels, or to offer a range of different products with specific attributes. Airbus has gradually been encircling Boeing with the progressive development of different models of civil aircraft.

- **Bypass attack** – where the attacker moves into areas not covered by the opponent. Direct Line is a classic example of an organisation penetrating an existing market by exploiting technology to develop a new and direct channel.

- **Guerrilla attack** – typified as a 'hit and run' attack and usually short term. In marketing, a series of tactical, short term measures such as price cuts and promotions to deflect a competitor.

## Strategies for defence

- **Position defence** – aims to build such a significant and sustainable competitive advantage that it is very difficult for an opponent to compete. Unilever and P&G use positional defence against other competitors, exploiting brand management, advertising and access to distribution to shut out competition.

- **Flank defence** – protects all of the business activities especially those seen as weaker or more vulnerable aspects. Tesco introduced its 'Value' range to defend against attack from the low cost supermarkets.

- **Pre-emptive defence** – attacking an opponent before it attacks. Market leaders may signal price cuts to deter competitors from attacking. Boeing announced enhancements to its 747 jumbo jet to deter Airbus, but it failed when customers responded unfavourably.

- **Counter-offensive** – responding when attacked. This is usually launched to reinforce a position defence, either immediately or when the attacker has expended some energy and resources and is therefore more vulnerable. British Airways and some of the other national flag carriers launched their own low cost brands in response to attack by low cost airlines.

- **Mobile defence** – switching to new areas of interest depending on the opportunities and threats at the time. In the late 1980s and early 1990s insurance companies in the UK bought independent estate agents to secure access to new business through this channel.

- **Contraction or withdrawal** – withdrawing from selected markets, retrenching into core business. The aim is to release resources to use elsewhere. For example, mobile phone companies no longer produce handsets.

## Strategies for position in a market

In the previous sections of this Session, we have described the various strategies available to organisations to develop competitive advantage. The key to success for any organisation is to select a strategy that is appropriate for the specific circumstances in which it finds itself. In this section, we therefore look at the range of strategies available to organisations operating in different positions within a specific market.

# Strategies for market leaders

Clearly we need to be careful where we draw the boundaries around a market when identifying the market leader. Market leadership is usually defined by market share but may also be defined in terms of technological leadership.

Holding the pre-eminent position in a market, the leader has both a strong position from which to develop further attacks and much to lose to determined competitors. A market leader can also attempt to consolidate the market by reducing the number of competitors and to expand the size of the market by encouraging increased usage or attracting new users.

If a market leader chooses to attack other competitors, it is likely to have the resources and strength to launch a frontal attack. However, in certain markets this may leave it vulnerable to attack from other competitors who may perceive the leader to be off guard.

Defence strategies available to the market leader are usually:

- **Position defence** – using its substantial resources to deter attack and defend its dominant position.

- **Flanking defence** – using price subsidies on weaker products to ensure a competitor cannot launch a successful attack against them.

- **Mobile defence** – switching to new activities as circumstances dictate.

- **Pre-emptive defence** – signalling significant retaliation in the event of attack by warning of price reductions.

- **Counter-offence** – being prepared to respond if attacked.

- **Withdrawal** – not usually considered in the early stages of attack but, if prolonged and highly damaging, ultimately an option.

# Strategies for market challengers

Market challengers are those competitors with the capability or intention to attack and displace the market leader. Throughout the 1980s Tesco challenged Sainsbury as market leader in the supermarkets sector, finally achieving leadership, which it has held since, in the mid 1990s.

Challengers will therefore adopt an aggressive posture. They may choose to attack the leader directly or to build their position by selectively attacking weaker competitors. The attack strategies they may adopt to undertake either of these objectives are:

- **Frontal attack** – perhaps on the market leader but more likely to be on weaker competitors.

- **Flank attack** – probing for and working on weaknesses in any competitor's armoury.

- **Encirclement attack** – gradually surrounding the market leader with a range of specific products of services and avoiding direct competition.

- **Bypass attack** – moving into those areas not occupied by the market leader and gradually building position there.

- **Guerrilla attack** – a quick attack carried out with maximum surprise, followed by withdrawal to avoid a punishing counter-attack.

## Strategies for market followers

Market followers lack the resources or intent to lead the market or challenge the leader. Usually third or lower in the market, followers tend to avoid any action that will invite counter-attack by the leader or a challenger and will usually offer similar products as the leader. In industries with high product development costs and risks, followers can be second to market having allowed the leader to make any mistakes and make the necessary investment in creating awareness.

Followers are unlikely to attack. Strategies available to them can be characterised as follows:

- **Follow closely** – mimicking the offer of the market leader in every detail, subject to patent and other legal protection available to the leader.

- **Follow at a distance** – using the idea but not the specific form of the leader's offerings, possibly providing additional features to differentiate them.

- **Follow selectively** – choosing which of the leader's products to compete against.

## Strategies for market nichers

A niche player operates in one or more specific segments where it seeks to satisfy the needs of specific target groups.

The niche player will specialise or segment:

- Geographically.

- By type of end-user.

- By product or product line.
- On quality/price spectrum.
- By service.
- By size of customer.
- By product feature.

The main danger for a niche player is that it attracts larger players which have more resources.

## Strategies for specific market conditions

Building on the concept introduced in the previous section of specific strategies for specific circumstances, we look now at the strategies available to organisations facing specific market conditions. These are declining and hostile markets and wear-out.

## Strategies for declining and hostile markets

The market conditions in which organisations operate are often hostile. While markets are growing, hostility is likely to be low as there is enough demand for all. Hostility arises when the market is static or declining and there is excess of supply over demand, declining profits and intense competitive activity.

The change in market conditions will arise for a number of reasons, which are derived from the external environment, for example technology and government policy. The responses available to organisations, summarised by Aaker (1998), are:

- **Generating growth** – the first reaction is to stimulate or find pockets of growth in the declining market. Ansoff's matrix illustrates the options available to breathe new life into the market. Market penetration – promoting increased usage. Product development – developing new products such DVD players to replace 'old' cassette players. Market development – finding new uses such as Lucozade, which is now a sport drink, or using the Internet to reach new customers.
- **Cutting costs** – by reducing fixed costs of operating, it may be possible to remain in the market using its 'cash cows'. This is the point at which an industry undergoes rationalisation, the result being fewer, larger competitors.

- **Withdrawal** – when all else fails, the only choice left is to withdraw from the market. There may be costs involved but these may be lower than remaining in the market. It may also be possible to recoup some of the investment by selling off products or licenses. The main challenge in executing an exit strategy is to maintain the confidence of stakeholders such as customers, bankers, shareholders and suppliers.

## Strategies for wear-out and renewal

The ability of the organisation to ensure that its strategy fits with the ever-changing environment is a key task if the organisation is to be successful. Scanning the environment is a key to success. However, once a strategy is no longer appropriate because customers or competitors have moved forward, then the strategy could be said to have 'worn out'.

Davidson (1997) suggests that this occurs because of changes in customers' needs, distribution changes, competitors launching new products and becoming more efficient, poor cost control and lack of investment.

Wear-out is often a sign of failure. Once a strategy has become worn-out, it is too late. So the emphasis has to be on prevention rather than cure. Steps the organisation can take to avoid wear-out include:

- **Adopting or maintaining a market orientation** – making sure the organisation has a culture of monitoring customers' needs as they change, developing offers that satisfy those needs and delivering satisfaction and loyalty.

- **Environmental scanning** – allocating resources to detect and recognise significant changes in the market and competitive environment.

- **Tight financial management** – keeping costs under control and measuring the effectiveness of activities.

- **Sustained and focused investment** – making sure investment is maintained in those products and activities that will lead to profitable customer satisfaction.

- **Strategic planning processes** – using a sound process for determining an appropriate balance between the capabilities of the organisation and the needs of its environment.

**Activity 10.4**

Your Managing Director has asked you to write a report on the dangers and causes of strategic wear-out.

In particular, your report should identify ways in which this danger can be avoided.

## Strategic choice

With so many strategies to choose from, making a strategic choice is a challenging part of the strategic process. An organisation will usually have more than one strategy from which to choose and each option should therefore be examined from a number of perspectives.

For Johnson and Scholes (1999), these are:

- **Acceptability** – how acceptable the likely outcomes from the option are likely to be to stakeholders.

- **Suitability** – how well the option fits the organisation's intentions, capabilities and circumstances.

- **Feasibility** – how feasible it is to achieve the desired objectives, given the various resources and constraints.

This is a useful starting point as it suggests that the strategy needs to address the ability of the organisation to build on its strengths and overcome weaknesses while focusing on the external issues. It also needs to be acceptable to all stakeholders and not alienate, for example, some customer groups by repositioning.

These can be developed into more specific terms and expressed as financial and non-financial criteria.

Firstly, financial criteria will include the usual performance indicators such as market share, profitability, liquidity, current and acid ratios, to name but a few. This suggests that the underlying objective is monetary, which follows logically from the overall corporate objectives. The costs of a strategy in terms of investment in capital equipment, staff training and marketing need to be balanced by the long-term potential. However, this is only part of the story and needs to develop to examine the broader issues of fit with the core capabilities of the organisation.

The impact of the strategies on the brand should be examined. For example, if a new product is being introduced the ability to stretch or extend the brand should be considered. The choice made by Volkswagen in buying Skoda clearly illustrated that it can be difficult to bring together two disparate brands and showed how it can be successfully completed. The likelihood of provoking a hostile response from the competitors should be considered. The balance of the portfolio to ensure the long-term growth of the organisation is a key issue.

A second approach to choosing between options is to use 'screening'. Screening is the use of a decision filter such as a portfolio model, e.g. the Shell directional policy matrix or GE screen. Dimensions such as 'option attractiveness' and 'competitive position' are used, with criteria specified for each dimension. By scoring and weighting each option, its relative attractiveness and competitiveness can be plotted on the matrix, in the same way as the elements of a portfolio are plotted during the analysis process. A choice can then be made of the strategy that is both most attractive and yields the strongest competitive position for the organisation.

Strategic choice contributes to the financial health of the organisation and ensures the closest possible match between the core capabilities of the organisation and the circumstances of its environment. The challenge is to evaluate each strategy fully and objectively.

# Case Study – Xbox

In May 2001 it was announced that Microsoft, a company with vast resources, planned to enter the games hardware market in November 2001 with its new Xbox games console. Priced at $299, each console contains a hard disk, DVD drive and Internet connection. Microsoft believes that the introduction of broadband technology will change the nature of the game market. In particular, individuals who play games with each other over an Internet connection will be able to talk directly to each other rather than typing messages to each other. In order to facilitate online gaming, Microsoft has formed an alliance with the Japanese Internet and Telecommunications Company, NTT Communications.

Microsoft aims to have 15-20 games titles available by the time Xbox is launched; also all the major software programming houses such as Sega and Electronic Arts have agreed to produce games for their console. The company aims to sell between 1-1.5 million units over the Christmas period.

Sony launched the PlayStation 2 last year and by May 2001 had already achieved sales of 9 million units and plans to sell another 20 million units by the end of the year. At the time of its launch 33 games were available and a further 63 have come on-stream since. The console can also operate many of the games originally designed for the first PlayStation console, so that individuals can upgrade to the new console without having to replace all their games software.

In response to the impending increase in competition Sony has taken several initiatives. It has formed an alliance with America Online (AOL) to enable fast Internet access through its games console. It has also linked up with the software company RealNetworks to allow its software product RealPlayer 8 to be installed on the PlayStation 2 to allow access to video on the Internet. A Netscape browser for the console is also under development along with other developments such as a hard disk drive, LCD display, keyboard and mouse. PlayStation 2 will be able to offer instant messaging, chat and email.

Nintendo plans to launch its GameCube in the United States on 5th November, 3 days before Microsoft introduces its Xbox console. The GameCube will have wireless control and is aimed at a slightly younger market. The GameCube console will not have the ability to play CDs or DVDs. However, Nintendo is also a software producer and has a reputation for providing some of the best games on the market and will be able to offer popular games such as Super Mario Brothers and Pokémon with the new console. It is currently assumed that it will be slower than Xbox but will be priced at $199.95, which may be attractive to many parents.

At the beginning of 2001 Sega, which makes the Dreamcast console, announced that it was ending production of games hardware and concentrating its activities on creating software products for this market. The Dreamcast console offered online gaming.

The world console market is estimated to be worth $20 billion a year. Microsoft plans to spend $500 million on promotion in the first year alone. It is estimated that Sony has spent $750 million promoting the launch of the PlayStation 2.

The games console market has some interesting dynamics. When Sony launched the PlayStation, as a financially strong consumer goods company it was able and prepared to discount prices in order to buy market share. The company lost money on every machine it sold but gained the largest share of the market. However, through licensing deals with the software houses it made money on every game sold and created large profits for Sony. The games companies were also content because they were making strong profits from a games market that was expanding due to lower priced consoles.

With the arrival of a new competitor to this market and three new product offerings, the outcome in this market over the next few years is far from certain.

**Source:** SMM Planning & Control Examination Paper, December 2001.

---

**Questions**

1. Any development in the games hardware market will have a major impact on the software companies. Therefore, as a contingency planning exercise, an independent games software company has asked you to evaluate the appropriateness of the actions Sony has taken, over the last 12 months, to defend its leadership of the games hardware market.

2. The software company has also asked you to write a report outlining what actions Microsoft will need to undertake to be a successful challenger in this market.

---

## SUMMARY OF KEY POINTS

In this Session, we have introduced strategies to develop competitive advantage and covered the following key points:

■ Competitive advantage is a position that an organisation achieves relative to its competitors by using the resources and capabilities available to it. To be sustainable, it should not be susceptible to being eroded by imitation by competitors or changes in the environment.

■ Sustainable competitive advantage can come from one large, or a number of smaller, advantages. Davidson lists ten sources that are important.

■ A range of development strategies is then available for organisations to develop and achieve competitive advantage. They include: generic strategies, alternative directions and alternative methods.

- Another range of strategies is available for specific purposes (such as attack and defence), for specific market positions (leaders, challengers, followers and niche players) and for specific situations (hostile markets and wear-out).

- Choice is a key part of the strategic planning process, based on assessment of suitability, feasibility and acceptability. The use of portfolio models in screening options is a valuable technique in selecting the most appropriate strategy.

## Improving and developing own learning

The following projects are designed to help you develop your knowledge and skills further by carrying out some research yourself. Feedback is not provided for this type of learning because there are no 'answers' to be found, but you may wish to discuss your findings with colleagues and fellow students.

### Project A

What are the sources of advantage of your organisation or one that you know well?

Try to be objective. Ask someone outside the organisation if they agree with your analysis.

Does the organisation's competitive advantage consist of one large single advantage or a number of smaller advantages? How could it increase its competitive advantage?

**Project B**

Investigate the strategies used by your own organisation or one that you know well.

Which generic strategy is it using?

Which direction(s)?

Which method(s)?

Is it using any of the strategies for specific positions or situations?

If possible, try to establish why and how these strategies were adopted.

**Project C**

Write short notes explaining how a major confectionery manufacturer might as market leader:

1. Establish a position defence.

2. Launch an encirclement attack on a challenger.

3. Conduct a pre-emptive defence against a major international player.

## Feedback to activities

### Activity 10.1

You should have been able to identify the nature of your organisation's competitive advantage. It may be a single large advantage or, more likely in today's markets, a number of smaller advantages that add up to a significant advantage. You may have considered the following sources:

■ Superior product or service.

■ Perceived advantage.

■ Global skills.

- Low-cost operator.
- Superior competencies.
- Superior assets.
- Scale advantages.
- Attitude advantages.
- Legal advantages.
- Superior relationships.

## Activity 10.2

Niche or focus strategy is one of Porter's three generic strategies where an organisation concentrates on a narrow market. This has a number of benefits for an organisation:

- Suited to organisations with limited resources.
- Reduces competition from large players that may deem the market too small to enter.
- It is possible to customise and use customised marketing approaches.
- Customers often pay premium prices to gain access to these specialised products.

This was Question 5 on the Planning & Control examination paper in December 2000. You can find a full specimen answer on the CIM student web site.

## Activity 10.3

The motivation is likely to be to maintain or develop competitive advantage. Organisations do not have the resources or goals to do everything themselves so alliances are a natural and increasingly common way to leverage additional resources and competitive advantage. In this example, the bank can broaden its product range and improve service, probably at a relatively low cost.

This was Question 6 on the Planning & Control examination paper in June 2000. You can find a full specimen answer on the CIM student web site.

## Activity 10.4

Strategic wear-out occurs when an organisation no longer satisfies customers' needs. It is usually gradual but may be sudden, caused by factors such as:

- Changes in customer requirements.

- Changes in distribution channels.

- Innovation by competitors.

- Lack of investment.

- Poor control.

There are a number of ways that this can be avoided. They boil down to effective monitoring of the external environment and review of activities that the organisation is undertaking.

This was Question 7 on the Planning & Control examination paper in December 1999. You can find a full specimen answer on the CIM student web site.

# Session 11

# Developing a specific competitive position

## Introduction

The previous Session explored the various approaches available to an organisation for creating strategic advantage, involving choices of strategy, direction and method. In this Session we move to examine how an organisation can now develop a specific position in the market using techniques of segmentation, targeting, positioning and branding. This Session defines the terms, describes the process and introduces the techniques involved in each of these steps in developing a specific competitive position.

---

## LEARNING OUTCOMES

At the end of this Session you will be able to:

- Define segmentation and outline the purpose of, and stages in, the segmentation, targeting and positioning process.

- Identify criteria for effective segmentation and use various bases for segmenting consumer and industrial markets.

- Select appropriate segments to target.

- Use positioning techniques to recommend appropriate position(s) to adopt in chosen segments.

- Create a distinctive identity for a product or service that is consistent with targeting and positioning decisions.

- Synthesise a brand policy across all the products and services of an organisation.

---

## The concept of segmentation

The development of Western markets in the 1960s and 1970s was typified by mass production and volume sales. By the 1990s, supply exceeded demand in most markets and consumers were searching for a greater sense of individualism and identity. Customers today are demanding, discriminating and less willing to settle for a mass-produced standard item, whether in consumer or industrial markets. Many are searching for something special or different, something that emphasises the buyer's sense of being an individual. The increase in competition due to globalisation and changes in people's lifestyles are two of the factors contributing to the fragmentation of markets.

This all means that market offerings need to provide their prospective customers a diverse choice. Most organisations now realise that segmentation is essential for their marketing strategy and 'customised marketing' is replacing 'mass marketing' as the way to do business in the 21st century. Segments are getting smaller and smaller – for example Tesco have segments of just two consumers – highlighting the trend toward mass customisation.

## Segmentation, targeting and positioning

At a fundamental level, marketing strategy is about markets and products. Organisations make decisions primarily about which markets to operate in and which products/services to offer to those markets. With those essential decisions made, the organisation has to decide on the position from which to compete in that chosen market. Segmentation is therefore at the heart of strategic marketing decision making.

Kotler et al (1999) define market **segmentation** as:

"Dividing a market up into distinct groups of buyers with different needs, characteristics or behaviours, who might require separate products or marketing mixes."

Segmentation can be beneficial to organisations for a number of reasons:

- **To meet customers' needs more precisely**. Segmentation should increase benefits to the consumers by providing a closer match with their needs. An organisation can gain deeper market and customer knowledge so that the market offering is tailored to the selected segment.

- **To increase profits.** By grouping customers based on their needs, organisations can obtain the best price for their products and services.

- **To gain segment leadership.** Most organisations are concerned with creating a specific competitive position and the leader's position confers benefits in the form of higher profits and ROI. Focus on a specific segment can also avoid competition with larger players.

- **To retain customers.** By providing specific products and services focused on specific needs, an organisation is more likely to foster the loyalty of customers.

- **To focus marketing communications.** Segmentation enables a firm to identify those most likely to buy and therefore avoid waste in terms of communications and promotional effort.

Once the organisation has identified prospective segments, it is then necessary to evaluate them and decide which ones it will serve or target. Kotler et al (1999) define **targeting** as:

"The process of evaluating each market segment's attractiveness and selecting one or more segments to enter."

Targeting involves evaluating market opportunities against their strategic fit with the organisation. Do they align to the organisation's competencies and assets and is there a synergy with a particular market segment?

Once target markets have been chosen, an organisation then has to decide the position from which it will compete. Kotler (1999) defines positioning as:

"Arranging for a product to occupy a clear, distinctive and desirable place relative to competing products in the minds of target consumers. Formulating competitive positioning for a product and a detailed marketing mix."

In short Segmentation, Targeting and Positioning (STP) encompasses the decisions made by organisations to develop a specific competitive position:

- How do we define the market?

- How is the market segmented into different customer groups?

- How attractive are the alternative market segments?

- How strong a competitive position could we take based on our current and potential strengths?

The process we can use for STP is as follows:

1. Identify the segmentation variables and segment the markets.
2. Develop profiles of each segment.
3. Evaluate the potential and attractiveness of each segment.
4. Select the target segment(s).

5.     Identify the positioning concept within each target segment.
6.     Select and develop the appropriate positioning concepts.
7.     If appropriate, develop branding concept and strategy.
8.     Develop the marketing mix.

## Customer behaviour and segmentation variables

Successful segmentation relies on a clear understanding of the market and customers' buying behaviours. This holds true whether the customers are consumers or buyers in a business, industrial or organisational context.

Segmentation involves identifying and grouping customers with similar needs. We are trying to define segments within which customers:

- Will respond in a **similar** way to a particular offer.

- Will respond in a **different** way to the particular offer from other groups of customers.

- Constitute a group large enough to generate an acceptable ROI for the organisation.

- Are identifiable and accessible at an operational level.

## Consumer segmentation

Consumer buyer behaviour relates to the **end customer**; those individuals who purchase products and services for personal consumption. There are many influences on consumer behaviour: social, personal, psychological and situational.

- Social influences – behaviour is largely learned so the traditions, values and attitudes of the society in which individuals are brought up will influence their behaviour. **Cultural norms** form the codes that direct behaviour – what might be quite acceptable in some cultures will be totally unacceptable in others, e.g. eating in the street or pictures of a couple kissing in an advertisement. Research proves that **social class** is also another important influence on consumer behaviour with individuals in lower social groups generally being seen to be more culture-bound. However, there can be wide discrepancies in purchasing patterns within social groups so this demographic information is only part of the picture. **Family** or **reference groups** also play a large part in an individual's attitude or behaviour. For example, it appears that a high percentage of people tend to use the same washing powder and toothpaste as the household in which they grew up.

- **Personal influences** – personal attributes will influence purchasing behaviour. **Age, occupation, financial situation, family life cycle stage** and their **lifestyle** in general are all factors that affect the pattern of an individual's purchase and consumption decisions.

- **Psychological influences** – factors such as **motivation, perception, learning, attitudes** and **beliefs** will all affect the way people decide on their purchases. This type of psychographic information, along with the demographic data (gender, age, socio-economic grouping, occupation, income etc.) gives the marketer a more rounded picture of the customer and the tools, at least in theory, to segment even more closely to the needs of consumers in that group.

- **Situational influences** – **situations** also influence how or what a consumer buys. High involvement purchases require a lengthy search for information and evaluation. Spontaneous purchases may have minimal involvement and may need to be ubiquitous and always available, adhering to the Coca-Cola advertising adage of 'being at an arm's length from desire'.

These influences on consumer behaviour yield a range of segmentation variables, or bases for segmentation, that can be used in these markets. They are:

- **Profile variables** – these are variables in the way that individuals live their lives. The main attraction to the marketer is that they are tangible.

  - **Demographic** variables include measurable or quantitative data on age, gender and family life cycle.

  - **Socio-economic** variables include data on individuals' occupations, education and income.

  - **Geographic** variables include data on consumers' location and geo-demographics (the demographics and socio-economic data on a particular area).

- **Behavioural variables** – these are variables in the way that consumers behave when buying or using the product.

  - **Benefits** sought are the reasons why an individual purchases the product.

  - **Usage** is how the consumer consumes or uses the product.

  - **Purchase occasion** is the type of occasion on which a purchase is made.

- **Psychographic variables** – these are variables in the attitudes, interests, personality and lifestyle characteristics that might reflect in buying behaviours and choices. The frameworks used (AIO, VALS and Monitor) are research-based and, while broader than single profile or behavioural variables, are culturally biased.

## Segmentation in business markets

Although segmentation was developed and used originally in consumer markets, it is now widely recognised as valuable in industrial, organisational and business markets. Organisational buyers, like consumers, rarely buy on price alone and are constantly seeking added value for their organisations. The essential differences in behaviour from consumer markets are as follows:

- Organisations often appoint a buying team with specific roles rather than relying on an individual. This is known as the decision making unit. (You should already be familiar with the roles within the DMU covered in Session 6 so it is not covered again here.

- The buying process is usually more formal and structured and buyer behaviour usually has higher involvement and is more rational and considered.

- Approaches to segmentation tend to be based on the characteristics of organisations, not individuals.


A range of segmentation variables, or bases for segmentation, can be used in business markets. They are:

- **Demographic variables** – these are variables in the way that organisations operate or are located. These variables are also referred to as 'macro-segmentation' variables.

  - Industry sector.
  - Organisation size, as an indicator of volume and type of needs and ability to pay.
  - Location.
  - End-use application or technology.

- **Decision making variables** – these are variables in the make-up and operation of the decision making unit. These variables are also referred to as 'micro segmentation' variables.

  - Structure of the DMU.

  - Nature of relationship with the seller.

  - The decision making process.

  - Decision making criteria.

  - Structure and policies of the buying function.

  - Personal characteristics of decision makers, including risk profiles.

  - Buy class (new buy, straight re-buy or modified re-buy).

  - Degree of urgency.

  - Attitudes towards innovation.

## Tests of an effective segment

Once we have identified some possible segments, the final step at the segmentation stage is to compile profiles of customers in the main segments. These profiles enable you to test how effective and successful these segments are likely to be. A test might consider the following attributes of each segment:

- **Distinctive** – the segment must have a significant difference from the rest of the marketplace.

- **Tangible** – the marketer must be able to demonstrate some tangible difference.

- **Viable** – the segment should be large enough to be financially viable.

- **Accessible** – the organisation must be able to access the segment through its distribution and communication channels.

- **Defendable** – the organisation must be able to specialise in an area and develop a competitive differential.

---

**Activity 11.1**

Evaluate how a company of your choice segments in a consumer market and choose another company to evaluate in an industrial market.

---

# Selecting target segments

Once potentially successful segments have been identified, the next step is to evaluate the different segments to see which segments the organisation should target.

This is the critical stage in the segmentation process at which we match the capabilities of the organisation to the opportunities available in the various segments. The 'targeting' decision should be based on a systematic review of:

- Attractiveness of the competing segments – this will be based on criteria such as the potential to create a sustainable marketing position, the ability to satisfy the segment with current resources and structures, the 'fit' with the corporate mission, and consistency with organisational culture. Will there need to be a change in structure to service the market effectively?

- Competitive capabilities – this it the organisation's comparative ability competitively to address the needs of that segment. It should always be judged relative to the competition. It will be based on an assessment of criteria such as brand awareness, communications effectiveness, product quality, relative production costs, access to distribution, levels of innovation and expertise in product development.

As introduced in the previous Session, a valuable tool to help in making choice decisions is one of the 3x3 portfolio model such as the GE matrix or the Shell directional policy matrix.

Targeting the segment allows attractive segments to be identified and marketing mix strategy to be developed.

- **Undifferentiated marketing** is used by organisations who standardise their marketing mix and target the whole market, thus assuming that customers are "typical". This can allow other organisations to take advantage of potentially less price-sensitive niche markets.

- **Differentiated marketing** is when the organisation identifies various attractive markets and tailors the marketing mixes according the requirements and needs of each segment.

- **Focus** or **niche marketing** is when an organisation disregards much of the standardised marketplace and focuses on one specific segment by developing expertise and tailoring their marketing mix accordingly.

**Activity 11.2**

Within your own organisation, or an organisation of your choice, analyse which market segment has been targeted and identify the company's rationale behind their decision.

What are their core competencies and assets in regards to the competition?

# Positioning

Positioning is not about what you do to a product but what you do to the mind of the prospective customer. It follows that you should position products in the minds of the prospective customer. With customers inundated with over 2,500 advertising messages every day, the key issue for the organisation is how to combine its assets and competencies to create a distinctive offering to the customer. This is where positioning comes in.

Customers will, if left to their own devices, position a product in their mind relative to other products in the market. They base this on their perception of its key attributes. However, this could be a very dangerous situation which may result in confused positioning or that the position is out of line with the corporate or marketing strategy. An equally dangerous situation is when an organisation is 'pushed' into a position by its competitors. So, the organisation should be in control of positioning.

Positioning decisions are made once segments have been identified and target segments selected. The process of strategically positioning the products of an organisation involves the following steps:

- Selecting a strategic market position that is credible to the customers to pursue over the long term. This can be shown on a perceptual map – a two (or more) dimensional illustration of the position to be adopted, expressed in terms that matter to the target customer.

- Implementing the positioning strategy through products to support the position and branding policy.

- Communicating the position to the marketplace in such a way that it successfully differentiates the product in the mind of the customer.

Here are examples of the associations used by some household names to position their products.

- Volvo has traditionally positioned its cars on product benefits such as safety and durability. More recently, campaigns have attempted to reposition the cars on luxury and high performance.

- Skoda has successfully managed to shrug off its low quality image with the backing of VW and has won many quality awards to reinforce its new quality position in the marketplace. The car industry in general tends to use product benefits as their position statement.

- Heinz positions its products on the attributes of no artificial colouring, flavouring or preservatives. This is by-product attribution.

- Kit-Kat (the chocolate snack bar) is positioned by usage occasion.

- Starbucks have targeted by-users – in this instance, ethical consumers – with their 2-year Fairtrade deal with poor Brazilian coffee producers.

- There are other associations that organisations can use to develop their position: by personality, by origin, by competitor, by symbol and by product class.

These are various methods that can help an organisation sway consumers' perceptions of the product offering but to achieve successful positioning, organisations must be aware of four factors (Jobber 1995):

- **Credibility** – customers must believe that the organisation's position is viable.

- **Competitiveness** – the product must be competitive in all senses and offer the consumer benefits that competitors are not supplying, e.g. the Dyson vacuum cleaner.

- **Clarity** – the positioning statement is straightforward, showing a clearly differentiated position – e.g. Nescafé and their 'Simply the best' campaign.

- **Consistency** – consumers do not like to be confused and therefore the organisation must formulate a long-term position in the marketplace so that there is a consistent perception of the organisation's position.

The emergence of 'customised marketing' as a replacement of 'mass marketing' was introduced earlier in this Session. This approach, where customers are treated as individuals and the marketing mix is tailored to each customer, has been used in business markets for many years but is now being translated into the consumer markets as the trend towards mass customisation develops. The advent of the Internet has allowed many companies such as Amazon.com to customise their presentation and service and so position slightly differently to each individual consumer.

---

**Activity 11.3**

Discuss the following proposition with your colleagues: "Positioning is not what is done to a product but what is done to the mind of the customer".

Using current examples, describe a successful company and an unsuccessful company in terms of their position in their chosen marketplace.

---

# Branding

Branding is an important tool that can be used in developing a specific competitive position. Brand building normally requires a significant amount of investment and reinforcement through the use of marketing communications over a long period. However, there are examples of brands, such as Amazon.com and lastminute.com, that have become established more quickly during the period of rapid growth in e-commerce in recent years. The success of these brands has probably been due to a lack of direct competition in the early period of growth of e-commerce, linked to the effective use of public relations as a tool of marketing communication.

The American Marketing Association defines a brand as:

"A name, term, sign, symbol, or design, or a combination or them, intended to identify the goods or services of one seller or group of sellers and to differentiate them from those of the competition."

Brands are generally used to develop a three dimensional personality in a product that is difficult for the competition to replicate. Successful brand development is reliant on far more than just creating a strong image through the marketing communications mix. A brand consists of both visible (like the symbol and communications) and less visible elements as crucial ingredients in a strong brand. Factors such as providing product quality, continuous product development, innovation and high levels of service are potential components of a successful brand yet are not visible as elements of the communications mix.

# Branding decisions

The overall aim of branding decisions is to create an identity for the product or service that is distinctive and consistent with the targeting and positioning decisions already taken. Organisations should strive to produce a brand equity that delivers value to the consumer. This will result in the customer either showing greater brand loyalty or being willing to pay a premium price for the product.

# Brand equity

Brand equity according to Aaker (1991) is:

"A set of assets and liabilities linked to a brand's name and symbol that add to or subtract from the value provided by a product or service to a firm and/or that firm's customers."

The term 'equity' is used in financial accounting and, given the importance of brands to some organisations, it is not surprising that there are initiatives within the accounting profession and in companies to value brands and show that value in annual reports and accounts. Traditional methods of valuation attempt to quantify future cash flows from an asset and this is the approach being used to value brands. Such a valuation will take into account those factors that affect the magnitude and longevity of cash flows, such as:

- Type of market in which the brand is operating.
- Share of the market.
- Presence in markets other than local or national markets.
- Future appeal of the brand – a brand that will 'tire' over time will have a lower value than one that will remain a market leader.
- Stretch or extension potential.
- Legal or other forms of protection.

# Brand name strategy

An integral part of any product policy is the question of how the organisation's brands are managed. An organisation has to decide its policy for naming brands across all of its products and services. Branding decisions for any new products can then be taken into this framework. In essence, there are four types of brand name strategy that can be pursued:

- **Corporate umbrella branding**, where the company's name is offered to cover the wide range of products and services, e.g. Ford, Kellogg's and Cadbury's.

- **Family umbrella branding** to cover a range of products in a variety of markets. For example Marks & Spencer's use of the St Michael brand which has now been dropped.

- **Range brand names** that link products within a specific market sector, e.g. Mars with Mars bars, a Mars drink and Mars ice cream.

- **Individual brand names** that are used for one type of product in one or more markets, e.g. Snickers, Bisto and Marmite.

## Exploiting brands

There are four principal options open to an organisation to exploit brands. These are:

- **Brand development** – an organisation can build on an existing position to create a distinctive perception of the brand by consumers.

- **Brand extension and brand stretching** – having established the attributes that are most important to the consumer, the organisation can see if there are any unoccupied positions that are desirable in consumers' minds and therefore offer viable opportunities.

  In **brand extension**, an organisation will try to extend the use of the brand name to new products in the same broad market. Brands with high brand equity are especially suitable for brand extension, as they have the ability to increase the attractiveness of the new products, e.g. easyJet has started up a car hire business, which complements its flights.

  In **brand stretching**, an organisation stretches a brand into new unrelated markets, e.g. Virgin who have moved from the record industry to airlines. Another example of brand stretching is given by some of the major supermarkets that have moved into financial services. As long as the original brand values are compatible with the aspirations of the new target group, this policy is likely to be successful.

- **Brand repositioning** – due to changes in factors such as consumer behaviour, or where perhaps there has been a failure of the original positioning, it may be necessary to reposition the brand.

**Repositioning** can be difficult to achieve as customers have already formed perceptions of the brand that first have to be 'unformed'. The successful campaign for Mars bars of 'a Mars a day helps you work, rest and play' has been redundant for many years. In an attempt to attract more female and health-conscious consumers (whose relationship with chocolate is a complex, psychological one we are told), Mars are trying to reposition the bar as a 'healthier option'.

- **Brand revitalisation** – a brand that has become 'tired' in its traditional markets can be stimulated by taking it into new markets or segments, or by increasing product usage.

Kellogg's has in recent years attempted to revitalise Kellogg's Corn flakes. Under pressure from supermarkets' own brand corn flakes and seeing sales declining as consumers no longer sit down to breakfast, Kellogg's attempted to increase usage by appealing to older consumers who used to have corn flakes for breakfast as children but who gave up.

---

**Activity 11.4**

Identify companies who have adopted the different types of brand name strategy. How successful have they been?

---

# Case Study – Freeplay Energy

This case study was used in Session 9 to explore issues in setting mission and objectives. We are using it again here, this time to explore segmentation.

In the early 1980s Trevor Bayliss, the British inventor, developed the concept of a self-powered radio. Electricity for the radio would be provided by an integral wind-up generator. Bayliss's idea was that this self-powered radio would allow people in remote villages across Africa to gain access to news and information from around the world. In 1994 the South African based BayGen Power company (later renamed Freeplay Energy) signed an exclusive agreement with Trevor Bayliss to develop and commercialise the product.

Although Trevor Bayliss no longer has an active involvement with Freeplay Energy, the partners who run the company are still driven by the desire to improve the lives of individuals in the less developed world. The company's Cape Town factories are co-owned by local charities that represent the disabled, single mothers and former offenders. Around one third of the company's employees are from these disadvantaged groups.

The first commercial version of the wind-up radio was the FPR1 and this was distributed to villages by aid agencies. Very early on, it became apparent that the radio was too heavy, too fragile and more crucially too expensive for its intended market. Villagers appeared to be more willing to spend £2 to £3 a month on batteries, than an initial £29 on a radio that did not require battery replacements. The product however, began to develop sales in more affluent markets. In the UK the Design Council awarded the wind-up radio 'Millennium Product' status. One national newspaper went as far as naming it the most significant invention of a generation.

Freeplay Energy began to realise that volume sales could be developed by concentrating on the European and North American markets. Sales growth in these markets has allowed Freeplay to invest further in the technology, and as a result develop products that are smaller, lighter, more durable and less expensive. The FPRI had to be wound for 20 seconds in order to produce 30 minutes of playing time. The FPR2, which Freeplay launched in 1997, weighs less, is more compact and supplies an hour of playing time after being wound for 20 seconds.

In 1999 the company added to the radio range with the launch of a new model, the Freeplay S360. The company also launched the 20/20 flashlight, which contains an integral energy storage unit to generate power for instantaneous or later use.

Currently Freeplay Energy has a £30m turnover and was forecast to produce 1.2 million units in the year 2000. Around 70% of its sales are in the United States of America and 25% in Europe, with Africa and the Middle East making up the balance. The company's promotional budget is around £3m.

Through market research the organisation has identified that the product is positioned differently in the various international markets. In Germany the product appeals to the consumer's strong environmental consciousness. In the USA and Japan, where there is a strong outdoor culture, the product is bought as a component of tornado or earthquake survival kits. In the UK, the company's biggest market per capita, the general public is proud of the fact that the product was invented there.

The company still has an aspiration to create products that will bring modern forms of communication to individuals in remote rural villages. However, they believe that entering into the European and North American markets has allowed them to develop much larger manufacturing volumes which in turn has enabled them to gradually lower prices.

Freeplay Energy has a number of new product ideas under investigation. One initiative is the concept of a satellite telephone that can be charged with energy provided by a 'self-powered' generator rather than costly disposable batteries. The company believes this product would overcome some of the problems faced by African economies. Some African states cannot afford to develop the landlines and other facilities needed for a modern telecommunications infrastructure. This approach would allow these states to make a technology leap and allow individuals access to the global communications network. Other product ideas include self-powered pull cord lights, water purification systems and even heartbeat monitors.

The company's philosophy is to attempt to create a range of products that will help improve communication across the less developed world. This is reflected in its tagline, 'Powered by You'.

The company now has to consider how it plans to develop over the next five years. There are a number of strategic choices to be made. It could move away from making its own products or it could carry on some manufacturing but license out its technology to mobile phone manufacturers such as Nokia, Ericsson and Motorola.

**Source:** SMM Planning & Control Examination Paper, December 2000.

---

## Questions

1. Outline the process the company should follow in order to successfully undertake segmentation, targeting and positioning.

2. Explain the associations that Freeplay Energy can use to position a brand such as S360 or 20/20.

## SUMMARY OF KEY POINTS

In this Session, we have introduced the concepts of segmentation, targeting, positioning and branding, and have covered the following key points:

- Segmentation is the process of dividing a market up into distinct groups of buyers with different needs, characteristics or behaviour. Different variables are used to segment consumer and business markets.

- Targeting is the process of evaluating each market segment's attractiveness and selecting one or more segments. The attractiveness of, and the ability of the organisation to develop a competitive position in, the available segments are assessed, and one or more segments chosen for the organisation to operate in. Portfolio models can be used to aid decisions.

- Positioning is the process of arranging for a product to occupy a clear, distinctive and desirable place relative to competing products in the minds of target consumers. There are many ways in which products can be positioned. The position can be shown on a perceptual or positioning map.

- Branding is a valuable tool for developing a specific competitive position. Brand name strategy, brand equity and valuation, and the various approaches to exploiting a brand are important techniques for developing and managing brands.

## Improving and developing own learning

The following projects are designed to help you develop your knowledge and skills further by carrying out some research yourself. Feedback is not provided for this type of learning because there are no 'answers' to be found, but you may wish to discuss your findings with colleagues and fellow students.

### Project A

Discuss with a colleague some good and bad examples of consumer and business market segmentation.

Why is segmentation as an approach used less widely in business markets?

---

**Project B**

Find out how your organisation, or one that you know well, segments its markets and selects its target segments.

Examine how well you think the target segments match the core competencies and assets of the organisation. If you discover a mismatch, ask yourself what the organisation should do: find new segments or develop its capabilities further.

---

**Project C**

Make a list of 10 to 20 brands with which you are familiar. Consider brand extensions for at least one brand (e.g. a cottage cheese product from Häagen-Dazs) and evaluate this against the brand personality and attributes.

Describe the positions they have established and identify the associations used to position them.

---

## Feedback to activities

### Activity 11.1

The principles of segmentation in consumer and industrial markets are the same. However, the main difference is the higher profile role and significance of the DMU in industrial markets. Segmentation, originally developed in consumer markets, is a more recent development in b2b markets where it is being used effectively. Your evaluation should show the difference between the approaches in these two types of market.

### Activity 11.2

Targeting is a decision that should take into account a range of relevant factors. Tools such as modified GE screen or Shell matrix are frequently used for this purpose as they allow organisations to define criteria relevant to their specific context and show clearly and easily the relative positions on the grid of the options being considered.

The targeting decision should take into account the extent to which options are able to exploit and develop the core competencies of the organisation and the fit between the option and the organisation's goals and culture. It is therefore important that you should identify the competencies and assets that the organisation is using to compete.

## Activity 11.3

Positioning is essentially about customers' perceptions of a specific product or service. These can position the product or service relative to their ideal or relative to competing products or services. The two main features of positioning are:

■ It takes place in the mind of customers that make up the market.

■ The position they perceive for the product or service is likely to be developed anyway to reduce uncertainty and complexity when buying. It is better that the provider should influence the customer to perceive the product or service in a position that is favourable to the company.

The examples you have used may be drawn from a consumer market and advertisements for products you have seen. Alternatively it may have been drawn from your own industry.

## Activity 11.4

Examples were given in the text. In addition to examples from your own industry or experience, well known brands include:

■ Corporate brand – Virgin.

■ Range brand – Heinz 57 covers a range of tinned foods. Heinz itself is an umbrella brand.

■ Individual brand – product brand names for various washing powders and cleaning products from Unilever and P&G.

# Session 12

# Products, innovation and service

## Introduction

This Session continues with the theme of developing a specific competitive position. In the previous Session we explored how organisations use techniques of segmentation, targeting, positioning and branding strategy to make decisions about, and plan, the specific positions they are going to develop. In this Session we explore how organisations can realise and fine-tune a competitive position through the new product development, innovation and customer relationships.

---

### LEARNING OUTCOMES

At the end of this Session you will be able to:

- Explain the New Product Development process (NPD) process and criteria for success.

- Define innovation and discuss its relevance to organisations.

- Describe a range of techniques that facilitate innovation.

- Assess the value of, and describe the main difficulties in, building relationships with customers.

---

## The product as a 'bundle' of benefits

One view of a product is as a 'bundle of benefits'. Kotler et al (1999) defines a product as having three levels:

- **Core product** – defines the fundamental need that the product meets. Whilst fundamental needs are generic in nature, the core product might vary between international markets. For example, a bicycle is seen in China as a form of transport, whereas in Western countries its function is as a fitness or leisure item.

- **Actual product** – is the product that we recognise as meeting the specific need. The actual product has attributes such as performance features, branding and packaging, that satisfy the benefits expected by customers or users.

- **Augmented product** – enhances the actual product through features such as after-sales support, interest free credit and the like. The features of the augmented product are important since they provide the basis for differentiating the product from others in its category or class. Over time however, the features of the augmented product are gradually integrated into the actual product and lose their power to differentiate. This is one of the many reasons for product development.

Product development needs to take place at each one of these levels and the organisation must understand their core product(s), especially when they may differ in international markets.

## New product development

While approximately 90% of all new products fail, it is essential in markets as competitive as today's global markets that organisations develop them. Indeed, product development and innovation – the activities that shape the future of the business – are the 'lifeblood' of any organisation. The development of a successful product is the outcome of many strategic decisions – allocation of resources for building core competencies, matching resources to market opportunities and co-ordinating activities across functional boundaries are all accepted strategic activities which normally determine the success or failure of products.

In essence, the term product covers five different offerings:

- Tangible goods.
- Services.
- People.
- Ideas.
- Venues.

Many products will be a combination of these five things but the most important part of the product development strategy is to understand the target market's needs and create value for the customer by delivering benefits.

But what is a new product? Research by Booz and Allen found that new products come in a number of different guises:

- Products new to the world and which then go on to create a completely new market, e.g. the facsimile machine.

- Products new to an organisation (rather than new to the world) or additions to existing product lines.

- Improvements, replacements, upgrades and minor modifications to existing products.

- Repositioned products that allow the organisation to target new markets.

Based on Kotler's work (1997) it is generally accepted that there are eight main stages in the new product development process:

- Idea generation.

- Idea evaluation/screening.

- Concept development.

- Market strategy development.

- Business evaluation.

- Product development.

- Test marketing.

- Product launch.

These are sometimes combined to produce fewer steps – for example, Drummond & Ensor combine marketing strategy development with business evaluation and test marketing with product development, to give six stages. Each stage consists of activities and reviews followed by a decision to proceed. This process can be viewed as a 'trumpet' with many ideas entering the wide end and few new products reaching launch at the narrow end. The decisions made during the process are how weaker, less viable ideas and products are filtered out.

With more and more pressure on companies to get products to market quicker and achieve returns on their investments, there are temptations for organisations to bypass some of the steps in the process or run them in parallel. Organisations in which product development is strategically important have been investing in developments such as multi-functional team working, customer involvement and knowledge management to address some of the problems and reduce the 'time-to-market', sometimes abbreviated to TTM.

Brands like L'Oreal launch over 2,000 products every year. Their target markets are diverse and many products are suitable only for specific markets. For example, a special hair dye has had to be created for the Asia Pacific market because the density of people's hair in that region is different from that of consumers in the West. Lifestyle trends and fads dictate in L'Oreal's cosmetics markets where products need to be introduced to the market at an exceptionally fast speed. However, L'Oreal are aware that they have to take care in not diluting their brand image by confusing their consumers with such a vast array of new product launches.

Despite the best endeavours of organisations, a large proportion of products still fail. There are five main reasons for this:

- Under-investment, either in the development of the product itself or in marketing to sustain a position in the market.

- Failure to deliver customer benefit, leading to rejection by prospective customers. Innovative high technology products can sometimes suffer this fate as they appear as solutions looking for a problem to solve.

- Forecasting errors – either over-optimistic or pessimistic forecasts of levels of demand, time and money needed for investment or product performance can all damage a product's chances.

- Internal politics – since effective co-ordination of teams across departments is essential to successful product development, inter-departmental conflict can be the death warrant for a new product.

- Negative or unsupportive response by channels and outlets which fail to embrace the new product and share the organisation's goals.

---

**Activity 12.1**

Evaluate the alternative means by which the new product development process could be organised by an organisation which manufactures electrical cooking equipment for both domestic and commercial customers.

---

## Innovation

An innovation is the generation and implementation of an idea. An innovation can be anything – from a novel 'Post-it' note developed by 3M, to a new postal delivery service, to a truly genuine response to a customer's need. The innovation is in the eye of the receiver and therefore does not have to be novel to the sender of the communication. Nor does it have to be new – it may have existed for some time before the receiver became aware of its existence.

For example, in 2001 Hilton Hotels launched a new service for tired Executives at conferences. They launched a 'neck and shoulders massage' service which caused some excitement at the first offering. This was an innovation in the hotel industry but Virgin had been offering this service on its first class flights for quite some time. Innovation is not necessarily about high-technology products.

Innovation is frequently linked in marketing with product development – the concept that innovation and new products are inextricably linked. But this is to hide an important distinction. On one hand, an innovation may result in a new or modified product; on the other hand, innovations can also be made to processes used within an organisation to make them more efficient or more effective. So we need to bear in mind that innovation is about both:

- Developing and modifying products.
- Developing and modifying processes.

## Innovation in product development

In a market-led organisation, marketing will be at the forefront of the NPD process, making sure that product developments are carried out to meet market needs. However, in a technology- or product-led organisation, products are more likely to be developed as a result of breakthroughs in technology and the role of marketing may be to find a market. The first approach is likely to be more effective.

The NPD process needs both marketing and technology disciplines and they have to work together. The professional capabilities of the people working with the technology, usually in an R&D or an engineering department, will depend on the organisation. Chemists, engineers, food technologists might be encountered in the R&D departments in a pharmaceutical company, a computer manufacturer and a processed food manufacturer respectively.

Pearson's uncertainty map (see Drummond & Ensor) shows how the organisation can integrate the uncertainties associated with the technology on which the product is based with the uncertainties about how the market is likely to react. Drummond & Ensor show its relevance to marketers but it is also used as a tool for managing a portfolio of projects in an R&D department. As in any portfolio model like BCG, the organisation needs projects in more than one quadrant to provide a balance of short-term gains, continuity and strength in depth. In a computer company, the spectrum of R&D, from 'Exploratory research' in quadrant 1 to 'Market penetration' in quadrant 4, may span only two or three years; in a pharmaceutical company, this could be up to 20 years.

What is important is that marketers work closely with technologists through the various stages of the NPD process. The higher the technology, usually the greater the demands on the skills of the marketer required to understand the features of the technology, therefore the benefits the product will offer, and contribute to the process. This is one reason that technologists, rather than marketers, tend to lead NPD in high technology organisations and why these organisations are more likely to be technology-led.

## Innovation in processes

Processes are the sets of co-ordinated activities conducted by an organisation that should ideally meet a customer requirement. Since the environments in which most organisations operate are changing, the processes they use should adapt. Organisations are continuously exploring ways of improving their processes so that they are more **efficient** (produce outputs with fewer inputs) or are more **effective** (produce better outputs for the same level of inputs).

Over the last ten or so years there has been a whole range of management approaches aimed at improving processes. Some of the better known ones are:

- Business Process Re-engineering (BPR).
- Total Quality Management (TQM).
- Quality circles.
- Continuous improvement.
- Learning organisations.

What they all have in common are some basic principles about the customer being the focal point for all activities within the organisation, learning from past performance by measuring what teams within the organisation do, and seeking continuously to improve what people do. While the principles are sound, organisations have experienced significant difficulties in achieving the levels to improvements to which the organisations aspire. We explore some of these difficulties in the next section.

## Innovation and the organisation

"Innovation is crucial to a company's long-term performance and marketers have to be the catalysts." (*Marketing Business,* January 1999.) There is no question that innovation is essential for any business, but stable and efficient day-to-day operations are necessary to accomplish basic tasks effectively. In the 1990s, many organisations placed a high priority on eliminating waste, reducing costs and optimising the use of assets but it can be argued that innovation requires support in the form of time, resources and finances. Innovation has to lead to operational effectiveness but it also has to recognise the constraints imposed by the needs for operational efficiency.

Organisational culture has a strong influence on the level of innovation and generation of ideas in organisations. The values inherent in the organisation will determine how creative and flexible staff can be. It is important for new ideas to be given support, commitment and resources if they are to be effectively implemented. A culture, for example, that does not tolerate failure is hardly likely to encourage staff to come forward with or experiment with new ideas, simply because they fear what will happen to them if their idea does not work out.

Innovation often means change, a potentially uncomfortable position for many employees. Managers have an important role in encouraging ideas and experimentation, fostering sound internal communications to keep their staff in contact with what is happening in the business, and facilitating change.

We have already noted earlier that, despite the use of innovation, a large proportion of new products fail for a variety of reasons. Some of the common reasons for failure identified above are to do with the way organisations manage (or perhaps fail to manage) innovation. Integrating teams from different departments and professional groups, vital to the success of NPD for example, is difficult for organisations to do well.

# Making innovation work

Marketing Managers in particular, while not solely responsible, have a key role to play in helping their organisations to adapt to their external environments and exploit opportunities through innovation. They have to ensure that market information is gathered and presented. They have to identify new products. They have to lead or be involved in the new product development process. As leaders of teams, they should also be focusing on the processes their teams use, innovating where required to improve the effectiveness and efficiency of those processes.

The first step is to **understand**. Marketing Managers might wish to undertake an **innovation audit.** This was covered in Session 4. The audit can be used to explore issues such as:

- What is needed – new products or process innovation?

- How much innovation is needed – where are profits coming from? Now? In 3 years' time?

- Who are the change agents and opinion leaders, both in the organisation and in the market?

- What are the resource, organisational and cultural barriers to innovation?

- How creative are the organisation and its people?


With a full understanding of the organisational context, Marketing Managers can then plan the innovations needed. Like any other plan, this involves setting objectives and a strategy for overcoming the constraints identified to achieve the desired outcomes. This could involve internal marketing to encourage people to buy into any changes.

Then comes the time to act. Introduction of innovation will usually involve initiatives and activities at the individual level, operational level and strategic level. These might include:

- Developing teams, often in different departments, and getting them to work together in a culture of co-operation as self-directed (i.e. no management involved) or directed groups.

- An organisational culture promoting a creative and flexible attitude to work in a 'no-blame' environment in which failure is tolerated.

- Motivating employees to exchange ideas with internal and external customers and suppliers in an attempt to develop innovative new ideas.

- Using market intelligence to assess trends in customer buying behaviour and developments in the external environment.

- Undertaking training and development in areas such as creativity.

- Making time available in the busy organisational day to innovate. At 3M employees are allowed 15% of their working time to work on their own ideas.

- Establishing recognition of innovations by individuals and teams, perhaps involving rewards.

These activities and initiatives all require marketing (and other) Managers to demonstrate leadership. Their plans may take them across the boundaries of marketing into the organisation as a whole, so here they will be acting as change agents.

---

**Activity 12.2**

An international high technology company has recognised that in the last three years it has brought fewer new products to market than its rivals. It also suspects that the time taken to develop its new products is longer than its competitors.

Write a briefing paper advising the organisation on how it can increase both the quantity and pace of its innovation.

---

## Relationship marketing

Relationship marketing is another set of techniques that an organisation can use to develop a specific competitive position. It is worth remembering that one of the recognised sources of competitive advantage is superior relationships. These may be with suppliers or other players in the market, not necessarily just customers. The benefits that organisations can gain from Customer Relationship Marketing (CRM) include:

- Improved customer retention.

- Improved cross-selling.

- Improved profitability (per customer and in general).


The concept of relationship marketing takes marketing back to basic principles. It recognises the fundamental importance of sustaining customer relationships in order to generate customer loyalty and repeat business. It recognises that this is more than just delivering a product that fulfils expectations. It is generally agreed that it is around six times cheaper for an organisation to keep its existing customers or 'voluntary re-purchasers' than to find and acquire new ones. Yet there are still some sales-oriented companies that reward their representatives on transaction-based incentive schemes where the emphasis is on the short-term sale, rather than a longer-term relationship. Reichheld and Sasser (1990) have illustrated that relatively minor improvements in customer loss can generate significant profit improvement. So, effective relationship marketing can save organisations money and can lead to its best customers becoming advocates for the business.

Technological developments have helped in enhancing relationship marketing. CRM software and customer information systems help to obtain, integrate and analyse customer information more easily so that organisations can tailor their marketing mix or communications offerings accordingly. Forces such as globalisation, technological change and the rising power of the customer have been stimulating marketers to find new ways to retain, satisfy and work with customers so that their needs can be anticipated and products and service customised more accurately.

It is essential to understand what the consumer requires from the relationship. High involvement purchases, both in industrial and consumer markets, lend themselves perfectly to relationships since a greater understanding of the customer's needs will reduce the risk on their part. Internally, it is essential that organisations recruit and retain customer-focused individuals. Geoff Birch in his book "Resistance is Useless" (2001) talks about employees as either 'ambassadors' or 'assassins' for an organisation. He goes on to suggest that organisations should recruit on personality traits (like customer service orientation) rather than skills, as skills can be taught in the fullness of time.

Customers need to feel valued if they are going to remain loyal to a company and its products and part of the 'valued' feeling is that they are being listened to by the organisation. Non-price issues may well be more important to certain segments of the marketplace and mutual developments will bring mutual benefits and competitive advantage to both companies.

Identifying when to develop relationship marketing is essential for any organisation if the strategy is going to succeed.

- Not all transactions are relational in nature – impulse buys do not usually require relationship development. In fact, this might aggravate customers in certain situations.

- New data protection legislation designed to protect the privacy of individuals may impose constraints on the way that organisations obtain and use information about customers. Permission is a key requirement for holding and using data, giving rise to the term 'permission marketing'.

- Some customers are cynical about relationship marketing and either do not want relationships at all or want to be in control. This is where 'Customer Managed Relationships' (CMR) is starting to become established in place of CRM.

The key to developing a successful relationship marketing plan is listening to your customers. Market research is essential as customers may be placing emphasis on the different elements of the 'bundle of attributes' (Kotler et al 1999) that the organisation's market offering depicts. Therefore, understanding customer expectations and sensitivities is an integral part of developing the relationship marketing plan.

In summary, organisations must:

- Use relationship marketing appropriately, not as a blunt weapon for all situations.

- Establish what the relationship drivers are.

- Build customer value and develop a customer retention culture within the organisation.

The business environment is changing. Customers may be more willing to collaborate and actively recommend brands and companies – recent research suggests that 60% of all new customers for service organisations such as insurance companies have been developed by word of mouth. This, of course, is very difficult to quantify in real terms but the opposite, equally, must be true. Culturally dextrous companies with customer-focused employees can profit enormously from relationship marketing. Collaboration is the way of the future.

As a final point, it is worth noting that customers are only one of the 'markets' with which an organisation has relationships. Relationships with employees and suppliers are also extremely important. A major life insurance company recently reorganised its internal departments and combined its human resources department with marketing, reflecting the importance it places on maintaining relationships with both customers and employees.

## Service quality

Relationship marketing is linked in most marketers' minds with customer service. When it was introduced, relationship marketing was seen by many companies as an opportunity to differentiate an organisation's offer – a feature of the augmented product. However, over time in many markets it has become in customers' minds a part of the expected offer and therefore in many cases no longer has the power to differentiate. All the more important then for organisations to make sure that the service they provide is of the highest quality.

Research undertaken by Parasuraman et al highlighted five main dimensions of customer service, or service quality ('Servqual', as it is sometimes referred to). They are:

- Reliability – consistency and dependability of performance.

- Responsiveness – the ability and readiness to provide service.

- Assurance – guaranteeing the security and effectiveness of the deliverable.

- Empathy – the ability to communicate with, understand and deal with customers in an appropriate manner.

- Tangibles – the physical evidence of the service.

Organisations should measure and monitor their service quality at frequent intervals. Innovative measures and methods may even highlight new opportunities in the market. This is particularly important for organisations that compete on the basis of service quality.

---

**Activity 12.3**

How can an information technology company in the business to business (b2b) sector build a relationship marketing programme?

---

## Case Study – The wet shave market

Gillette is launching a new wet shave razor system, called Mach 3, onto the global market. This product cost £460 million and took seven years to develop. The company aims to spend around £215 million launching this product globally, of which approximately 10% will be spent in the UK. The main feature of this shaving system is that it has three blades. The key benefit is that it cuts 40% more hair than Gillette's previous shaving system Sensor Excel, and gives an extra-smooth shave. It also exerts less friction, making shaving more comfortable. The Mach 3 is forecast to generate 17% category growth over two years, equivalent to selling 1.2 billion blades globally.

Wet shave customers can buy a shaving system or a disposable razor. With shaving systems the customer buys a razor handle which is refillable with blades that they can buy separately. The three main competitors in the wet shave market in the UK have the following market shares:

| | Number of users of Wet Shave Razors (Millions) |
|---|---|
| Gillette | 9.0 |
| Wilkinson Sword | 2.8 |
| Biro Bic | 2.6 |

The UK market is split between 54% on systems and 46% on disposables. 74% of blade and razor purchases (shaving systems and disposables) are made by men for themselves. The male grooming market has grown over the last two years by £50 million. The shaving systems market alone is worth £113 million. This is broken down as follows:

| | | |
|---|---|---|
| Gillette | £105m | 65% |
| Wilkinson Sword | £32m | 20% |
| Biro Bic | £11m | 7% |
| Other brands, retailers' own label | £13m | 8% |

When Gillette launched Sensor (a new razor system) in 1989 it went on to generate £3.65 billion in worldwide brand sales and sold nearly 400 million razor handles and 8 billion blades. At the same time, because Sensor was an innovative product, Gillette was able to charge a high price for the product. The fact that there was little interchangability of the blades with other systems meant that the customer was restricted to purchasing Gillette blades. Previous launches of new systems have typically been priced 15% higher than the most expensive product available. The Mach 3 will be around 35% more expensive. Replacement blades will cost £1.12 each.

The aim with the Mach 3 is to capture new users into the Gillette franchise, to encourage millions of current Gillette users to trade up to the new system, and to move current users of disposables into the refillable shaving systems sector.

Advertising for the Mach 3 will be identical globally. Television advertisements will use the same film from Asia to Europe, with only minor modifications to the script. The aim of the campaign will be to steal customers from its competitors (Wilkinson Sword in particular, as it is the only major competitor in the systems market) and to aggressively grow the sector. Prior to the launch of the Mach 3 Gillette ran a television advertising campaign with the aim of persuading customers to move from disposable razors to the Gillette system.

**Source:** SMM Planning & Control Examination Paper, June 1999.

---

## Questions

1. Explain the benefits of an innovation audit and how it should be carried out.

2. As a Marketing Manager for Wilkinson Sword write a briefing paper to your Marketing Director explaining why Gillette continues to spend large amounts of money on new product development and promotion.

---

## SUMMARY OF KEY POINTS

In this Session, we have introduced techniques for developing a specific competitive position through new product development, innovation and relationships, and have covered the following key points:

- NPD is a key process for the organisation to produce products with augmented features that provide a potential source of differentiation. In organisations other than market-led ones, marketing should still be involved in the NPD process. Relationships with technologists responsible for the development of new products are key.

- Innovation is the generation and realisation of ideas. Organisations can use innovation both in their new products, to make them more competitive, and in their processes, to make them more efficient and more effective.

- Relationships with customers can also be a source of advantage if planned and used wisely. Relationship marketing is not easy to apply since not all customers want relationships, employees have to be capable of delivering them and constraints imposed by data protection legislation have to be taken into account.

- Service quality is closely linked to relationship marketing. The five dimensions that an organisation can use to monitor service quality are: reliability, responsiveness, assurance, empathy and tangibles.

---

## Improving and developing own learning

The following projects are designed to help you develop your knowledge and skills further by carrying out some research yourself. Feedback is not provided for this type of learning because there are no 'answers' to be found, but you may wish to discuss your findings with colleagues and fellow students.

---

**Project A**

Identify a new product development either in your own organisation or an organisation with which you are familiar.

Identify what type of new product development it is. Has it been successful?

Can you trace the steps of the NPD process that the product might have been put through?

---

**Project B**

Define the type of organisational culture that encourages innovation. If you need an examplar, look at the culture within 3M.

Does your organisation or an organisation of your choice possess such a culture?

If not, what changes would it have to make to introduce such a culture?

---

**Project C**

Evaluate the relationship marketing policy of your company, or a company with which you are familiar, from the perspective of a customer.

What do you see as the strengths and weaknesses of relationship marketing in this situation?

---

## Feedback to activities

### Activity 12.1

Companies are always trying to improve the 'time to market' for their new products. Ways to optimise the NPD process include:

- Cross-functional teams.
- Involving customers.

- Parallel development.

- Strategic direction.

- Knowledge management.

This was Question 6 on the Planning & Control examination paper in December 1999. You can find a full specimen answer on the student web site.

### Activity 12.2

This is about both the organisational climate for innovation and the NPD process itself. 'Pace' is about the effectiveness of the NPD process while 'quantity' is probably more about innovation. Remember that innovation affects both products and process. To improve the climate for innovation, you would consider:

- Teamwork.

- Cognitive styles of Senior Managers.

- Policies and practices, support and systems.

- Rewards.

- Exchange of information.

- External inputs.

This was Question 3 on the Planning & Control examination paper in June 2001. You can find a full specimen answer on the student web site.

### Activity 12.3

The focus of relationship marketing is, as the name implies, on the relationship with the customer rather than the purchase transaction and maximising the lifetime value. Steps in implementing this kind of programme will include:

- Identifying customers with whom relationships should be established.

- Deploying appropriately skilled relationship Managers.

- Allocation of responsibility for RM to one individual.

- Development of a plan detailing the steps necessary.

This was Question 7 on the Planning & Control examination paper in June 1999. You can find a full specimen answer on the student web site.

# Session 13

# Strategic marketing plans

## Introduction

In the first twelve Sessions of this Companion, we have covered the analysis, objective setting and strategy formulation stages of the strategic planning process. In this Session we cover the output from that process – the strategic marketing plan. We look at its relationships with other plans in the organisation, the structure of the plan and common barriers to planning found in organisations.

---

**LEARNING OUTCOMES**

At the end of this Session you will be able to:

- Explain how marketing planning fits into the strategic planning process.

- Describe the structure of a typical marketing plan.

- Prepare an effective and realistic marketing plan incorporating appropriate strategic and tactical marketing decisions.

- Identify common obstacles found in organisations to effective planning and explain how they might be overcome.

---

## Marketing planning as part of strategic planning

Let's quickly recap how marketing planning fits with corporate or business planning.

In developing a strategy, Managers analyse what is taking place in the organisation's external environment and how the environment is likely to develop both in the short and the long term. Managers also look objectively at what the organisation is capable of achieving or delivering and understand the expectations of the organisation's various stakeholders. A corporate and then a marketing strategy can be developed, so matching the capabilities of the organisation with opportunities in the market.

It is generally accepted that there are three levels of activity in an organisation. These are more explicit in larger organisations but do still exist in smaller organisations. They are:

- Corporate level.
- Business or divisional level.
- Functional level.

## Corporate or business planning

The relationship between corporate or business planning and marketing planning is a hierarchical one with corporate planning and strategy at the top and marketing planning and strategy below. Thus marketing decisions are not taken in isolation but within a framework of guidelines and priorities that already determined by corporate management.

The corporate plan will define the objectives for the whole of the organisation and should co-ordinate the various business or functional strategies (marketing, operations, human resource management, finance, etc.) to deliver the overall corporate objectives. The corporate plan, which defines the corporate strategy, then feeds into the marketing strategy (and operations, finance strategies etc.) producing objectives, which in turn translate into specific tactical marketing objectives and actions.

## Marketing planning

Marketing planning consists of three main activities:

- Analysing and evaluating the organisation's environment and competitive capabilities and then using this information to develop forecasts of future trends in areas of interest.
- Influencing business objectives and formulating strategy on which the marketing objectives and strategy will be based.
- Choosing target markets and strategies, developing positioning strategies to meet target market needs and developing plans for implementing these through appropriate marketing mixes for each market.

Marketing objectives should be stated as quantified targets. If the corporate objective is to increase profits, a related marketing objective might be to increase market share in a premium segment. In formulating product-market strategy, techniques such as product life cycle analysis can help management to select suitable strategies for developing existing and new products, and existing and new markets (Ansoff).

Planning should be systematic, structured and involve three key elements:

- What has to be achieved – objectives.
- Defining how the objectives are to be achieved – strategy and tactics.
- The resources required to implement the strategy – resource implications.

Devising a marketing strategy involves identifying target markets and customer needs and planning products which will satisfy those needs and organising marketing resources to complete the objectives in the most effective way in terms of cost and service level satisfaction. A marketing strategy can be written down in a plan (usually long-term) to achieve the organisation's objectives by specifying:

- What resources should be allocated to marketing activities across the organisation.
- How those resources should be used, given the current and predicted macro environmental and microenvironmental situation.

From the overall marketing strategy, tactics for each level of the marketing mix need to be developed.

## The planning cycle

Most organisations operate on an annual cycle geared to the end of the financial period and requirements for publishing or filing reports on financial performance. Let's illustrate how this might work in a large organisation with a financial year end on 31st March.

| August | Corporate centre issues to SBU heads the view of current position and market outlook for the period, corporate objectives, planning assumptions and guidelines for the 3 year 'strategic plan'. |
|---|---|
| October | SBU heads present their business objectives, strategies and investment requirements for the 3 year strategic plan to corporate centre. Marketing in each SBU carries out the market analysis and contributes to outline plans. |

| November | Corporate centre confirms or modifies SBU objectives to fit overall corporate plan. They issue planning assumptions and guidelines for the 1 year operating plan. |
| --- | --- |
| December | SBU management teams lead the planning process. Functional plans are prepared to contribute to SBU objectives. SBU budgets are drawn up. |
| January | SBU heads present their objectives, action plans and budgets for 12 months starting 1st April to corporate centre. They negotiate with centre over their objectives and budgets. |
| March | Corporate centre issues a consolidated plan that confirms the SBUs' targets and budgets. Minor adjustments may be necessary to reflect the 'closing position' at the end of the financial year. |
| April | SBUs and corporate centre start working to new plans. |

In this example, the organisation has a 3 year 'strategic plan' and a 1 year operating plan. A small team of planners working for the CEO's office at the corporate centre, who may include strategic marketers, drives the process. Marketers within each SBU are involved in preparing strategic plans, the SBU operational plan and their own functional plans. In this example, there is no strategic marketing plan: this is embraced within the strategic plans for each SBU and the overall corporate plan.

---

**Activity 13.1**

Identify the plans that your organisation, or an organisation with which you are familiar, uses to specify its strategy and operations.

Evaluate how the marketing plan relates to the higher level plans and the role of marketing in the preparation of these plans.

---

## Structure of the marketing plan

When we talk about a 'strategic marketing plan', it may take one of a number of forms:

- It may be part of the business or corporate strategic plan, as in the illustration above.

- It may be a functional plan, covering the strategic aspects of the business plan and the operational plan for marketing activities.

- It may be a discrete plan. However, this is not common in organisations.


Whichever of these forms the marketing plan takes, it should include objectives, strategy, action programme, budget and controls. We will now look at this structure in more detail.

Each marketing plan is specific to each organisation and its stakeholders but there are elements that have to be covered in every plan. Kotler puts forward his framework as follows:

- **Situation analysis** – including various analyses and forecasts.

- **Objectives and goals** – what the organisation aims to or needs to achieve. These would be in measurable terms, e.g. increase in market share or 'bottom line' profits and returns.

- **Marketing strategy** – including the selection of target markets, the marketing mix and the marketing expenditure levels.

- **Action programme** – how these various strategies are going to be achieved.

- **Budgets** – developed from the action plan and usually including capital investment.

- **Controls** – to monitor the progress of the plan and the budget at regular intervals so that the company can analyse the variance between budget and actual results and put in place a corrective action plan earlier rather than later.


Certainly, an organisation's plan would be expected to cover:

- **External analysis** – of the industry and the market that the organisation is in. You will remember from earlier that this consists of macro and microenvironmental analysis.

- **Internal analysis** – of the organisation's competencies and resources. These are sometimes referred to as 'strengths and weaknesses' but should be much 'deeper' than this.

- **Opportunity** – those that exist for the organisation within its selected market segments.

- **Strategic intent** – defining mission and setting appropriate objectives.

- **Strategy** – formulation of strategy.

- **Actions** – what is being proposed as tactical marketing activity.

- **Implementation and control** – measures to ensure effective implementation and control of the plan.


The exact format of the written marketing plan will vary depending on the organisation and the industry but the following headings are generally accepted as a typical format that may be used:

- **Executive summary** – this covers all of the major issues and should analyse where the organisation is now and how it will achieve its future objectives.

- **Corporate strategy** – this is where the corporate mission and objectives are stated along with a summary of the overall organisational position and the developed corporate strategy.

- **External and internal analysis** – provides an overview to the industry or market sector in which the organisation operates, highlighting macro environmental elements and outcomes from the competitor, industry and customer analysis. Internally, it would summarise available assets and competencies and look at forecasts of future trends and may finish with a SWOT analysis.

- **Marketing objectives** – highlighting financial targets so that the objectives can be translated into measurable marketing objectives e.g. market share, customer retention, etc.

- **Marketing strategy** – examine segmentation, targeting and positioning strategies and how competitive advantage is going to be achieved. This should include the marketing mix and the specific marketing tactics that will be used.

- **Implementation** – includes a schedule of key activities, allocating resources, setting budgets and developing contingency plans.

- **Control** – includes measures of performance to highlight the progress of the plan. This section usually includes detailed forecasts.

---

**Activity 13.2**

Obtain a copy of the marketing plan for your organisation or an organisation of your choice.

Examine the content and headings used and compare them with the structure discussed here. Take note of the content under each heading of the plan. If the structures are different, why might this be? Make some notes on the recommendations you might make to the organisation and on what you have learned by comparing a 'real' marketing plan with the outline shown here.

Note: If you are unable to obtain a copy of a plan from an organisation, visit the CIM student web site (www.cimvirtualinstitute.com) and look up a Specimen Answer from any recent Analysis & Decision case study examination. This will include an outline strategic marketing plan that you can use for this activity.

---

## Effective and realistic plans

Marketing and business plans are produced for different purposes. The common ones are:

- **Time-driven plans** – plans, usually revised annually, that define the objectives, strategies and actions for an organisation for a given period. The illustration above describes plans prepared for this purpose. They are prepared to a set timetable.

- **Event-driven plans** – plans for a specific event or activity such as market entry, new product launch, setting up a new channel, or joint venture business launch. These are prepared when a particular event is planned.

Marketing plans produced for either of these purposes can take two forms – strategic and tactical. They are often confused and may differ in definition from business to business or Manager to Manager.

As you can see from the illustration of planning in an organisation, the distinction is that strategic plans take a longer-term view of the organisation's future and, in organisations with a market-led orientation, broadly define the organisation's marketing activities (Drummond and Ensor, 2001). This type of plan seeks to develop effective responses to a changing business environment based on an analysis of markets, segmentation and evaluation of competitors to position products and so gain a competitive advantage.

Tactical marketing takes a shorter-term view (probably 12 months or less) and highlights the day-to-day marketing operations and activities. It translates strategy into specific actions and deals in detail with the individual elements of the marketing mix.

An organisation needs a strategic marketing plan in order to adapt to a changing business environment (Drummond and Ensor, 2001). The pressure for companies to be more and more customer-centric – that is re-engineering business processes as well as products and services to benefit the customer more by adding more value at each link of the value chain – means that organisations must continually adapt and develop to remain successful and profitable. Strategic marketing facilitates this process and provides robust solutions in an increasingly competitive world (Drummond and Ensor, 2001). The aim of the plan is to provide the organisation with a framework which will rely on market research and analyse how best to optimise the organisation's assets.

The marketing plan is also a framework for informing, communicating and motivating involvement of the staff. In true total quality management style, a well-defined plan can be fed into employee communications to help staff understand the marketing strategy, how they are involved in the links of the chain and what future timetables for development and change they should be planning for. This can be a useful 'buy-in' mechanism when it comes to employee commitment and must not be underestimated.

In order to prepare effective and realistic marketing plans incorporating appropriate strategic and tactical marketing decisions, organisations typically carry out the following marketing activities:

- Internal review and evaluation of current capabilities and performance.
- External market research, amongst other things to monitor buyer behaviour and trends.

- Collaborating with customers to forecast future demand and trends.

- General environmental scanning and market intelligence.

Some organisations have a marketing information system into which this kind of information is fed for analysis and storage.

---

**Activity 13.3**

List the main benefits of planning to your organisation, or one that you know well. Evaluate the benefits your organisation gains against those quoted by Drummond & Ensor (p239).

---

## Planning in organisations

Planning in its truest form provides a framework for an organisation's employees and Managers within which to develop and implement a strategy. It is intended to stimulate effective action and provide a fundamental basis for success. The main benefits for an organisation to use planning are:

- It helps them to identify and adapt to changes in the environment.

- It provides a process for balancing the resource needs of the environment and the capabilities of the organisation.

- It provides a common and consistent basis within an organisation for undertaking and evaluating activities.

- It should integrate activities throughout an organisation so that the parts are working together, rather than pulling against each other.

- It provides a common message to be communicated to stakeholders.

- It defines the desired level of performance for all to see and against which to measure actual performance.

Recently however, the value of planning as a business discipline has been questioned. This is due in part to the fact that it is difficult to plan in conditions of uncertainty and volatility, very much characteristics of today's global marketplace. Stacey and Arthur in their book *Managing Chaos* (1993) suggest that anything useful about the long-term future is essentially unknowable and that, because of this, regular strategic planning meetings serve a ritual rather than a functional purpose. In many organisations, the planning process described in this Session places a heavier emphasis on establishing short-term targets than on long-term strategies.

This points to the existence of barriers to successful planning, listed by Drummond and Ensor (2001). Often, these barriers are more to do with the human aspects (the 'soft' issues) of business management. They involve people, politics, skills and culture, to a greater degree than formal systems, methodology and data. Whatever the issues, it is true that the majority of organisations experience problems both in developing and in implementing marketing plans. These arise for some of the following reasons:

- An unfocused environmental analysis relies on incorrect assumptions or an overestimation of the organisation's marketing capability.

- Timescales or resource budgets are optimistic.

- The plan contains too much detail (so is too rigid) or too little detail (so does not provide the direction and co-ordination required).

- Objectives set out in the plan are inconsistent or conflict with objectives in other parts of the organisation or distribution chain.

- Employees who are responsible for delivering many of the activities in the plan do not feel any ownership of the plan, often because they have not been involved in its preparation. This causes irritation and may lead to objectives not being met.

Clearly there are actions that the organisation can take to remedy these mistakes and overcome the difficulties. Drummond and Ensor (2001) highlight five areas of common barriers to effective planning:

- **Culture** – make sure that the organisation recognises and accepts a marketing orientation. Managers need to be seen to be endorsing the strategy and not just paying lip service to it.

- **Power and politics** – different Managers' vested interests make for interesting viewing by staff and can absorb a lot of wasted time and effort. Make sure that the marketing strategy and planning associated with it is agreed and consistent so that there are no (or very few) potential conflicts of interest within the business.

- **Analysis not action** – much wasted time and effort can be released if over-analysis of the situation is eliminated. Globalisation, quick market entry and flexibility are drivers in expecting faster delivery of implemented plans and corrective action programmes, and so organisations must refrain from over-analysis.

- **Resource issues** – resources, whether human or financial, are always in demand particularly since the downsizing and cost reduction programmes of the 1980s and 1990s. A key role of Managers here is to balance the level of resources available with the business objectives to be met.

- **Skills** – some Managers and other employees may not be trained to deliver and implement a marketing plan, so it becomes reduced to a minor working document or disregarded totally. Just like any marketing communications document, it must be credible and those who are responsible must be supported and knowledgeable about the outcome objectives.

---

**Activity 13.4**

What are the potential problems faced by your organisation, or an organisation of your choice, attempting to make marketing planning effective?

How can the impact of these problems be minimised?

---

# Case Study – Marketing in a downturn

## Marketing strategy

Don't cut your marketing costs in a downturn, says Allyson Stewart-Allen, a Director of International Marketing Partners. "Keep investing because when the economy rebounds, your brand will have remained on the eyeballs of your target markets."

But the board may order cuts to protect cash flow. So start by making sure board members understand the pay-off from marketing spend. Support your case with statistics culled from PIMS' database and other sources (e.g. some firms which kept spending during a recession grew market share three times faster when recovery came than those that cut back).

If the board still orders cutbacks, start by looking at the productivity of sales calling. Re-qualify customers and prospects ruthlessly. Downgrade marginal customers from a personal to a telephone call. Upgrade more promising prospects. Focus on key accounts where there is potential to grow new business. Look for ways to aid valued customers going through difficult times, such as providing more generous payment terms. Seek out markets which avoid the downturn or even grow. These may be geographic or industry sectors. Find ways to make products or services more attractive in these markets.

Demonstrate to the board that the Marketing Department can perform better by reviewing admin costs. Use the Pareto principle – the 80/20 rule – to focus on where most revenue comes from. Then adjust marketing spend accordingly. Watch key performance indicators as the recession deepens. If your sales decline is behind the market as a whole you're holding your own. Monitor average account spend per customer. Even keeping that stable means you're gaining share in a falling market.

Seek out new opportunities for alliances and partnerships. Joint promotions are a way to keep marketing visibility while sharing spend. Remember that alliances can be used to open new channels to market as well as promote brands. Understand when what started as a temporary downturn looks like a permanent seismic shift in the market (e.g. could budget airlines now replace flag carriers as the market leaders?).

## Market research

Expenditure on market research has grown consistently during the past decade at around 10% year on year. But the downturn plus September 11 has put a blip in some budgets – especially American and FMCG brands. The key question is how to continue developing a customer relationship strategy when there's less money to spend, says Ruth McNeil, a Director of Response Consulting.

Start by considering what you need to know about your customers in these difficult times. How have their perceptions of your market and its products been changed by recent events? Is the change temporary or permanent? Look beneath the surface to the underlying attitudes which may drive new purchasing behaviours. Use more qualitative research techniques to do this. Switching some budget from quantitative to qualitative techniques can also save money.

Other money-saving tactics: use smaller samples but more in-depth ones, take space in omnibus surveys, and experiment with Internet research. Find out about the new dynamics of your market. What will drive customer purchasing decisions in future? Pay attention to the way people are reacting to the messages you use in advertising and marketing literature. Find out what they think about the language you couch your messages in. Probe to find what ways your customers might want to be treated differently both as a result of the downturn and September 11. Companies that pitch the tone of their communication with customers appropriately are likely to score.

If your market is declining, pay special attention to brand tracking. Are customer perceptions rising or falling? Use this data to adjust the tone and targeting of your customer communications. Use research to identify new geographic or vertical markets for existing products or services. Reconsider new product launches in the light of research data. In uncertain times, people often like the comfort of sticking with the familiar. "There is a lot of anxiety in people's lives at the moment," says McNeil. "They are tending to batten down rather than look outwards. Probably companies need to reflect that."

## Advertising

Fortune favours the brave, suggests Marilyn Baxter, Chairwoman of advertising agency Hall and Partners. "If you are a strong competitor in a market and you are reasonably courageous about your strategy, then you will win over weaker rivals who either don't have deep pockets or are more cautious." Trouble is, not every company has deep pockets, so advertising is one of the first cost cuts in a downturn. But be clear about the implications of advertising cuts. Be blunt with the board about the likely impact on short-term sales and long-term brand building. Argue the case for maintaining ad spend and making cuts elsewhere, if this is the tactic you favour.

To make remaining budgets work harder, target key market segments and loyal customers. Achieving higher density in important markets could be more effective than making a smaller noise everywhere. Prioritise those products and services – or brands – which should keep advertising. Use advertising to maintain share in those markets which will be important for your company in the future. Look out for bargain prices in the media. Space costs are falling in newspapers, magazines and posters. In television, the cost of a typical slot is around 12% lower than last year.

Become cleverer about using the budget. For example, consider more half and fewer whole pages, 20-second rather than 30-second TV slots. Even if you're cutting advertising, watch for the upturn and plan ahead. Be first to step up advertising when the market grows. Listed companies often have the biggest difficulties in a downturn, suggests Mark Palmer, Managing Partner of media buyers OMD. They have to maintain dividends which may mean cutting short-term advertising budgets to conserve cash.

## Public relations

In past recessions, some companies have switched a portion of their marketing budget from advertising to public relations. PR looks like a less costly way of achieving profile. There is some truth in that but PR, like other spending, works best as part of a well-balanced marketing mix.

And there are plenty of opportunities for saving money on PR during a downturn. As with other marketing activity, make sure priorities about markets, audiences and messages are clearly understood. Align messages with markets and audiences more tightly.

If your company has both in-house PR staff and uses a PR agency, look at the balance of the work between the two. Could more be handled in-house, saving on agency fees? Examine the performance of the agency closely. What has it actually contributed in essential strategic advice and hard measurable results?

Consider renegotiating fees with your agency. It may be prepared to accept less for a period rather than lose your account completely. Look for ways of saving money on how your account is operated. PR agencies waste significant sums writing and distributing press releases and articles of no interest to the press. Use a reputable and independent monitoring agency to gauge the impact of press and broadcast PR. Evaluate your PR campaign's effectiveness in getting across your key messages to target audiences, including your own employees. "There are no one-size-fits-all campaigns," says Jon Aarons, president-elect of the Institute of Public Relations. "Because every company is different it needs access to good PR advice and skills."

## Direct marketing

Direct marketing has changed dramatically since the last recession at the beginning of the 90s, says Colin Lloyd, president of the Direct Marketing Association. The Internet and call centres are the two biggest changes. So there are strategic questions your company may want to consider in this downturn, such as whether it's possible for you to sell more to end-customers, cutting out retailers or distributors. And if you could, whether there is long-term business pay-off, taking into account the reaction of current intermediaries.

Whether your company is new to direct marketing or an existing user, it pays to conduct a fundamental review in the light of fast-moving changes. Look with a fresh eye at mail, telephone, Internet and the new Wireless Application Protocol (WAP) technology, which makes it possible to deliver marketing messages to mobile phones.

To raise response rates consider three critical points. One, target outbound communications more precisely using data about previous buying habits. Two, time mailings or calls just before likely buying decisions. Three, make messages appropriate to the recipient. Tailor standard texts or call centre scripts to take account of specific needs. Give close thought to how an offer can be made more attractive by adding extras with low cost to you but high perceived value to the recipient. Pay attention to the writing and creativity in mailshots – fresh ideas are needed to raise generally declining response rates.

Organise to receive and deal with responses effectively. Many companies still don't. Make sure that fulfilment is taken care of. Use reliable third party suppliers – remember they are your link with the customer. Never forget that direct marketing is about targeting. "We have long moved from the shotgun to the rifle, but today's rifle has a laser sight," says Lloyd.

## New media

There is an explosive growth in audience available through new media, says Danny Meadows-Klue, Chairman of the Internet Advertising Bureau. He expects Internet advertising to have held up in the first six months of this year, but won't make predictions about the second half of 2001. Even so, Internet advertising is worth considering as part of the marketing mix. It's now relatively straightforward to buy through specialist Internet advertising agencies. It's possible to monitor response levels through techniques such as click-throughs to your web site. But don't overlook the Internet's growing brand-building potential.

As you develop your own web site remember that new media changes the ground rules of marketing – customers choose to contact you and control the dialogue. Ensure your web site is easy to navigate and invite comments from users so you can carry out continuous improvement on the site. Provide enough information about your product and services to satisfy even inquisitive enquirers but make sure the detail is accessible through succeeding levels, so that casual visitors are not put off by overloaded screens.

Make it easy to contact your organisation by any medium the caller chooses – email, telephone, fax or mail. Assign responsibility for handling incoming emails – one of the most badly performed new media marketing tasks at present.

Research by Plymouth University shows that of 1,000 companies who were emailed queries, only 45% replied. Use outbound email marketing responsibly. Seek permission to send email information to customers and prospects. Recipients who have given permission are as much as five times more likely to respond.

**Source:** Marketing Business, December/January 2002.

---

### Questions

1. What specific factors does marketing need to take into account when planning during a downturn?

2. When planning for the coming year, how would a Marketing Manager go about handling a 10% cut on last year's communications budget imposed by the MD or Financial Director?

---

## SUMMARY OF KEY POINTS

In this Session, we have introduced strategic marketing plans, and covered the following key points:

- Corporate and business plans set the framework of objectives and strategies that marketing and other functional plans have to achieve.

- Marketing is likely to be involved in preparing strategic plans, particularly in organisations with a strong market-led orientation. They will be responsible for preparing functional plans for marketing.

- Plans, although different in different organisations and at different levels, tend to follow a common format consisting of an understanding of the current situation, objectives, strategies and tactics, action plans and measures for control (including budgets).

- There are a number of benefits to planning, reasons that organisations should persist with planning despite the uncertainties of today's global environment.
- There are a number of obstacles to effective planning in organisations.

## Improving and developing own learning

The following projects are designed to help you develop your knowledge and skills further by carrying out some research yourself. Feedback is not provided for this type of learning because there are no 'answers' to be found, but you may wish to discuss your findings with colleagues and fellow students.

### Project A

Look at the objectives in corporate, business or marketing plans over a three or five year period for your organisation, or one that you know well.

Compare the results achieved at the end of each period with the objectives.

What do any long-term patterns tell you about the planning process used by the organisation?

Make any recommendations you think necessary.

### Project B

Examine the process by which plans in your organisation, or one with which you are familiar, are prepared. Prepare your thoughts on the following points and discuss them with a colleague:

- Why are the plans produced? What are the main motives – are they internal or external?
- How effective are the plans that emerge from the process in terms of defining targets, resources, key actions and co-ordinating mechanisms for all members of the organisation?

- How effective is the scanning and analysis of the external environment in which the organisation operates?

- How objective and thorough is the evaluation and analysis of the organisation's performance, capabilities and resources?

- How much time is spent reviewing and reconsidering marketing strategy? Why is this so high or so low? Is it anything to do with the motives for planning or the orientation of the organisation?

- What recommendations would you make to improve the process?

---

**Project C**

If you have never written one, write a marketing plan for your organisation or one with which you are familiar.

Use the headings provided in this Session and either make assumptions or use real business objectives that the plan has to meet.

---

## Feedback to activities

### Activity 13.1

Your investigation may have revealed the existence of some or all of the following plans in the organisation:

- Business plan – an annually updated plan for the business or business unit with a 1-3 year outlook. In some organisations this plan is split into two separate plans: a one-year operating plan and a longer-term 'strategic' plan. The horizon of the strategic plan will depend on the industry and length of the business cycle, so high technology may be less than 3 years; the nuclear industry up to 20 years.

- Corporate plan – in an organisation consisting of multiple businesses, a corporate plan will provide the overall plan for the corporation. Its contents and function will depend on the type of organisation. In a diversified organisation in which businesses enjoy autonomy, the plan is likely to be financial; in an organisation where all the businesses are related through a single brand or high levels of inter-trading, the plan will also contain overall strategies and co-ordinating mechanisms.

- Marketing plans – the nature of the marketing plan will depend on the orientation in the organisation. At one end of the spectrum, it may be a simple operational plan to support the business with marketing activities; at the other end is may be a company-wide plan co-ordinating the marketing activities conducted in the separate businesses.

If you are in a small or young and fast-moving organisation, then you may have found no formal plans. In this case, did you find any evidence of plans being made informally between the Senior Managers and communicated as targets and budgets alone?

How involved marketing is in preparing these plans will again depend on the orientation of the organisation. In a market-led organisation, marketing will have a significant input into the business strategy and plan; in a sales-led or production-led organisation, marketing may have little input, perhaps other than some basic research.

### Activity 13.2

As we have seen, the structure and content of a plan will depend on the nature of the organisation and its orientation. The format of plan described in this Session is more likely to be found in a market-led organisation. In a production-led or sales-led organisation, the plan may not contain any external view of the market and competitors or details of strategies. The emphasis may be on short-term targets and budgets.

Looking at an organisation's plans can reveal much about its orientation, culture and management style.

### Activity 13.3

The main benefits quoted for planning include:

- Helps an organisation to monitor and adapt to change.
- Provides a framework for identifying resource needs and making allocations.
- Integrates the activities of the organisation into a coherent and consistent whole.

- Communicates intentions and motivates Managers and employees who are charged with achieving objectives.

- Provides a structure for control so that, during a period, the organisation knows how far it has come.

How much these benefits are recognised in the organisation you investigated will depend on the organisation itself. Some organisations do not communicate plans widely; some organisations produce plans because they are required to by the head office but do not use this as an opportunity for a thorough analysis and evaluation of their current position in the market.

## Activity 13.4

We have covered the barriers to effective planning in this Session. You may have identified some of these as existing in the organisation you looked at.

The examiner is keen that you should be able to find and explain practical ways to overcome barriers like these. So your recommendations are important.

- An internal marketing plan can sometimes help – we cover this in the next Session.

- Sometimes it is a skills issue and you either need to develop or bring into the organisation the skills required, e.g. marketing research skills.

- More often the barriers are cultural and 'political', possibly even reflecting the wider corporate culture that does not place importance on plans. Your recommendations might therefore be about building a case, and winning the argument, for developing a stronger market orientation.

# Session 14

# Implementing the plan

## Introduction

In the previous Session, we covered strategic marketing plans – the outcome from the planning process. Having developed its plan, the organisation now faces the problems associated with making it happen. 'Making it happen' is treated by the syllabus for this module under two headings: implementation, which is covered in this Session, and control, covered in the final Session.

A military maxim says that no plan ever survives contact with the enemy. In other words, no matter how good a plan might be, the unexpected or deliberate activity by competitors is likely to impede the organisation in trying to achieve its objectives. This Session explores some of the reasons that plans fail at the implementation stage and introduces principles and techniques, including internal marketing and project management, which can be used to anticipate and overcome problems.

## LEARNING OUTCOMES

At the end of this Session you will be able to:

- Identify the key elements of implementation.

- Assess the likelihood of success at implementation.

- Use internal marketing as a technique to support implementation.

- Describe project management techniques that can be used to implement a marketing strategy effectively.

## Key elements of implementation

The key elements of implementation defined in the syllabus are:

- Leadership.
- Internal marketing.
- Project management (systems and skills).
- Management of change.

Drummond and Ensor (2001) define the following factors for successful implementation:

- **Leadership** – this can be learned or intrinsic to an individual's personality. Whether leaders are born or made, a strong leader with good interpersonal, negotiation and delegation skills can balance the conflicting needs of the task, team and individuals to implement the plan effectively.

- **Culture** – there has to be a good 'fit' between the culture, or shared values and beliefs, of the organisation and the strategy: where this is not the case, implementing the strategy is going to be inherently more risky. In cases where the strategy requires a change in culture, techniques for managing change are needed. These are covered later.

- **Structure** – a structure must be developed which clarifies lines of responsibility and enhances, rather than blocks, effective communication. The structure will also define how various teams or departments relate to each other. Various forms of organisation structure are available including the functional form (organised by department or function), product form (organised by product) and matrix form (organised by both product or region and department, with employees having two Managers). Each form has its strengths and weaknesses.

- **Resources** – resources are always in demand in organisations. To ensure successful implementation, appropriate levels and types of resources have to be in place at the required time.

- **Control** – effective monitoring and control systems must be in place to identify gaps, or variances, between planned and actual results so that corrective action can be taken as soon as is practicable.

- **Skills** – technical/marketing skills, human resource management skills and project management skills are all essential to ensure effective implementation. In a situation of change, people's basic need is one of security (Maslow). Even if there is no threat of changing conditions for the worse, people's anxieties cause worry and may create obstacles to the proposed change. It is a fact that despite successful implementation, businesses see an increase in staff turnover after change has taken place. Project management skills are needed to ensure that the organisation is on track.

- **Strategy** – Managers involved in creating strategy have to communicate their plans to employees. They also have to keep the strategy under review, making changes as and when performance indicators show they are needed. This may take the form of short-term operational changes or longer-term strategic changes to keep the organisation in balance with its environment.

- **Systems** – effective systems must be in place to support the strategy and the implementation. Most organisations already have some systems in place: these may be appropriate for a new strategy or plan. Equally however, they may need to be modified to reflect changes in priority, activities being undertaken or measures used to control the plan. In short, the systems have to be compatible with the objectives and strategies being pursued.

The marketing plan is the vehicle that enables the marketing strategy to be effectively implemented. It is well documented that some organisations divide the two roles of writing and implementing the marketing plan. This is a recipe for disaster as there may be confusion or a misunderstanding of some very basic issues. Therefore, as well as defining detailed operational actions, the marketing plan needs to provide detail of the actions that will be necessary to ensure effective implementation.

Bonoma (1985) identified four distinct corporate-level skills relating to the successful implementation of marketing plans:

- Recognising and diagnosing a problem – are poor results due to a weak plan or poor implementation?

- Assessing the company level where the problem exists – is it a strategic, operational or policy problem?

- Implementing plans – Managers need to have good interpersonal and organisational skills to allocate and monitor the implementation of the plans.

- Evaluating implementation results – marketing management must possess well-developed skills of evaluation that can be applied to the control process.

---

**Activity 14.1**

Evaluate with specific examples whether your organisation, or one with which you are familiar, has a management culture that can combine excellent leadership, human resource management and project management.

---

## Causes of failure

One of the general features of corporate cultures is that they do not like to admit failure. While there are many noted examples of the failed implementation of plans, few are well documented. Research on failures during implementation have highlighted the following common reasons:

- Implementation took more time than originally allocated.

- Major problems surfaced during implementation that had not been identified beforehand.

- Co-ordination of implementation activities was not effective enough.

- Competing activities and crises distracted Managers from implementing decisions.

- Capabilities of employees involved were insufficient for the task.

- Training and instructions given to lower level employees were inadequate.

Whenever a plan fails at implementation, it can be either a weak plan or a failure to overcome difficulties experienced during implementation. The first two points above may be seen as weaknesses in the plan itself: plans that were unduly optimistic or insufficiently detailed. The remaining four points above are typical of the difficulties experienced during implementation that Managers have been unable, or unwilling, to resolve. These often boil down to the Managers' commitment to the original plan.

The difficulties, or barriers, that organisations encounter during implementation may have their origins in the external environment or internal environment.

We can illustrate the types of difficulties experienced as sudden or unexpected changes in the external environment. These difficulties may arise as a result of the organisation's ineffective attempts to monitor changes in its external environment or its complete failure to do so.

- **Social factors** – changing demographic and social patterns, employment patterns (the slide from manufacturing domination to service industry domination of the market), class structure, socio-economic groupings can all contribute to implementation failure. This is particularly true when the marketing plan is involved with many international and fragmented markets where accurate market information and data are hard to find.

- **Legal factors** – an increase in international and indigenous business legislation (including consumer protection, data protection and company law) also have an impact on successful implementation and will continue to do so in the future as consumers grow more and more litigious.

- **Economic factors** – demand levels, purchasing patterns, and competition (particularly from countries with low labour costs) can affect sales revenues and profits during the plan implementation.

- **Political factors** – governments' role in business, taxation and trade can affect activities in both domestic and international markets.

- **Technological factors** – new manufacturing developments and capabilities and, of course, the development of e-business have brought significant change in the last five years. Speed of market entry and competitors who would otherwise be unable to compete in an organisation's home market have been empowered by this new technology, making many markets even more competitive.

Internal barriers too may affect the successful implementation of marketing strategy. There are many forms of organisational culture and few of these are truly customer or market-focused. In the organisation with a non-market oriented culture, chances of successfully implementing a truly customer-focused plan will be severely limited. This is an example of the absence of the strategic 'fit' necessary between strategy and culture. In some organisations, the structure creates walls and barriers to communication. In others, the lack of project management skills leaves the organisation without essential skills to plan and implement marketing programmes.

## Managing change

Implementing change is complex and uncertain. Managers need to be aware of barriers to change within an organisation so that they can overcome them by negotiation, communication and implementation. This is why the human resource management issues, commonly referred to as 'soft' issues, need to be highlighted and confronted during implementation.

In order to assess the challenges facing an organisation during implementation we must look at how easily the strategy will fit into current activities. In general, the narrower the scope of change, the higher the likelihood of successful implementation, but this does not guarantee success. Drummond and Ensor (2001) use two dimensions, the level of change and the importance of change, in a 2x2 grid to suggest four degrees of change:

- **Overhaul** – a high level of change and high importance of change may lead to a high degree of resistance and risk as the new strategy has only a limited fit with current activities.

- **Synergy** – a low level of change and high importance problems should lead to a high degree of co-operation or synergy.

- **Limited impact** – a low level of change and low importance should be tackled as incremental change with limited resources only being allocated to it.

- **Overkill** – a high level of change and with low importance is likely to cause unnecessary conflict in the organisation and questions the need for the change in the first place.

Successful implementation requires Managers to appreciate the nature of change and its impact on individuals and the organisation. According to Drummond and Ensor (2001), Managers must assess the level of change associated with a project and deploy strategies relating to the management of change. For example:

- **Justification** – publish hard evidence and facts to support the change.

- **Commitment** – involve as many people in the change as possible. Opponents can be brought onto the management's way of thinking with good communication skills.

- **Learning** – an open culture that readily acknowledges its mistakes will encourage people to experiment and learn from their experiences.

- **Incrementalise** – divide strategy into smaller, manageable ongoing projects.

- **Operations** – ensure that change is reflected in operational activities through the appropriate systems, structure, policies etc., so that the change becomes permanent. Change is complete only when people are consistently exhibiting the desired behaviours.

Various authors have written on the steps involved in planning and managing change in organisations. Some common steps are:

- Develop a clear concept and proposal that people can buy into.

- Win senior management commitment as a first priority. They should be fully committed to seeing the change through all the difficulties, not just paying lip service to it.

- Develop a plan for at least two years. Changing behaviour takes a long time, so plans should reflect this.

- Win over supporters first and recruit them to help winning over neutrals and opponents.

- Communicate, communicate, communicate to keep everyone informed and clear about the objectives and methods.

- Celebrate successes and progress through appropriate recognition and rewards.

---

**Activity 14.2**

A national hotel chain has decided to embark on an internal programme to develop more fully into a market-led organisation. Prepare a briefing paper advising the senior management team on how they can overcome any resistance to this development that may stem from internal cultural barriers.

---

## Internal marketing

Internal marketing is a technique to help organisations in managing change. It focuses on the relationship between the organisation and its employees. It attempts to smooth the working relationship between functional areas of the organisation and, in so doing, to establish the organisation as an integrated whole, rather than an aggregation of disparate and opposing units (CIM 2000). We should recognise at the outset that this approach is more likely to be used by organisations that have a stronger market-led orientation and are implementing strategic marketing plans.

Berry and Parasuraman (1991) define the process in terms of viewing employees (or groups of employees) as internal customers. It is readily accepted that, to support implementation or organisational change, Managers need to be aware of the issues relating to internal marketing.

Drummond and Ensor (2001) suggest that by applying the marketing concept internally, it may be possible to enhance the likely success of the project. Internal segmentation and application of the 'marketing mix' will have roles to play. An internal marketing plan may have a similar structure to an 'external' marketing plan. However, some elements of the plan will need special treatments:

- Segmentation of the target audiences can be based on expected behaviour or reaction to change. A simple approach is to segment into 'supporters', 'opponents' and 'neutrals'. Alternatively, it could be done using a variable such as the training needs of Managers, administration staff and shop floor.

- Product is the change or plan that the organisation is trying to 'sell' to its employees. Like any product, it should have a number of benefits for the target audience.

- Price is the cost that the individual is going to pay in embracing the change. This could be due to differing working conditions, a different position in the structure, different (high-technology) systems or different corporate values. These can be seen as psychological, social or financial costs.

- Promotion plays a vital part in communicating and winning support from employees who are 'opponents' or 'neutrals' to the project.

- Place defines the methods and channels of communication to be used.


Drawing on their work at McKinsey & Co., Waterman, Peters and Phillips (1981) argue that effective organisational change depends on the effective assignment of seven variables that have become known as the 7Ss or 7S McKinsey framework:

- Structure.
- Strategy.
- Systems (and procedures).
- Style (management style).
- Staff (people).

- Skills (corporate strengths and skills).

- Shared values.

Thus Waterman, Peters and Phillips (1981) have developed an assessment tool for corporate capability. It is widely used as a method of assessing how capable organisations are of using internal marketing to implement change successfully. Drucker points out that efficiency or productivity is now less related to the productivity of manual labour or machinery, and more related to the increasing role of 'knowledge management'. This lies in the work of Managers, Researchers, Planners, Designers and Innovators. Thus many Managers have seen the importance of internal marketing and good people or human resource management and believe that the only opportunity left for competitive advantage lies with their staff and employees.

---

**Activity 14.3**

Using the 7S McKinsey framework, evaluate the capability of your organisation, or one that you know well, for successful implementation of organisational change.

---

## Project management

It has been repeatedly stressed that project management skills are important for any Manager involved in implementing marketing strategy or other organisational change. Effective communication, controlling multiple related activities, meeting deadlines, and effective human resource management all play a huge part in successful implementation.

Project management skills are transferable and can be applied to any given situation. Essentially, project management is the planning, supervision and control of a collective and co-operative activity designed to achieve a pre-determined objective. Efforts tend to focus on integrating activities, building teamwork and monitoring progress against the plan. Marketing projects are normally quite complex and often have to achieved while overcoming unforeseen problems and barriers. This is the role of an effective Manager who must manage these problems as and when they arrive.

Typical tasks that may be undertaken as part of a project are:

- **Objective setting** – SMART objectives must be clearly set at the outset.

- **Planning** – the implementation of the strategy or plan must be broken down into manageable activities, each being delegated or allocated to an appropriately skilled person with adequate resources. Techniques such as critical path analysis, Project Evaluation and Review Technique (PERT), Gantt charts, and computer software like Microsoft Project can be used for more complex projects.

- **Delegation** – tasks need to be shared and good organisation of resources combined with good communication and control.

- **Team building** – motivating and encouraging staff to work together and for each other is a large part of a Manager's role. Managers should find and maintain the balance between the needs of the task, of the individuals and of the group or team. They should encourage a positive and supportive environment where mistakes can be acknowledged and learnt from. They should link individual reward to group performance.

- **Crisis management** – good Managers will be able to deal with unforeseen circumstances in a calm and reassuring way and communicate the way forward to the team.

- **Monitoring and control** – project planning techniques provide a sound framework for monitoring the completion, level of resources and costs of activities that contributes to the control of the overall project.

In summary, project management is one of the techniques available for an organisation to turn strategy and plans into action. A good project management process will:

- Establish clear standards of performance.

- Establish clear standards of quality.

- Ensure that results are achieved within the minimum time and cost.

- Establish objective setting, planning and delegation which will facilitate a workable framework for the implementation of strategy.

---

**Activity 14.4**

Explain how your organisation, or one that you know well, might use project management techniques to assist in managing change or implementing marketing programmes.

---

# Case Study – The Lens Shop Ltd.

The Lens Shop Ltd (TLS) is a camera retailer based in the UK. It currently has 15 outlets based in the major centres of population.

There are two types of retailer selling cameras in the UK. On the one hand, stores that sell a limited range of cameras amongst a range of other electrical and domestic appliances. These are mainly large department stores and electrical retailers that sell computers, hi-fis, televisions and cameras. Then there are specialist camera stores that only sell photographic products. TLS is one of the major retailers in this more specialist camera sector.

TLS sells the majority of the leading brands. It also is the largest and most well established outlet for discontinued products, used by all the distributors to clear their shelves of 'old' product lines. These products are discounted heavily by TLS. TLS are able to buy in bulk and as a result can negotiate extra discounts.

All TLS stores are small and located on less expensive secondary sites, in the city centre but away from the main, high rent, shopping centre locations. As the outlets are small they need less stock for display purposes and have very limited stock room space. Management feel that small stores have a better atmosphere, are less formal, and are hectic, yet friendly.

TLS's main promotional vehicle is a colour catalogue, which is described as '16 great pages of bargains.' This is very much seen as a 'fun' brochure promoting products in a positive light-hearted way by mixing illustrations, technical details and humour. The catalogue is distributed in a number of ways; to people coming into the stores, from racks outside the store, by 'freephone' telephone hotline and via a database of past customers. Media advertising is also used. Typically, camera magazines will carry a five-page advertisement which highlights current bargains and often contains a promotional voucher for discounts or free accessories.

Prices are highly competitive, often discounted below recommended retail levels. The customer is provided with a price guarantee that TLS will beat any current local price by £10 for a similar brand of camera. TLS also offer a three year extended warranty at an extremely low price. Additionally, their warranty offers a unique guaranteed buy-back service for customers wishing to upgrade their photographic equipment. Management see this as a genuine customer service which will hopefully encourage customer loyalty. All goods are subject to a 14-day exchange.

The company also aims to give high levels of customer service. Members of staff have a high degree of product knowledge. Sales assistants are particularly helpful, advising on the best purchases for any given budget. Staff are also happy to demonstrate the equipment. Selections of recent reviews from camera magazines are also available in the store to provide further information to customers.

To maintain required levels of customer service, all customers are given a short questionnaire and asked to return them to the Managing Director of TLS by freepost. The Managing Director reviews all comments relating to customer service, and responds where appropriate.

**Source:** SMM Planning & Control Examination Paper, December 1998.

---

**Questions**

1. Explain the benefits of an internal marketing programme in implementation of the marketing plan.

2. Explain to the Managing Director of TLS how an internal marketing programme might be implemented.

## SUMMARY OF KEY POINTS

In this Session, we have introduced some of the techniques and approaches for overcoming the problems facing organisations in implementing their strategic plans. It has covered the following key points:

- Key success factors in implementing plans and strategies include leaderships, culture, structure, resources, control, skills, strategy and systems.

- Implementation can fail due to poor plans or weaknesses during implementation. These weaknesses have their origins in external and internal barriers to effective implementation that organisations face, that test Managers' abilities and commitment.

- Managing and implementing change is complex and uncertain. Winning support from employees throughout the organisation is essential to success and much of the 'management of change' literature deals with the 'soft' issues (staff, skills, shared values and style) as distinct from the 'hard' issues of systems, strategy and structure in the 7S McKinsey model.

- Techniques such as internal marketing and project management can be used to facilitate managing change in organisations.

- Internal marketing involves treating employees as customers and using traditional techniques of marketing planning and communication.

- Project management is a philosophy and set of techniques for objective setting, planning, delegation, crisis management and control.

## Improving and developing own learning

The following projects are designed to help you develop your knowledge and skills further by carrying out some research yourself. Feedback is not provided for this type of learning because there are no 'answers' to be found, but you may wish to discuss your findings with colleagues and fellow students.

## Project A

Using your own organisation, or one with which you are familiar, examine the implementation of a plan or strategy or an attempt to introduce change.

Using the frameworks and techniques identified in this Session, evaluate how successful the organisation was and why this was so.

## Project B

Prepare an internal marketing plan for the implementation of a business or marketing plan in your organisation or one that you know well.

The plan should identify target segments and appropriate elements of the marketing mix.

The budget should be realistic for the change being introduced.

## Project C

Do a little more reading about project management techniques in a practical management textbook. Identify and describe how the following are used to plan and control a project:

- Work breakdown structure.
- PERT, Gantt or critical path analysis.
- Resource budgets.

# Feedback to activities

## Activity 14.1

This part of the syllabus builds on the Effective Management for Marketing (EMM) module at Advanced Certificate level. Even if you did not study the EMM module, you are expected to be familiar with its content.

The three features mentioned – leadership, HRM and project management – are all characteristics of strategic management because they are essential for managing change. That is not to say that, just because it is good at all three of these, an organisation uses a strategic management approach. However, if your evaluation has shown that the organisation is weak in all three areas, then it is unlikely to be using strategic management effectively. It is likely to have problems in identifying and recognising the need for change, maintaining high levels of resistance to change and difficulty implementing change.

## Activity 14.2

A marketing tool available to overcome cultural barriers to a market orientation in the organisation is the internal marketing plan. Internal marketing is a planned effort to effect change through communication, motivation and training. As such, close involvement with HR is essential to success. It is likely to be used most effectively in organisations that already possess a strong marketing orientation.

Segments in the organisation include: supporters, neutrals and opposers. The internal marketing plan should specify the marketing mix for each of these groups or segments.

- Product – the change itself.
- Price – the cost of change to the individual.
- Promotion – the mix of communications media to be used.
- Place – the methods to be used, e.g. training.

This was Question 2 in the P&C exam paper in June 2001. You can see a full specimen answer on the CIM student web site.

## Activity 14.3

The 7S model provides a helpful framework in analysing the capabilities of an organisation in embracing and implementing change. The 7 elements of the organisation cover all the perspectives of the organisation's ability to identify and recognise the need for change, plan appropriate change and implement change effectively.

Your evaluation could use the following matrix to identify key strengths and weaknesses from which your final conclusions can be drawn.

|  | Identification and recognition | Planning | Implementation |
|---|---|---|---|
| Strategy |  |  |  |
| Shared values |  |  |  |
| Structure |  |  |  |
| Staff |  |  |  |
| Skills |  |  |  |
| Systems |  |  |  |
| Style |  |  |  |

## Activity 14.4

Project management is a set of techniques designed for the performance of specific and one-off tasks or projects. In most (but not all organisations) the tasks are routine and performed over and over. Project management deals with activities and tasks that are performed once or just a few times. Change, although becoming continuous in organisations today, is often treated as a discrete and one-off activity, so lends itself to project management techniques. Because organisations are used to routine, projects usually contain higher uncertainty and can even be uncomfortable for some people. The skills and approach to projects are therefore different to those required for the routine running of the organisation.

The key elements of project management that you should have covered are:

- Planning – this covers objective setting, identification of activities required, resource requirements and scheduling (e.g. PERT or Gantt) to meet objectives, taking into account resource constraints.

- Team building – forming, motivating and directing the team charged with delivering the project, often from a range of disciplines within the organisation.

- Control and reporting – the nature of project plans makes it easy to monitor progress towards objectives and taking appropriate action.

If techniques like these are not used effectively, projects can fail through poor planning, a lack of planning, or poor implementation.

# Session 15

# Controlling the plan and evaluating success

## Introduction

In this final Session we explore mechanisms for controlling and evaluating the success of the plan. We cover the principles of control systems and then how organisations use such systems, particularly in the context of marketing. Finally, the Session covers measurement, an increasingly important aspect of marketing as marketers attempt to demonstrate the value that brands and other marketing activities add to organisations.

---

### LEARNING OUTCOMES

At the end of this Session you will be able to:

- Explain the principles of control systems.

- Explain how organisations use management control processes and discuss their implications for marketing.

- Explain how these principles can be applied to provide effective feedback on marketing activities.

- Initiate control systems for marketing planning.

- Explain how measures are used to evaluate marketing.

---

## Principles of control systems

Control mechanisms aim to translate strategic plans into specific actions (Drummond and Ensor 2001). Their purpose is to ensure that behaviour and operations conform to the corporate objectives and policy. Marketing Managers need to be aware of a range of control variables, financial measures, budgetary controls, performance appraisal and benchmarking as tools available to them in the control process.

Basic control theory proposes that most organisations need to measure, compare and analyse variances from plan so that timely corrective actions may be taken to keep implementation on track. Control compares what should have happened with what has or is likely to happen in the near future. In business, performance is usually measured against objectives – corporate, business or marketing – and budgets.

Quantifiable measures are typically used but they must be the relevant to the business rather than those easiest to measure. The ideology behind control systems is that, by monitoring performance, they enable Managers to identify problems before a situation becomes critical. Many of the basic principles of control systems are inherent in concepts such as total quality management and continuous improvement.

Basically, the process is broken down into a series of simple steps:

- Set the target(s) – quantified objectives or a budget. Budgets can be historical information based, zero based or activity-based.
- Determine the method(s) of measurement.
- Measure results at the end of each period, usually monthly or quarterly.
- Compare results against the targets and identify any variances.
- Identify and implement any necessary corrective action.


Any process uses inputs and outputs. Drummond & Ensor argue that the measurement of output alone constitutes 'inspection' as opposed to control. Addressing inputs as well as outputs allows Managers to optimise the process and take a strategic view.

Inputs are measured and controlled to enable Managers to allocate appropriate levels of resources to particular processes or activities, and to adjust those levels as required. Typical inputs include:

- Finance used for capital investment and to provide working capital for the organisation.
- Operations resources such as production or service capacity, materials, training, systems and other assets.
- Human resources in different quantities and with different types and levels of skills.

The resulting outputs are:

- **Efficiency** – measures of how well the organisation uses its inputs and assets. Typical measures of efficiency include profit, contribution and value added, often expressed per unit of input: for example, sales per square foot or profit per employee. It is important that these measures concentrate on the efficiency of the assets and inputs that are strategically important to the organisation: for example seats on aircraft for airlines, retail space for supermarkets and service deliverers in professional service companies.

- **Effectiveness** – measures of the results that the use of the inputs and assets has in the market. Typical measures of effectiveness include sales revenues, market share and customer satisfaction ratings. Again, it is important that these measures concentrate on the performances that are strategically important. For example, sales revenue or market share on its own may be important in markets where economies of scale are significant; profits however, can also be a good broad indicator of effectiveness.

Organisations use a range of techniques to monitor and control their performance in the market. These typically include:

- **Financial analysis** – would include techniques such as ratio analysis, variance analysis, cash flow monitoring and capital expenditure monitoring.

- **Market analysis** – would cover total market demand and market share as well as marketing resources used.

- **Sales analysis** – if separate from market analysis, would include analysis of sales targets and selling costs.

- **Physical resource analysis** – would involve analysis of plant and equipment utilisation, and other measures of productivity and product quality.

- **Systems analysis** – would look at the effectiveness of strategic implementation and analysis of marketing resource application.

Organisations have traditionally used purely financial measures of performance, which tell them what has happened. Their weakness is that they do not necessarily reflect the strength, effectiveness and efficiency of the organisation at some point in the future. The balanced scorecard was developed to overcome this one-sided view of the organisation.

---

**Activity 15.1**

Explain the rationale behind control systems.

---

## Effective control systems

Drummond and Ensor (2001) propose that the following principles should be adhered to if a system of control is to be effective.

- **Involvement** – it is important to encourage participation in the process. Staff at all levels should be encouraged to contribute to target setting. These targets could include their own development needs. It has been suggested that ensuring the involvement of staff results in increased levels of commitment and morale and a sense of ownership.

- **Target setting** – targets should be objective and measurable. They should also be achievable but challenging. Budgets can be developed for all areas of the organisations' operations.

- **Focus** – it is important to distinguish between the **symptoms** and the **causes** of problems. Identifying the cause and tackling this rather than just the symptoms will prevent the problem recurring in the future and save time and money.

- **Effectiveness** – organisations should measure **effectiveness** as well as **efficiency**. Effectiveness is concerned with doing the right thing (a goal of the professional marketer) while efficiency is concerned with doing things right (the goal of most management and financial accountants). It is important that you measure those elements that are important rather than those that are easiest to measure.

- **Management by exception** – this approach sets the limits within which performance can vary against the target before management intervention. The process involves setting tolerances and standards for normal operations and management intervention only takes place when these pre-set measures are breached.

- **Action** – an effective control system does not just measure performance in a passive way. It promotes action when necessary, such as resource adjustment or corrective action in reply to a variance report.

---

**Activity 15.2**

Discuss the management control processes used in your organisation or one that you know well.

Are they adequate? Where would you suggest improvements?

---

# Control mechanisms for marketing

Control mechanisms are just as important to Marketing Managers as they are to all departmental and functional Managers in an organisation. An old adage in management is 'You can't manage what you can't measure'. The implication for Marketing Managers is that they have to measure the efficiency and effectiveness of their marketing activities to make decisions about the type of activities to undertake in the future in order to achieve specific objectives.

A second reason that measurement is increasingly important to Marketing Managers is that organisations are keen to establish the return they get from their investment in marketing. An important part of most Marketing Managers' roles today is to show how much value marketing activities add to the organisation and how they impact on the bottom line. If they are unable to do this, marketing is always a potential target for cuts in leaner times.

A third reason for marketers to be involved in measurement is that there are moves afoot in accounting standards to introduce the valuation of brands and other marketing assets into annual financial reporting. It is easy for the Marketing Manager to leave this task to the financial accountants; however, they need to be aware of the issues and need to be involved in the process.

So, Marketing Managers need to use measurement for control. They have four main tools available to them: benchmarking, financial and management ratios, performance appraisal and the balanced scorecard. These are described in turn below.

# Benchmarking

Many companies set out to benchmark their core operational standards against the very best in the business. This does not necessarily have to come from the same industry sector, just the same discipline. It is a valuable tool for marketing in an industry that is traditionally not market-led: a firm could benchmark itself against a Marketing Department in a market-led industry to identify areas for improvement.

Benchmarking is the process of comparing performance of all or part of an organisation to that of leading performers in a relevant field. It was developed by the Japanese after World War II. It is part of the process of continuous performance (which includes TQM and kaizen) and is used as a control mechanism to ensure that the organisation is operating effectively and efficiently in comparison with the 'best of breed' in the industry or profession.

Benchmarking can be used in two different ways:

- **Process benchmarking** – this compares performance in one or more processes in the organisation with one or more organisations of a similar size or type. Alternatively, as already discussed, this type of benchmark may be used to ascertain the difference between your operations and one of a standard to which you aspire. Data or information exchange has to be open and honest.

- **Competitor benchmarking** – this compares performance in key areas against that of competitors. It is usually more difficult to obtain valid and reliable information for this purpose.

## Financial and quantitative measures

Marketers often allow themselves to be blinded by figures and ratios. However, they are simply tools to measure, control and make decisions about the use of marketing activities and assets.

The information needed will usually be obtained from monthly or weekly management accounts. These will usually show budgets, actuals and variances against each budget heading. These reports often contain a lot of data and not enough information. The Marketing Manager has to take responsibility for obtaining the relevant measures and measuring the right things.

A selection of financial ratios and measures can be used to measure the effectiveness and efficiency of marketing activities. Marketers need only use a subset of the ratios available, which can be summarised as follows:

- **Profitability ratios** – measure the effectiveness of the use of available resources. Typical profitability ratios include **gross margin**, **nett** or **operating profit**, **'contribution'** (sales revenues minus cost of goods/services sold minus sales and marketing costs), **return on capital employed** and **return on investment**.

- **Liquidity ratios** – measure the capacity to pay short-term debts and are used in assessing the risk to future objectives. Typical liquidity ratios include **liquid** or **quick ratio** and **debtor payment period**. Liquidity ratios are not usually the concern of marketers, with the possible exception of debtor payment period and stock holding period. However, marketers should understand their use and implications.

- **Solvency (or capital structure) ratios** – measure the ability to meet long-term financial commitments and are used in assessing the impact of longer-term commitments and risks to future cash flows. Like liquidity ratios, solvency ratios are not usually the concern of marketers. Typical solvency ratios include **gearing** and **times interest covered**.

- **Investment ratios** – measure the attractiveness of the company to investors and shareholders. They indicate potential levels and sources of financing for the organisation. Again, they are not usually the concern of marketers. Typical investment ratios include **earnings per share, yield** and **price/earnings ratio**.

In addition to the financial ratios, Marketing Managers can also use management accounting ratios to measure the effectiveness and efficiency of marketing activities. There are no set measures to use, each organisation using slightly different measures. Typical quantitative measures will include:

- Measures of effectiveness of marketing campaigns, e.g. levels of response.

- Measures of resources levels used, e.g. marketing people and costs per campaign or period.

- Measures of achievement, e.g. £ profit or £ sales achieved per £ spent on marketing. By comparing this with past periods or other organisations, the Marketing Manager can decide how effective the marketing activities are.

- Measures of value of marketing assets, such as brands and customers. Assets are usually valued in terms of the future cash flows they are capable of generating. For example, marketing might produce a sales forecast for each customer over, say, a five year period and calculate the contribution as the basis for valuing the customer base. The Finance Manager would usually assist in this type of calculation.

## Performance appraisal

Performance appraisal is about achieving better results from groups and individuals. A performance appraisal framework is based on planned objectives, levels of individual and team achievement and competence (Drummond and Ensor 2001). The focus is on the development and control of staff and is critical to project implementation.

The purpose of appraisals is to encourage and motivate the individual, the group and therefore the organisation to do a better job. At the same time it should review the skills level of the individual for the tasks in hand and provide appropriate opportunities for development and advancement. Effective performance appraisal requires Managers to have good 'people' skills and appraisal feedback should be constructive rather than destructive. Appraisal has to be objective and visible for both the individual and the Manager: measurable objectives and variance analysis will contribute to this.

The Manager must review the performance as part of a continuous and regular management activity, give feedback by highlighting 'hard' measurable results, and counsel if necessary. In the marketing area this feeds back into the implementation plan in a positive way, with all individuals and the group as a whole knowing their roles and actions plans for the future.

## Balanced scorecard

The balanced scorecard was introduced as a tool for organisations to assess their performance across a wider dimension than just financial performance, which tends to provide a backward looking view of the organisation. As a control technique, its strength is that it starts with objective setting and selection of strategies. It encourages organisations to develop measures of performance from four key perspectives:

- **The customer perspective** – this is how the customer sees the organisation. This encourages the organisation to measure performance such as customer satisfaction and retention.

- **The internal perspective** – this perspective includes the major processes that are involved in delivering satisfaction to customers. Measures will be based on the main outputs from these key processes, for example levels of awareness of the brand.

- **The innovation and learning perspective** – this perspective covers the ability of the organisation to create value by innovating and learning. This is particularly relevant to marketing, including as it does measures of idea generation, product development and improvements in campaign performance.

- **The financial perspective** – this important traditional perspective is retained, representing the view of the organisation from the shareholders' perspective.

---

**Activity 15.3**

How might an organisation you know use benchmarking in the control process?

Use relevant examples of where it may be appropriately used.

---

## Using control to make things happen

Control is defined as 'ensuring that the desired results are obtained'. Planning without control simply means that the organisation has some intentions but no means of knowing whether they have been achieved or not. Control systems are essential to make sure that the organisation drives the content of the plans and achieves its objectives in the market.

Marketing activities are inherently volatile (Drummond and Ensor 2001) due to a constantly changing business environment driven by the needs and wants of the market and the resources the organisation is prepared to allocate. Measuring marketing performance is a process of determining appropriate criteria by which to judge activity. Kotler (1997) identifies four main areas associated with the control of marketing activity:

- **Annual plan** – evaluates successful achievements, focusing on aspects such as sales, market shares, expenses and customer perception.

- **Efficiency control** – concerns gaining optimum value from the marketing assets. Managers are worried about obtaining value for money from their marketing activities and whilst sometimes PR, customer loyalty schemes etc. may seem a high investment for the organisation's accountants, as long as they are planned and measured against expenditure targets and revenue targets, marketing can be deemed as a worthwhile cause.

- **Profitability control** – is focused on optimising and controlling profit. Analysis of profitability will allow strategic marketing decisions of product, customer or channel elimination, brand strategies and communications strategies whilst looking at different segments and geographical locations.

- **Strategic control** – ensures that marketing activities are directed towards strategic goals and are an integral part of the overall process of delivering value.

The essence of control is the ability to measure and take actions precisely and in a timely way. In marketing terms, there should be a balanced view of what is required from the measurement and control, what actions should be taken when a variance analysis is highlighted and how the corrective action may impinge on the rest of the organisation, distribution channels or the marketplace itself.

Marketing is about a long-term view, not a short-term increase in sales which might damage corporate image or positioning in the future. This is particularly true in international marketing where it is not always possible to control the execution of marketing plans as precisely as in the home market. This is because the environment scanning and feedback required from potentially volatile international markets, where information flows may be distinctly poor or substandard, may be just too difficult to achieve. Flexibility is therefore required and corrective actions need to be taken on a regular basis.

---

**Activity 15.4**

As an external Project Management Consultant to a sportswear manufacturer you have been asked to write a report outlining the general principles that need to be followed in establishing an effective control system.

The company has also asked you to illustrate the potential problems that control systems can create.

---

# Case Study – Database marketing at a click

David Murphy reviews the latest technology of interest to marketers to enable them to plan and execute successful campaigns.

'Keep control in the Marketing Department, rather than enlisting the help of those in IT.'

Take an established business with a clean, well-maintained customer database. There's no shortage of sophisticated database management and mining tools available to help the company cut and slice its customer list any way it wants. However, in a bid to keep control in the Marketing Department, rather than enlist the help of those in IT, MarkIT Information Services' *MarkIT Manager* software is designed for marketers.

The software is especially well suited to companies carrying out ongoing direct marketing activity, either with a large database of over 250,000 prospects and customers, or with a smaller database but one that is marketed to with above-average frequency.

Based on Alterian database technology, *MarkIT Manager* is a software program which contains a series of key processing modules built around a central data management and campaign control capability.

## Campaign planning

There are four elements to the software: Design, Selection, Execution and Evaluation.

In the Design section, the marketer can build a campaign, using some or all elements used in previous campaigns to speed the process up. The marketer can specify the elements to be included in the campaign. He or she can also set frequency and start and end dates. Crucially it is also possible to calculate cost and profit for the campaign based on expected response rates. The cost of running the campaign is entered, including any incentives, along with the profit value of each sale resulting from it.

According to Roger Luxton, head of consultancy at MarkIT, this is a key consideration. "People run campaigns that should never have been run. We estimate that 40% of campaigns that fail never had a chance of succeeding."

In the Selection section, the Campaign Manager can begin profiling and segmenting the database to select their target prospect. New queries can be generated and saved for subsequent use and saved previous queries can be applied to the database again. So in a couple of mouse clicks, a database of say, 200,000 prospects can be segmented into unmarried, female property owners. A suppression module removes from the list recent complainers, those mailed in the last three months, or whatever other criteria the marketer sets.

Execution brings the Design and Selection sections of the system together to enable the marketer to roll out the campaign. The entire campaign can be created and the database profiled and segmented in advance, ready to run at a pre-specified date using the data on the database at that point in time.

Post-campaign, the Evaluation tool helps assess the results of the campaign, slicing the data any way the marketer likes in order to analyse cost per response, profit per response, number or percentage of responders and the campaign's overall profit.

The data can be presented in a variety of ways to make it easy for the campaign Manager to extract top-level results and import data into Excel spreadsheets or PowerPoint presentations and share it with colleagues and Directors.

"Post-campaign evaluation is a bit of a chore so a lot of people, even heavy direct marketers, don't do it," says Luxton. "Here it happens at the click of a button."

## Customer comment

One of the first customers to sign up for the system was Britannic Assurance. This company is using the system to uncover high-quality leads for follow-up by its direct sales force, automating the quarterly campaigns that form a central plank of the company's marketing strategy.

"MarkIT's comprehensive analysis of our customer data enables us to profile our highest value customers and provide leads to our direct sales staff in those that are likely to purchase other products from us," says Britannic Assurance's market research and Database Manager, Simon Wigley. "By taking a more personalised and targeted approach to our direct marketing, we hope to increase our cross-sell ratio significantly and expect to see a rapid return on our investment."

**Source:** 'Database Marketing at a Click', *Marketing Business,* November 2001.

---

### Questions

1. Explain the various types of marketing and financial information that are useful within a marketing control system.

2. From the Case Study, explain the measures that can be performed by the 'Evaluation' tool of the software described.

## SUMMARY OF KEY POINTS

In this Session, we have introduced the principles and techniques of control, and covered the following key points:

- Effective control systems involve the measurement of inputs as well as outputs.

- The control process involves: setting the target(s); determining the method(s) of measurement; measuring results at the end of each period; comparing results against targets and identifying variances; and identifying and implementing corrective action.

- Effective control systems have focus, involve people and promote action.

- Management control extends to cover establishing and maintaining performance benchmarks, financial and quantitative measures of efficiency and effectiveness, performance appraisal and balanced scorecard.

- The marketing management team will be particularly focused on the annual plan, profitability control, control of the efficiency of marketing activities and strategic control.

## Improving and developing own learning

The following projects are designed to help you develop your knowledge and skills further by carrying out some research yourself. Feedback is not provided for this type of learning because there are no 'answers' to be found, but you may wish to discuss your findings with colleagues and fellow students.

### Project A

Find out and examine the types of control used in your organisation or one that you know well.

Explore what information is routinely generated within the organisation and used by Managers for control purposes.

Discuss with a colleague how effective the information and decision making processes are.

---

**Project B**

Prepare a short report for the Marketing Director or Manager that recommends appropriate measures for the control of marketing activities in your organisation or one that you know well.

---

**Project C**

Write a project proposal to use benchmarking to identify standards of practice for your organisation's marketing activities.

Your proposal should explain what is involved and the benefits to the organisation as well as the main activities and costs involved.

---

## Feedback to activities

### Activity 15.1

Control is the basis for monitoring progress towards objectives in an organisation. Used proactively, it is the feedback that allows learning and improvement to take place.

The elements of a control system are:

- Process, with inputs and outputs. This might be a marketing activity such as brochure development with its various inputs (e.g. customer requirements) and outputs (e.g. the brochure).

- Measures, usually of the outputs. In this example, measures might include date of delivery, quality and costs incurred.

- Comparator – these measures then have to be compared with some pre-set standards or target. In this example, the delivery date and requirements would have been set by the 'customer' (the Sales Department) against which delivery on time and quality of the brochure (whether it meets the customer's requirements) will be measured. The budget may have been set in the plan for the year, against which cost incurred will be measured.

- Decision process decides whether the process is working or has worked effectively. If it has not, some action may need to be taken to adjust the inputs or process for the next iteration.

## Activity 15.2

You identified the elements of a control system in an organisation in the last Activity. Here you have evaluated how effective the system is in a specific organisation. Problems typically encountered in control systems include:

- Not using measures or pre-set standards/targets.

- Measuring the wrong things. Many organisations measure efficiency (whether they are doing things right) at the expense of effectiveness (whether they are doing the right things).

- Measuring too much so that the organisation spends too much time and energy measuring and controlling what it does, rather than getting on with it.

Your recommendations may therefore have been on overcoming some or all of these problems, depending on what your investigation revealed.

## Activity 15.3

Benchmarking is an effective tool for control because it should link back to objectives and compare performance against an external measure. The main steps in using benchmarking are:

- Identifying key performance measures for the business function or process.

- Identifying competitors or organisations that exemplify best practice against which to benchmark.

- Collecting measurement data for the 'benchmark' organisation and your own organisation.

- Identifying areas of competitive advantage by comparing performance levels.

- Designing and implementing plans to improve one's own performance on key issues relative to performance.

## Activity 15.4

Principles to be followed:

- Involvement of staff.
- Target setting should be SMART and agreed in advance.
- Focus on cause, not symptoms.
- Measure the right things – effectiveness as well as efficiency.
- Management by exception.
- Action, not just measurement.

Typical problems:

- Expensive and time-consuming.
- Demotivating on staff.
- Emphasis on measuring efficiency because it is easier to measure.
- Deals with symptoms, not causes.

This was Question 7 in the Planning & Control examination in December 2001. You can see a full specimen answer on the CIM student web site.

# Glossary

# Glossary

**Above-the-line** – advertising for which a payment is made and for which a commission is paid to the advertising agency.

**ACORN** – A Classification of Residential Neighbourhoods: a database which divides up the entire population of the UK in terms of housing in which they live.

**Acquisition** – one company acquiring control of another by purchase of a majority shareholding.

**Added value** – the increase in worth of a product or service as a result of a particular activity. In the context of marketing this might be packaging or branding.

**Advertising** – promotion of a product, service or message by an identified sponsor using paid for media.

**AIDA** – Attention, Interest, Desire, Action: a model describing the process that advertising or promotion is intended to initiate in the mind of a prospective customer.

**Alliance** – an agreement of two or more organisations to co-operate to pursue a defined strategy or activity.

**Ansoff matrix** – model relating marketing strategy to general strategic direction. It maps product/market strategies.

**Asset-based approach** – a view of the organisation in which the base for developing competitive advantage consists of its various tangible and intangible assets.

**Asset-based marketing** – an approach to developing strategy and conducting marketing activities in which opportunities in the organisation's environment are found to match its assets and capabilities rather than the other way round.

**Attack strategies** – see *offensive strategies.*

**Balance sheet** – one of the three parts of a financial statement showing the assets, liabilities and shareholders' funds of the company at a point in time, usually the end of the period on which the report is being made.

**Balanced scorecard** – a technique allowing a company to monitor and manage performance against defined objectives. Measurements typically cover financial performance, customer value, internal business process, innovation performance and employee performance.

**BCG matrix** – a model used for product portfolio analysis based on relative market share and market growth.

**Below-the-line** – non-media advertising or promotion when no commission has been paid to the advertising agency.

**Benchmarking** – the process of comparing performance of a specific activity with that of a similar activity performed in one or more organisations, usually with the aim of making improvements to the process.

**Brand** – the set of physical attributes of a product or service, together with the beliefs and expectations surrounding it.

**Brand equity** – the 'value' of the name and image of a brand in terms of its assets and liabilities. It is essentially a measure of the additional cash the organisation can generate through its brand.

**Brand extension** – extending the use of a brand to other products in the same market.

**Brand stretching** – taking a brand into a new, unrelated market.

**Brand valuation** – the process of determining the financial value of brand for the purposes of accounting for it on the balance sheet.

**Break-even analysis** – a technique used in decisions about cost, volumes and pricing of products and services. The break-even point is the point at which revenues based on a given price result in neither a profit nor a loss.

**Budget** – a plan in monetary terms of activities for a future period. Each department, function or unit in an organisation will usually have a budget against which its performance is measured. There are various forms of budget in organisations.

**Business plan** – a strategic document showing cash flow, forecasts and direction of a company.

**Business strategy** – the means by which a business works towards achieving its stated aims.

**Business-to-business (b2b)** – relating to the sale of a product for any use other than personal consumption.

**Business-to-consumer (b2c)** – relating to the sale of a product for personal consumption.

**Buying behaviour** – the process that buyers go through when deciding whether or not to purchase goods or services.

**Capabilities** – a collective term for the assets and competencies of an organisation.

**Cash flow statement** – one of the three parts of a financial statement for a company, showing the main inflows and outflows of cash over a period.

**Centralisation** – the tendency in an organisation for information to flow towards its centre or head and for the majority of decisions to be taken by top management.

**Channels** – the methods used by a company to communicate and interact with its customers.

**Competencies** – the skills that are contained within an organisation. Core competencies provide the foundation for competitive advantage.

**Competitive advantage** – see *sustainable competitive advantage.*

**Competitive intelligence** – information of value to an organisation about its competitors and their activities that may be used in decision making.

**Competitor analysis** – the process of analysing information about existing or potential competitors to inform decisions about future actions of an organisation in its markets.

**Confusion marketing** – controversial strategy of deliberately confusing the customer.

**Consumer** – individual who buys and uses a product or service.

**Consumer behaviour** – the buying habits and patterns of consumers in the acquisition and usage of products and services.

**Contribution** – also known as *unit contribution*. It is revenue minus direct costs of production, promotion and delivery and is usually expressed per unit. It is used to calculate break-even in cost-volume-profit analysis and pricing decisions.

**Control** – the process of ensuring that actions taken to achieve a strategy or plan conform to the requirements or standards laid down.

**Corporate identity** – the character a company seeks to establish for itself in the mind of the public.

**Corporate reputation** – a complex mix of characteristics such as ethos, identity and image that go to make up a company's public personality.

**Cost leadership** – one of Porter's three *generic strategies* in which the organisation takes on a wide market and attempts to achieve lower costs than its competitors.

**Cost-volume-profit** – a term describing the relationship between the three key variables modelled when determining the break-even point for a given price. Used during *pricing decisions*.

**Costing** – the process of determining costs and attributing them to the various activities undertaken in the organisation.

**Critical success factors** – those aspects of the business or process which must result in order for objectives to be achieved; factors that are critical to success.

**Culture** – a shared set of values, beliefs and traditions that influence prevailing behaviour within a country or organisation.

**Customer** – a person or company who purchases goods or services.

**Customer analysis** – the process of collating and analysing information about customers in a market in order to identify opportunities for a particular organisation.

**Customer loyalty** – feelings or attitudes that incline a customer to return to a company, shop or outlet to purchase there again.

**Customer Relationship Management (CRM)** – the coherent management of contacts and interactions with customers.

**Customer satisfaction** – the provision of goods or services which fulfil the customer's expectations in terms of quality and service, in relation to price paid.

**DAGMAR** – Defining Advertising Goals for Measured Advertising Response, a model for planning advertising in such a way that its success can be quantitatively monitored.

**Data Protection Act** – a UK law which makes organisations responsible for protecting the privacy of personal data.

**Database marketing** – whereby customer information stored in an electronic database is utilised for targeting marketing activities.

**Decision Making Unit (DMU)** – the team of people in an organisation or family group who make the final buying decision.

**Defensive strategies** – competitive strategies analogous to military strategies that an organisation may adopt to defend itself from attack by other players in the market. They include position defence, flank defence, pre-emptive defence and counter-attack.

**Delphi technique** – a forecasting technique in which the view or estimate for the future is compiled from inputs by a number of individuals, usually experts in their field, working independently of each, usually in successive rounds.

**Demographic data** – information describing and segmenting a population in terms of age, sex, income and so on which can be used to target marketing campaigns.

**Differentiation** – ensuring that products and services have a unique element to allow them to stand out from the rest. Specifically one of Porter's three *generic strategies* in which the organisation takes on a wide market and exploits perceived uniqueness.

**Direct marketing** – all activities that make it possible to offer goods or services or to transmit other messages to a segment of the population by post, telephone, email or other direct means.

**Direct Product Profitability (DPP)** – the technique of using *contribution* to make decisions about price and monitoring performance of the organisation's assets, such as channels and production or retail space.

**Discounted Cash Flow (DCF)** – a method, used in making *investment decisions,* for calculating the present value of capital expenditure and future revenues for a project based on a *discount rate.*

**Discount rate** – the rate used in *DCF, IRR* and *payback method* to discount future values to calculate the present value of an investment. It is either the interest rate or cost of capital.

**Distribution (Place)** – the process of getting the goods from the manufacturer or supplier to the user.

**Diversification** – an increase in the variety of goods and services produced by an organisation. Diversification may be related to current goods and services, or unrelated.

**E-commerce** – business conducted electronically.

**Efficiency** – a measure of output in relation to input.

**E-marketing** – marketing conducted electronically.

**Employee Relationship Management (ERM)** – an approach based on CRM in which an organisation recognises and treats its employees as 'customers' and uses marketing techniques to communicate and maintain loyalty.

**Environmental analysis** – the process of collating and analysing information about the environment an organisation operates in, usually as an early step in the strategic management or planning cycle.

**Environmental scanning** – the process of monitoring and evaluating the organisation's environment on a continuous and routine basis to detect events that may have significance for the organisation and the way it operates.

**Ethical marketing** – marketing that takes account of the moral aspects of decisions.

**Export marketing** – the marketing of goods or services to overseas customers.

**External analysis** – study of the external marketing environment.

**Field marketing** – extending an organisation's marketing in the field through merchandising, product launches, training of retail staff, etc.

**Financial statements** – statements made by a company that presents a 'true and fair view' of its financial position at the end of a period, usually one year. They consist of a *profit and loss statement, balance sheet and cash flow statement.* Under company law in UK, all companies are required to submit financial statements annually to Companies House; companies above a certain turnover have to submit accounts that have been independently audited.

**Five forces model** – an analytic model developed by Michael E. Porter which analyses the competitive environment and industry structure.

**Fixed costs** – costs in an organisation that do not vary with the level of activity or sales. They are usually fixed over a certain period.

**FMCG** – Fast Moving Consumer Goods such as packages food and toiletries.

**Focus** – one of Porter's three *generic strategies* in which the organisation focuses on one segment or a narrow part of the market and exploits either perceived uniqueness or low costs.

**Forecasting** – estimation of the probability and scope of future events and performance. A forecast is usually used as the basis for a budget.

**Franchising** – the selling of a licence by the owner (franchisor) to a third party (franchisee) permitting the sale of a product or service for a specified period.

**Gap analysis** – the process of identifying the gap over a period of time between an organisation's objectives and the projected results of its current or potential objectives. The gap is then filled by one or more strategies or courses of action.

**Generic strategies** – the term used to describe Porter's three competitive strategies available to organisations to develop and maintain advantage *(differentiation, cost leadership* and *focus).* Failure to develop a clear strategy will usually result in an organisation becoming 'stuck in the middle'.

**Geo-demographics** – a method of analysis combining geographic and demographic variables.

**Grey market (silver market)** – term used to define a population over a certain age (usually 65).

**Industrial marketing (or business-to-business marketing)** – the marketing of industrial products.

**Innovation** – development of new products, services or ways of working (processes).

**Innovation audit** – the process, conducted usually as part of the *internal analysis,* of investigating and evaluating an organisation's innovations capabilities and performance.

**Internal analysis** – the study of a company's internal marketing resources in order to assess strengths, weaknesses and opportunities.

**Internal customers** – employees within an organisation viewed as 'consumers' of a product or service provided by another part of the organisation.

**Internal marketing** – the process of eliciting support for a company and its activities among its own employees in order to encourage them to promote its goals.

**International marketing** – the conduct and co-ordination of marketing activities in more than one country.

**Internal Rate of Return (IRR)** – a technique used in making *investment decisions* to determine the percentage rate at which the *net present value* of an investment equals zero, in other words when the project break-even taking into account the time value of money. If the IRR is higher than the *discount rate* then the investment is worth considering; if it is less than the *discount rate*, the project will not break-even.

**Investment decisions** – the decisions made in organisations by Senior Managers on investments in assets and capabilities of the organisation, based on the calculation of net present value of capital expenditures and revenues.

**Joint venture** – a business entity or partnership formed by two or more parties for a specific purpose.

**Jury technique** – a forecasting technique in which a group of people, usually experts in their field, working together make a forecast.

**Key account management** – account management as applied to a company's most valuable customers.

**Knowledge management** – the collection, organisation and distribution of information in a form that lends itself to practical application. Knowledge management often relies on information technology to facilitate the storage and retrieval of information.

**Logo** – a graphic usually consisting of a symbol and or group of letters that identifies a company or brand.

**Macro environment** – the external factors which affect companies' planning and performance, and are beyond its control. (SLEPT).

**Margin** – a generic term used to express profit as a percentage of sales. Gross margin is gross profit as a percentage of sales, net margin is net profit as a percentage of sales.

**Market development** – the process of growing sales by offering existing products (or new versions of them) to new customer groups.

**Market orientation** – a business culture whereby customers' needs and wants determine corporate direction.

**Market penetration** – the attempt to grow ones business by obtaining a larger market share in an existing market.

**Market research** – the gathering and analysis of data relating to markets to inform decision making.

**Marketing research** – the gathering and analysis of data relating to marketing to inform decision making (includes product research, place research, pricing research, etc.).

**Market segmentation** – the division of the marketplace into distinct sub-groups or segments, each characterised by particular tastes and requiring a specific marketing mix.

**Market share** – a business' sales of a given product or set of products to a given set of customers expressed as a percentage of total sales of all such products to such customers in a market or segment.

**Marketing audit** – scrutiny of an organisation's existing marketing system to ascertain its strengths and weaknesses.

**Marketing communications (Promotion)** – all methods used by a firm to communicate with its customers and stakeholders.

**Marketing information** – any information used or required to support marketing decisions.

**Marketing mix** – the combination of marketing inputs that affect customer motivation and behaviour (7 Ps – Product, Price, Promotion, Place, People, Process and Physical Evidence).

**Marketing planning** – the selection and scheduling of activities to support the company's chosen marketing strategy or goals.

**Marketing strategy** – the broad methods chosen to achieve marketing objectives.

**McKinsey Seven S's of management (7S Model)** – a framework for considering business strategy with reference to seven interrelated aspects of the organisation: Systems, Structure, Strategy, Style, Staff, Skills and Shared values.

**Merger** – the formation of one company from two existing companies.

**Microenvironment** – the immediate context of an organisation's operations, including such elements as customers, competitors, channels to markets and suppliers.

**Mission statement** – a summary of an organisation's business philosophy, purpose and direction.

**Model** – simplified representation of a process, designed to aid in understanding.

**Net Present Value (NPV)** – the value in today's terms of expenditures and revenues associated with a specific set of activities or project over a period of time, discounted at a specific rate. The main method for arriving at a NPV for a project is *discounted cash flow.*

**New Product Development (NPD)** – the creation of new products from evaluation of proposals through to launch.

**Niche marketing** – the marketing of a product to a small and well-defined segment of the marketplace.

**Norms** – commonly understood rules, often defined culturally rather than formally, that provide guidelines for personal behaviour.

**Objectives** – an organisation's defined and measurable aims or goals for a given period. Objectives are usually defined at corporate, business or marketing level.

**Offensive strategies** – competitive strategies analogous to military strategies that an organisation may adopt to attack other players in the market. They include frontal attack, flank attack, encirclement and bypass attack.

**Packaging** – material used to protect and promote goods.

**Payback method** – a method used in making investment decisions. Expressed as a point in time, it is the point at which a project breaks even. When it is used with a *discount rate* it takes into account the time value of money and is therefore more precise.

**Perceptual map** – a two or more dimensional representation of customer perceptions of a product or service.

**Personal selling** – one-to-one communication between seller and prospective purchaser.

**PIMS** – Profit Impact of Marketing Strategies. A US database supplying data such as environment, strategy, competition and internal data.

**Planning** – the process of determining and defining the future actions over a specified period for an organisation. Formal planning results in a written plan that usually requires the approval of head office.

**Portfolio (and portfolio analysis)** – the set of products or services which a company decides to develop and market. Portfolio analysis is the process of comparing the contents of the portfolio to see which products and services are the most promising and deserving of further investment and those which should be discontinued.

**Porter** – Michael Porter known for his work in competitive strategy who developed a number of well known models, such as *Five forces model, value chain* and *strategic groups* model, used for analysing the competitive environment of an organisation.

**Positioning** – the creation of an image for a product or service in the minds of customers, both specifically to that item and in relation to competitive offerings.

**Pricing decisions** – decisions to determine the price at which products or services will be sold. There are a number of methods available to determine price taking into account the relevant costs.

**Product life cycle** – a model describing the progress of a product from the inception of the idea via the main people of sales, to its decline.

**Profit** – the amount that is left out of revenues at the end of a period once all the relevant costs have been deducted. Profit is measured at a number of levels including gross profit (after direct costs), operating profit (after all operating expenses) and retained earnings (after interest, tax and dividends).

**Profit and Loss (P&L) account** – one of the three parts of the financial statement for a company showing the revenues and costs over the period being reported.

**Project management** – the use of various management techniques to plan and control a set of activities designed to achieve a specific goal, often undertaken as a non-routine activity.

**Promotional mix** – the components of an individual campaign which are likely to include advertising, personal selling, public relations, direct marketing, packaging and sales promotion.

**Public Relations (PR)** – the planned and sustained communication to promote mutual understanding between an organisation and its stakeholders.

**Pull promotion** – addresses the customer directly with a view to getting them to demand the product and hence 'pull' it down through the distribution chain.

**Push promotion** – relies on the next link in the distribution chain, e.g. wholesaler, to 'push' out products to the customer.

**Qualitative research** – information that cannot be measured or expressed in numeric terms. It is useful to the marketer as it often explores people's feelings and opinions.

**Quantitative research** – information that can be measured in numeric terms and analysed statistically.

**Ratio analysis** – the use of financial ratios, usually as part of a wider analysis of an organisation and its current situation, to ascertain its performance and financial health. The analysis usually involves the use of profitability, liquidity, solvency, utilisation and investment ratios.

**Reference group** – a group with which the customer identifies in some way and whose opinions and experiences influence the customer's behaviour.

**Relationship marketing** – the strategy of establishing a relationship with a customer which continues well beyond the first purchase.

**Resource-based approach** – a view of the organisation, fundamental to strategy, as a 'bundle' of historically developed resources or endowments. This view provides the foundation for *asset-based marketing.*

**Return on investment** – the value that an organisation derives from investing in a project.

**Sales forecast** – a forecast of the sales revenues expected for a future period. It is significant in that it determines the level of activity for the organisation for that period and as such forms the basis for the other forecasts of costs generated by organisations. Considerable emphasis is therefore placed on its accuracy.

**Sampling** – the use of a statistically representative subset as a proxy for an entire population, for example in order to facilitate quantitative market research.

**Scenario planning** – a technique used in planning to identify the possible future scenarios for an organisation which can then be quantified and modelled and a view taken on the probability of occurrence of each. This technique is particularly useful to organisations facing high uncertainty.

**Segmentation** – the process of dividing customers in a market up into discrete groups, each group being unique and having identifiable and similar needs.

**Sensitivity analysis** – the modelling and assessment of the potential risks facing an organisation in a specific situation using the question 'what if?'. It is commonly used in planning at the forecasting stage, setting budgets and making investment decisions to take into account different circumstances and risks.

**Skimming** – setting the original price high in the early stages of the product life cycle to get as much profit as possible before prices are driven down by increasing competition.

**SLEPT** – a framework for viewing the macro environment – Socio-cultural, Legal, Economic, Political and Technical factors.

**SMART** – a mnemonic referring to the need for objectives to be Specific, Measurable, Aspirational, Relevant and Timebound. (Note: Variations exist in the specific terms used.)

**Stakeholder** – an individual or group that affects or is affected by the organisation and its operations.

**Strategic drift** – the gradual shift of an organisation's responses away from what the market needs which, if uncorrected, may lead to the organisation becoming uncompetitive and its strategy wearing out.

**Strategic groups model** – a model, developed by Porter, in which competitors in an industry are grouped according to similarities of the way they compete.

**Strategic Business Unit (SBU)** – a part of an organisation, irrespective of its size, that is a complete business with its own customers and strategies and contains all the necessary functions to operate independently. In organisations, SBUs may take the form of divisions, departments, operating companies

**Strategy** – the goals (vision, purpose, aims or objectives) and the means for achieving them. Originally applied to armies, the term was accepted into business use in the mid 20th century.

**Strategy formulation** – the process of determining the goals, identifying and evaluating options, and specifying actions. It may be part of planning or independent of it.

**Structure** – the way a group is organised such as reporting line, lines of authority, specification of roles (commonly shown on the organisational structure chart).

**Sustainable competitive advantage** – the advantage that an organisation can gain and sustain over its competitors, usually by offering higher customer value through the products, proposition or benefits it offers.

**SWOT analysis** – analysis to determine strengths, weaknesses, opportunities and threats; often used to summarise other parts of a detailed analysis.

**Targeting** – the use of market segmentation to select and address a key group of potential purchasers.

**Trend extrapolation** – the use of historical data to identify trends and extrapolate them forwards as the basis for a forecast.

**Unique Selling Proposition (USP)** – that benefit that a product or service can deliver to customers that is not offered by any competitor.

**Unit contribution** – see *contribution*.

**Value chain** – the primary and support activities undertaken in a firm to add value to materials and other inputs which it sells to customers.

**Variable costs** – costs that vary according to the level of activity or sales.

**Variance** – the difference between a planned or budgeted activity and the actual cost or result. A variance may be positive (or favourable) or negative (or adverse). Variance analysis is used to assess performance and identify when corrective action is required.

**Virtual organisations** – organisations that deliver products and services but which have few of the physical features usually associated with organisations.

**Vision** – the long-term aims and aspirations of the organisation for itself.

# Appendix 1

# Feedback to Case Studies

## Session 1

1.  Principles:

    ■ Marketing involves identifying customers' needs.

    ■ It involves grouping, or segmenting, customers by their needs, behaviours or characteristics.

    ■ It involves selecting and targeting one or more groups and positioning the organisation's offerings through a proposition and mix of marketing tools to be attractive to each segment.

    ■ It involves developing and sustaining competitive advantage through an effective position.

    ■ The result is profit for the organisation.

2.  These principles are difficult to implement in practice for a number of reasons:

    ■ The organisation may have priorities other than customers' needs. Some high technology companies, for example, focus on the technology and products to the exclusion of customers.

    ■ Understanding customers' needs is easier said than done. Needs are not always easy to identify and customers do not always know what they need.

    ■ Competitors are equally trying to gain advantage and only one company can be market leader.

    ■ Competitive advantage needs continuing investment in technology, marketing and innovation.

    ■ Markets mature and it becomes increasingly different to find and communicate points of difference.

    ■ Profits can be compromised over time if the organisation does not continually refresh its understanding of its markets and its positioning and mix.

3. Your list of rules might include:

- Focus – on customers and make sure that everything the organisation does is geared to satisfying customers' needs profitably.

- Understand – customers' needs and keep monitoring them as they change.

- Watch – for opportunities.

- Plan – set priorities, allocate resources and identify performance measures.

- Move quickly – when you spot an opportunity: time to market is key in many markets and is getting shorter.

- Communicate – clearly through the right media to the right target audiences, including employees.

- Innovate – in both products and services to stay ahead of the competition.

- Invest – in competitive capabilities and position.

- Integrate – activities across the business: 'marketing' involves every body in the organisation.

- Measure – performance against plan and take corrective action if it starts to fall short.

## Session 2

1. easyJet's capabilities are made up of its competencies and assets. We might see the following as its main capabilities.

- Clarity of understanding of target markets and customers' needs.

- Low cost approach achieved through low overheads, ticketing over the telephone and Internet system with posted tickets, using low cost airports, and rapid aircraft turnaround.

- Attractive and clearly communicated pricing policy.

- Emphasis on those elements of the service that matter: safety, reliability, and convenience.

- Offensive marketing strategy.

- Innovative marketing for marketing communications to date with easily identifiable brand, partnerships and promotional tie-ins with mass media, high profile PR strategy, PR stunts against British Airways etc.

easyJet would hope to be able to use these to replicate its success in other markets.

2.  You may have identified the **market-based approach** as the more appropriate for easyJet, based on the argument that its success in a competitive and regulated market will depend on knowing its customers, identifying opportunities and moving more quickly than competitors to exploit those opportunities.

    Alternatively, you may have preferred an **asset-based approach.** Now that easyJet is up and running, its success is due to some extremely effective capabilities. These capabilities are difficult for competitors to replicate and for easyJet to change. From now on, the argument might go, easyJet should look for opportunities that enable it to exploit these capabilities rather than having to go to the trouble and expense of developing new ones.

## Session 3

1.  Inmarsat has clearly undertaken some market analysis and auditing as part of defining its proposition and strategy leading up to flotation. It would have served a number of benefits including:

- Quantifying the market size.

- Identifying the main customer needs and 'grouping' needs and behaviours in order to identify segments the company can target.

- Identifying existing and potential competitors. This will involve understanding the function that satellite communications perform. For example, if its only competitors are mobile phone companies, that says one thing about the use of satellite communications. However, if landline-based networks and couriers are also competitors, this tells them something else.

- Identifying channels to market. These may be existing channels or new ones that the company can develop or exploit.

- Identifying trends in both customers and competitors.

2. Inmarsat faces a number of strategic issues including:

- Identifying its position in the market and the function that its products are going to fulfil.

- Identifying target segments.

- Developing an appropriate orientation within the organisation. As an ex-public sector organisation, its culture may lack a commercial edge.

- Developing the capabilities necessary to compete effectively in the product markets it chooses. This will require clear leadership, resources and finance; it will all take time.

## Session 4

1. The GE matrix is just one of a number of portfolio tools. In this example, it can be used to show the elements of Marks & Spencer's portfolio on two dimensions: business strengths versus market/industry attractiveness. It is important to recognise that there is no 'right' or 'wrong' answer for a question like this: the answer you come up with will depend on the criteria you have used for each dimension and your interpretation of the incomplete data provided in the mini case.

First, you have to identify the elements of the portfolio. We can identify the following candidates:

- Ladies' fashion wear.

- Ladies' functional clothing.

- Ladies lingerie.

- Designer menswear.

- Functional menswear.

- Children's clothing.

- Financial services.

- Weddings.

- Lingerie boutiques.

Candidates in the UK and those who have experience of M&S would also know that the company also offers food and home furnishings which are not featured in the case.

Second, list criteria under each dimension of the matrix that are relevant to this market. For example, **business strengths** might consist of market share, brand image, customer loyalty, relationships with suppliers, and opportunities to develop competitive advantage. **Market attractiveness** might consist of market growth rate, number and strength of competitors, potential for premium pricing, nature of competition, and fit with corporate resources and culture. You may wish to weight these criteria to reflect their relative importance.

Third, rate each product against the criteria and determine a score on each dimension. This enables you to plot each product on the matrix.

Fourth, evaluate the results to identify problems and areas for action. You can also use it later in the planning process to make decisions about the structure and direction of the future portfolio.

2.   The GE matrix is just one of many portfolio matrices available. Others include:

- BCG – market growth versus relative market share.
- Shell – prospects for sector profitability versus competitive position.
- Abell & Hammond – market attractiveness versus competitive position.
- AD Little strategic condition matrix – stage of industry maturity versus competitive position.

The BCG is arguably the weakest of these, relying on narrow measures of market growth as an indicator of attractiveness and share as an indicator of competitive position. GE, Shell and Abell & Hammond are similar and, depending on the criteria used for each dimension, the results would be also be similar. AD Little uses industry maturity, which would arguably make it less effective in this case where we are using the matrix to investigate the portfolio at the level of the individual products.

# Session 5

1.  As the case points out, many marketers have an in-built aversion to finance! So it is important they use financial information wisely in making decisions. Finance is important at the following steps on the marketing process:

    ■ Analysing the current position of the organisation and competitors.

    ■ Identifying and setting objectives that are relevant and achievable. Marketing is about adding value and you need to understand the cause-effect relationships.

    ■ Evaluating strategic options to determine which option will add most value and how it relates to the bottom line.

    ■ Making decisions about investments in marketing assets and capabilities, including identifying returns and deciding between competing projects when funds are limited.

    ■ Measuring marketing performance.

    In short, finance is a language of professional business people. As business professionals, marketers need to understand and to be able to speak this language. To do this, the article suggests that marketers should:

    ■ Understand what the 'bottom line' really is and what it means.

    ■ Understand how business decisions and activities, and which of these, affect the bottom line. Cash is crucial to this understanding: an easy way to remember it is to think about the 'cash pipe'.

    ■ Identify the marketing actions that will generate best returns and drive up value.

    ■ Use the 10 point checklist for helping you to understand and use value-based marketing.

2.  Notes as follows:

-   Shareholder value – a long-term measure and a key indicator of future value used in strategic decision making. Each business unit, or the business as a whole, is valued by calculating the present (discounted) value of cash flows each generates and its residual value less any debt associated with it. While it has merit as an overall measure, like any financial ratio, it can result in undue emphasis on finance and shareholders at the expense of strategy and customers.

-   Total Shareholder Return (TSR) – a measure of shareholder value over time. It incorporates the long-term growth in the value of shares and dividends that investors might receive along the way.

-   Economic Profit (EP) – the net operating profit for a period (total revenues minus all the costs of production) minus the capital employed, multiplied by the cost of capital. Capital employed covers the costs of the assets used (**capital assets** such as machinery and buildings and **intangible assets** such as training and development of people), which are charged over the life of those assets. It also takes into account the opportunity cost of capital, in other words the cost of the money that the organisation has tied up in its assets.

    If EP is positive, then the organisation is contributing to shareholder value. If EP is negative, the organisation has reduced shareholder value over the period.

-   Economic Value Added (EVA) – another term for economic profit.

The important consequences of using these measures are that:

-   Shareholders dominate other stakeholders, raising questions about where customers fit in.

-   They encourage the use of debt, rather than equity, to finance investments and projects.

-   They encourage a reduction in capital employed.

-   Investments are unlikely to be approved unless they generate a return very quickly (in three years or less), because of the use of discount factors. This contributes to short-termism.

# Session 6

1.  The Marketing Director has identified two key problems to which an effective environmental monitoring system may be able to contribute: the lack of information on how the company's market is going to develop and an unclear competitive stance. It has clearly been surprised by developments in its markets and actions by its competitors. An environmental monitoring system may deliver the following benefits:

    ■ Monitoring trends and detecting changes in customers' needs and wider market developments. While TMM has strong technical skills, it has perhaps not kept up with changing customer needs.

    ■ Making Senior Managers more aware of changes in the organisation's environment and possible scenarios.

    ■ Enabling opportunities to be identified and exploited faster than, or as quickly as, competitors. TMM has been outmanoeuvred by its SE Asian competitors.

    ■ Providing objective information on which plans, decisions and a clear direction for marketing can be based. This will also help to provide a case for moving towards a stronger marketing orientation.

2.  Information needs to be structured and gathered efficiently. TMM may cover the following types of information:

| Market intelligence. | ■ Market statistics (growth, size, etc.).<br>■ Customers and needs.<br>■ Competitors.<br>■ Prices.<br>■ Industry trends.<br>■ Orders and contracts. |
|---|---|
| Alliance intelligence. | ■ Information about potential alliances, JVs and mergers or acquisitions. |
| Technical intelligence. | ■ New technology and processes.<br>■ New products.<br>■ Licensing and patents.<br>■ Costs. |

| Environmental intelligence. | ■ Government legislation and directives.<br>■ Economic conditions.<br>■ Government intentions and policies. |
| Other. | ■ Suppliers.<br>■ Materials and other inputs.<br>■ Any other category of valuable information. |

This intelligence will come from a number of sources, both internal and external, and will be collected through a variety of different channels and resources. Data has to be analysed and evaluated to have any real value, so this step should be built in. The outputs may be a series of routine reports, e.g. a strategic update newsletter for Senior Managers, and market analysis reports and forecasts which will form the basis for strategic decisions and plans.

## Session 7

1.  Criteria that would be used to decide whether and how to respond to price-based attack might include:

    ■ How serious the company thinks the attack is.

    ■ Whether the attack is likely to be sustained. If this is price discounting to gain market entry, a strategic response may not be necessary.

    ■ The reasons for the success of the attack – for example, is it linked to TMM's poor recent record of innovation?

    ■ The opportunity to develop competitive advantage in a different way than has been used traditionally. We know the company is product and technology-led at the moment.

    ■ Options for response other than price such as increasing product and service benefits or more effective communication. TMM should be careful not to let this develop into a price war.

    ■ How to win back distributors. Loss of market share may be directly linked to the loss of the four large distributors.

    ■ Costs and the company's cost base – to see what scope there is for cutting cost.

Note: In answers to this type of question in the examination, it is important to explain why these criteria have been chosen.

TMM has three main options:

- To discount price in the short term to retain existing customers.
- To match the Asian competitors.
- To counter-attack by undercutting the competition. This risks a price war.

2. As the competitive threat appears to have taken TMM by surprise, the company needs to include competitive intelligence in its information gathering and analysis activities. It appears to have about 50 direct competitors (perhaps fewer with a clearer segmentation) and an unknown number of other competitors. The types of information the company should collect include:

- Financial information, annual reports and stock exchange information.
- Trade press articles on activities and orders.
- Trade shows, exhibitions and web sites to glean information about products, services, promotions, prices, etc.
- Industry and market research reports on their relative strengths and weaknesses.
- Sales staff and customers who are in contact with competitors.
- Recruiting staff from competitors with a good understanding of their customers, distribution chains and technologies.

## Session 8

1. One of the main benefits of scenario planning is that it identifies possible futures for an organisation. It does not necessarily attribute a probability to those futures. This has the effect of putting in front of strategists and Senior Managers a range of possibilities to which the organisation may choose, or have, to react. For example, some possible scenarios for Weetabix might be:

- A competitor successfully launches a 'me too' product which, so far, no competitor has achieved.
- Customers gradually move away from 'wet' cereals to the more convenient 'in hand' and 'snack' options.

- Cereals are shown by research to contain very high residual levels of pesticides, which accumulate in the livers and kidneys of consumers.

- Increasing competition and declining demand in the breakfast cereals market results in a price war.

It appears that a price war may have started with Weetabix being forced to respond with a 12% price reduction. It is not clear whether Weetabix foresaw this possibility.

2.   The current situation can be summarised as follows:

- The strategy appears to be multi-niche. The company is a leader in its chosen niches and No 2 in the market as a whole. Its profits have increased from 15.3% to 16.9% in 1999, even with the effects of a 40% increase in advertising and a 12% price cut.

- It does not compete head-to-head with Kellogg's, the market leader, but focuses on its niches.

- Weetabix is clearly concerned about the nature and style of competition. Although there is nothing specific, there are hints that more manufacturers are supplying own label and that this is having downward pressure on prices.

- While Kellogg's products are losing share to own label, Weetabix appears to be growing slightly. Weetabix supplies own label wheat biscuits, which may be protecting its position and contributing through higher volumes to higher profits.

- It has good relationships with its distribution channels because of the quality of service.

- Its key weaknesses, from an outsider's perspective, appear to be a lack of innovation and new product development. This leaves the company vulnerable with little sales revenue coming from new or recent products.

- It is being outspent in advertising by Cereal Partners (No 3 in the market). Nestlé's Shredded Wheat is growing rapidly, possibly because of the advertising, a possible reason for the increase by Weetabix.

# Session 9

1.  The key influences on mission and objectives are:

    ■ Corporate governance – whom the organisation exists to serve.

    ■ Stakeholders' expectations – of the main stakeholder groups including shareholders, customers and employees. These expectations may be in conflict with each other.

    ■ Business ethics – social responsibility as an organisation, an increasingly important aspect of the current business agenda affecting brand reputation.

    ■ Cultural context – the nature of the dominant orientation within the organisation and the priorities that result.

    The company also faces some key trade-offs when determining its mission and objectives.

    ■ Short versus long term.

    ■ Profit versus investment in competitive position.

    ■ Growth versus stability.

    ■ Developing share in existing markets versus seeking out new customers and new markets.

    ■ Risk taking versus risk avoidance.

    ■ Profit objectives versus non-profit (e.g. social responsibility) objectives.

    Freeplay Energy may feel a particular pull in opposite directions: it is a commercial enterprise that has to make a profit for its shareholders and the partners have a desire to improve the lives of individuals.

2.  Freeplay is still a young company with an interesting balance between commercial and social objectives. Its current situation is:

    ■ Its accumulated experience is enabling it to reduce prices, so reconsider what it sees as a key market – developing countries – to achieve its social objectives.

    ■ It appears to have the innovation and technical skills needed to develop new products.

- The product – a power source – can be applied to almost any small electrical device. This opens up possibilities of alliances with established brands and products.

- It has no direct competitors but many indirect competitors. However, to succeed, the product needs to match the convenience and light weight of traditional electrical devices.

- The constraint the company faces is a lack of financial resources relative to the opportunities and choices it has available.

## Session 10

1. Evaluation of the appropriateness of Sony's actions:

- Sony is the market leader and has to be active in defending its position.

- Strategies available to the market leader:

  - Expand the total market – by targeting non-users, increasing the rate of usage or discovering new applications for the product.

  - Guard existing market share – by strong positioning, effective customer relationships and loyalty, continuous innovation, advertising, and strong distribution channels.

  - Expand current market share – by developing new products, expanding distribution channels, aggressive pricing, geographic expansion or alliances.

Alternatively, the strategies available to the market leader can be expressed in terms of strategies for defence.

- Evaluation of Sony's actions – heavy advertising to expand the total market, its alliance with AOL and RealNetworks to expand share, and price discounting to guard existing share.

- On the basis of this, it appears that Sony's actions have been appropriate and effective in maintaining its leadership, both for the short term and for the foreseeable future. Being first to market may well convey benefits in that users will be reluctant to buy another console that does not play games they already own.

2. Microsoft can be either a 'challenger' or a 'follower'.

- The offensive strategies available to a challenger are:
  - Frontal attack.
  - Flank attack.
  - Encirclement attack.
  - Bypass attack.
  - Guerrilla attack.

These strategies can be realised through actions such as price discounting, cheaper product offerings, product innovation, intensive advertising, market development, developing a prestige image, product proliferation and cost reduction.

- Microsoft are probably engaging in frontal attack. To succeed, they will have to:
  - Possess or develop a sustainable competitive advantage (cost or differentiation).
  - Negate the leader's advantage, generally by being able to deliver the leader's key attributes at almost the same level.
  - Take advantage of an obstacle hindering the leader from retaliation. This may be a factor such as limited resources.

- If these conditions are not present, Microsoft would be better to attack players other than the leader (Nintendo).

## Session 11

1. First the company has to develop a segmentation and identify segments within the market. The variables for segmenting consumer markets are:

- Profile variables.
- Behavioural variables.
- Psychographic variables.

Then the company has to 'test' segments using the following criteria:

- Homogeneous.
- Exclusive.
- Substantial.
- Accessible.

Having defined segments, the company then needs to select its target segment(s). This is essentially assessing the segment's attractiveness and matching the segment to the company's capabilities (competencies and assets). Factors to consider would be: market factors, competition and environmental factors.

Finally, the company needs to develop a clear positioning proposition. The key factors to be considered are:

- Credence – attributes have to be credible.
- Competitiveness – benefits delivered should be those that competitors are not supplying – quite easy for Freeplay.
- Consistency – should be consistent over time.
- Clarity – it has to be clear in the minds of consumers in the target market.

2.  The associations that Freeplay Energy can use to position a brand such as S360 or 20/20 are as follows:

- Product benefits – this plays on its unique features.
- Usage occasions – they have made a play on this in Western markets, e.g. in the US where it is seen as a 'survival' product.
- Origin – its link to a less developed economy and disadvantaged employees could be used.
- Quality/value – as price comes down and no need for batteries or power bills.

# Session 12

1.  An innovation audit will tell a company like Gillette or Wilkinson Sword how effectively it is able to deliver the innovations needed. These can be in new products and services or in processes, such as marketing or production. The innovation audit looks at four areas of the business:

    ■ Quantitative measures of performance, e.g. numbers of innovations, proportion of sales from new products/services.

    ■ The organisational climate: its attitudes towards, and capacity for, innovation.

    ■ Policies and practices in the organisation.

    ■ The balance of styles of the senior management team.

2.  As market leader, Gillette has three strategies available:

    ■ Expand the total market – increase usage by getting people to use it more, or getting more people to use it.

    ■ Guard current market share – maintaining current position and competitive advantage.

    ■ Expand current market share – developing new products, finding new markets or using price.

    It appears that Gillette's actions will:

    ■ Expand the category.

    ■ Capture new users.

    ■ Encourage users to trade up.

    ■ Expand market share.

    High levels of expenditure on NPD and promotion are key to realising these goals.

# Session 13

1.  A 'downturn' or 'recession' occurs when customers, for a variety of reasons, collectively either reduce expenditure on a particular type of product or service or defer their purchase.

    In addition to the usual factors, marketing has a number of specific factors to consider. The organisation needs to maximise its revenues to cover its fixed costs and needs to cut as much cost as possible without impairing its competitive position. The additional factors marketing should consider are:

    - Are there any segments, sectors or regions where the recession is not going to have such a hard impact so revenues will hold up? These are candidates for priority for reduced promotional budgets.

    - Are there particular competitor weaknesses that can be exploited, possibly by maintaining promotion, to reinforce revenues?

    - Can demand be stimulated or maintained through a revised message or short-term price discounting without starting a price war?

    - What is the minimum that needs to be done to support the brand?

    - In what ways can marketing costs be reduced without reducing the level of activity? For example, are there other, cheaper ways of achieving the same objectives?

    - Which marketing activities are essential to maintain revenues and which can be reduced or deferred without affecting revenue?

2.  A cut in marketing expenditures should trigger a re-evaluation of marketing objectives and strategies. This involves re-examining priorities and choices of markets, audiences, messages and media.

    - Can the existing marketing objectives still be achieved? Will one or more objectives have to be dropped or modified?

    - Are the existing marketing strategies still feasible? Will they achieve the modified objectives? Are they still affordable? If not, which are the key market segments and loyal customers?

    - Are the existing media and campaigns still feasible? Do the cost reductions mean cutting the coverage of certain products and services, certain campaigns or the use of certain media? If so, which are the key products, campaigns and media? What effect will any cuts have on the integrated campaign?

- Is it possible to achieve the cuts through savings in agency fees, campaign development or campaign execution? For example, by using a 20-second rather than 30-second TV slots and paying 10% less for the slot.

This approach to decision making is businesslike but requires a good understanding of the cause and effect linkages between objectives and strategies, between strategies and media decisions, between media decisions and results. The Marketing Department therefore needs good records and accurate measures of its campaigns.

If the Marketing Manager does not have this information, he or she is left only with two weak options to achieve the savings: one, to make arbitrary decisions; or two, simply to cut back every activity by 10 per cent.

## Session 14

1. Internal marketing is planned effort to overcome resistance to change through effective communication, motivation and training. The benefits of internal marketing to TLS include:

- Better communication throughout the organisation, leading to more harmony and increased awareness.

- Employees are more market- and customer-oriented, critical in a service business like TLS.

- Increased motivation and purpose.

- Focus for TLS with better management ideas/awareness.

- Co-operation between employees/departments and integration with back-office systems.

2. Segments in the organisation include: supporters, neutrals and opposers. The internal marketing plan should specify the marketing mix for each of these groups or segments.

- Product – the change itself.

- Price – the cost of change to the individual.

- Promotion – the mix of communications media to be used.

- Place – the methods to be used, e.g. training.

Successful implementation of the plan will rely on three key skills:

- Persuasion.
- Negotiation.
- Politics.

Potential problems include:

- Time and cost involved in implementing programme.
- Staff turnover increases at a time of change. TLS could lose some good people.
- Opposers may have strong influence and can create convincing arguments.
- Retail staff may already be strongly customer-oriented and may be demotivated by the programme.

## Session 15

1. Various types of marketing and financial information are useful within a marketing control system. Measurable inputs include investment in marketing activities and campaigns.

   For the most part, organisations measure outputs in terms of efficiency (doing things right) and effectiveness (doing the right things). Examples of measures used are:

   - Profitability ratios, e.g. operating profit and ROCE.
   - Utilisation or efficiency ratios, e.g. profit per square foot, sales per employee and stock turnover.
   - Marketing outcomes – what marketing activities have achieved. E.g. cost per response generated by a direct marketing campaign; cost per order resulting from an integrated PR, advertising and sales campaign; and levels of brand awareness or recall following an advertising campaign.
   - Process measures – indicators of likely trends in outcomes for the coming months. E.g. a fall-off in the number of enquiries may signal a fall in sales revenues over the coming weeks and months.

- Qualitative measures – customers' perceptions and behaviours, e.g. customer satisfaction levels and brand perceptions. Again, these are likely to be indicators of future sales levels.

2. The Evaluation tool is used after the campaign to assess the results. The user has the option of grouping data any way in order to analyse standard measures such as cost per response, profit per response, number or percentage of responders and the campaign's overall profit.

The results can then be extracted into Excel spreadsheets or PowerPoint presentations for reporting and sharing with colleagues and Directors.

# Appendix 2

# Syllabus

# Planning & Control

## Aims and objectives

- Understand the theoretical concepts, techniques and models that underpin the marketing planning process.

- Build practical skills associated with the management of the planning process.

- Justify their strategic decisions and recommendations.

- Develop an understanding of the barriers that exist to effective implementation of strategy.

- Appreciate the need to tailor marketing plans and process to allow for the specific sector and situational factors that apply to any given organisation.

- Develop an awareness of the techniques that underpin innovation and creativity in organisations.

## Learning outcomes

By the end of this module, you should be able to:

- Understand and critically appraise a wide variety of marketing techniques, concepts and models.

- Conduct and evaluate a detailed marketing audit, both internally and externally.

- Identify the elements that can be used to create competitive advantage.

- Compare and contrast strategic options and specify a clear rationale when choosing between strategic alternatives.

- Prepare effective and realistic marketing plans and initiate control systems for marketing planning.

- Understand and evaluate the processes that can be used to overcome barriers to effective implementation of marketing strategies and plans.

- Evaluate a range of techniques that facilitate innovation in organisations.

## PART B – Answer THREE Questions Only

### Question 2.

A major supermarket chain is planning to enter the financial services market. Write a report identifying the key elements of a brand strategy and the criteria that should be used by the retailer in making a decision on whether to stretch its current brand name into this new market.

**(20 marks)**

### Question 3.

Evaluate the usefulness of portfolio models in helping managers to make strategic choices.

**(20 marks)**

### Question 4.

What are the causes of strategic wear-out in an organisation and how can this danger be avoided?

**(20 marks)**

### Question 5.

Your company, which supplies IT equipment and services to the business market, has just appointed a new Marketing Director whose background is in consumer markets. You have been asked by this new Director to write a report outlining the nature of organisational buyer behaviour and the resulting approaches that have been developed to segment organisational/industrial markets.

**(20 marks)**

### Question 6.

Outline and evaluate how scenario planning may assist a large regional electricity company to gain a better understanding of the future of its markets. What advantages does scenario planning have over traditional econometric models?

**(20 marks)**

### Question 7.

As an external Project Management Consultant to a sportswear manufacturer you have been asked to write a report outlining the general principles that need to be followed in establishing an effective control system. The company has also asked you to illustrate the potential problems control systems can create.

**(20 marks)**

# Appendix 4

# Feedback to specimen exam paper

The following do not represent full specimen answers to the Specimen Examination Paper, but look at:

- The rationale for the question – what the examiner is looking for.
- The best way to structure your answer.
- The key points that you should have included, and expanded upon.
- How marks for the question might have been allocated.
- The main syllabus area that is being assessed.

Note that many of the key points are represented here in the form of bullet point lists. All of these points should be expanded in your answer, unless the examiner specifically asks for a bullet point list.

The timings given for each part of each question allow a little time for reading the Case Study, planning your answers, and choosing which questions you will answer. Remember to follow the instructions on the paper.

## PART A

## Question 1.

The Case Study for this paper is about the response by Sony, the leader in this market, to Microsoft's launch of Xbox in competition with Sony's established PlayStation 2 and Nintendo's GameCube. In this case,

- Sony is clearly the market leader.
- Microsoft is a determined challenger.
- It is a dynamic market, both in terms of what customers are demanding and what technology can deliver, so no player can afford to stand still.

The important thing to remember about approaching the mini case questions is that you must apply the **concepts** that the examiner is looking for to the **context** and situation described in the case. With every question that is broken up into sections, you also need to consider how marks are spread across the various parts of the question, as this should dictate how much time you allocate to each part.

a.   The examiner was looking for an **evaluation** of the appropriateness of Sony's actions. Given the inclusion of **contingency planning** in the question, you should link your answer to it (but not make a major play on it). The format of the answer was not specified but, unless stated, it is good practice to use a **report** format.

Your answer should have been structured along the following lines:

- Introduction – recognise that Sony is the **market leader** and has to be active in defending its position.
- Strategies available to the market leader:
  - Expand the total market – by targeting non-users, increasing the rate of usage or discovering new applications for the product.
  - Guard existing market share – by strong positioning, effective customer relationships and loyalty, continuous innovation, advertising, and strong distribution channels.
  - Expand current market share – by developing new products, expanding distribution channels, aggressive pricing, geographic expansion or alliances.

Alternatively, you may choose to explain the strategies available to the market leader in terms of strategies for defence.

- **Evaluation** of Sony's actions – show with evidence from the case how the actions Sony has taken are appropriate in defending its position as leader. These might include heavy advertising, its alliance with AOL and RealNetworks and price discounting to establish share.
- Summary or conclusion – you should reach an opinion on how **appropriate** Sony's action have been and how this might help it to retain its position in the foreseeable future.

Of the 20 marks available for this question, there would be marks available for recognising Sony as the market leader (perhaps 3-4), the strategies available (perhaps 7-8) and a conclusion, supported with evidence from the case, on the appropriateness of Sony's actions (perhaps 8-10).

Syllabus area – 3.4.2 (defensive strategies and strategies for market leaders).

b.  In this part of the question, the examiner was looking for the strategies available to Microsoft as a market challenger. The question specifies **report** format.

Your answer might have used the following broad structure:

- Introduction – you might show that Microsoft can be either a challenger or a follower.

- Strategies available – the offensive strategies available to a challenger are:
    - Frontal attack.
    - Flank attack.
    - Encirclement attack.
    - Bypass attack.
    - Guerrilla attack.

These strategies can be realised through actions such as price discounting, cheaper product offerings, product innovation, intensive advertising, market development, developing a prestige image, product proliferation and cost reduction.

- Microsoft's approach – you should comment on what you conclude Microsoft are doing (e.g. frontal attack) and briefly give some evidence. To succeed they would have to:
    - Possess or develop a sustainable competitive advantage (cost or differentiation).
    - Negate the leader's advantage, generally by being able to deliver the leader's key attributes at almost the same level.
    - Take advantage of an obstacle hindering the leader from retaliation. This may be a factor such as limited resources.

- Alternatives open to Microsoft – if these conditions are not present, Microsoft would be better to attack players other than the leader (Nintendo). You may have already touched on 'market follower' in the introduction.

Of the 20 marks available for this question, there would be marks available for the strategies and ingredients available to a market challenger, a view on what Microsoft is doing, supported with evidence from the case, and an identification of what it has to do and the alternatives to market challenger available.

Syllabus area – 3.4.2 (offensive strategies and strategies for market challengers).

# PART B

## Question 2.

The examiner is looking for you to demonstrate not only your knowledge of the elements of **brand strategy** but also an appreciation of how it should be applied in the context of a **brand stretching** decision by a supermarket entering the financial services market.

Your answer might have followed a structure as follows:

- Introduction – what a brand is (product, benefits, what it communicates).

- **Brand strategies** – the strategies available with short notes about each, ideally related to the supermarket/financial services context set in the question:

  - Company brand.
  - Individual brand.
  - Company and individual brand.
  - Range branding.

- Brand stretching – what **brand stretching** is and the **criteria** for deciding in this context. These might include relevance, opportunities to add to (not detract from) value of brand, fit between markets for organisation, resources available and likely customer response.

- Conclusion – a closing statement highlighting the possible pitfalls and linking these to the criteria you have identified. As the question is general in nature and does not specify this, it is not necessary to offer a recommendation or opinion on whether the supermarket should go ahead with its decision to stretch its brand into the new market.

Of the 20 marks available, perhaps 8 would have been allocated to the brand strategies, with the remaining 12 available for the identification of criteria and explanation of how they relate to the stretching decision.

Syllabus area – 3.4.3 (branding strategy).

## Question 3.

In this question, the examiner is providing an opportunity for candidates to demonstrate their knowledge and understanding of the **range of portfolio models** and their **use** in making **strategic decisions**. It is not enough simply to pick a single model, such as the BCG matrix, and describe it.

Your answer may be built around the following points:

- Introduction – how and why these models were developed: to enable Managers in large organisations such as **Shell** and **GE** to compare different business units and make decisions about the allocation of resources to the stronger or more promising units.

- Models – list examples and briefly describe one or more models, preferably the 3x3 matrices.

- Benefits – portfolio models have made the following advantages:
  - Show that SBUs and products have different roles in the portfolio.
  - They represent the portfolio graphically in an easily understood form.
  - SBUs and products have different resource requirements and yields.
  - They are a useful aid to balancing the portfolio in a multi-business or multi-product corporation.
  - They can be used in setting strategic objectives and focus attention on management skills and reward systems.

- Drawbacks – they also have weaknesses:
  - They are time-consuming to collect information for and prepare.
  - While their simplicity aids understanding, they are perhaps too simplistic in taking just a single perspective.
  - Managers in businesses labelled 'harvest' or 'cash cow' may be demotivated.
  - A model like BCG places too much emphasis on market growth when many markets are mature or declining.
  - Even when weighted scores are used to evaluate criteria (as in GE and Shell matrices), the approach is subjective and open to question.

■ Conclusion – a short statement reaching a conclusion on the usefulness of portfolio models in strategic choices – perhaps that they can help but should not be used as the only means for making these decisions.

Of the 20 marks available, there might have been 4 marks for how the portfolio models were developed, 6 marks each for the benefits and drawbacks, and 4 for explaining how useful they are as part of the strategic decision process.

Syllabus area – 3.3.3 (portfolio analysis tools) covers the basic models themselves; 3.4 (strategy formulation and choice) covers their application in strategic choice.

## Question 4.

The examiner is looking for an explanation of what **strategic wear-out** is, what causes it and what organisations can do to avoid it. It is a straightforward question on a specific subject with no hidden 'traps'. These are 'good' questions for the well-prepared candidate.

Your answer may have contained some of the following elements:

■ Introduction – what strategic wear-out is (when an organisation no longer satisfies customers' needs); you may link it to 'strategic drift' – a gradual shift over time away from the customers' needs.

■ Causes – the causes of strategic wear-out are:
   – Changes in the external environment, often new legislation.
   – Changes in customer needs or expectations.
   – Changes in distribution channels or the development of a new channel.
   – Developments by competitors.
   – Failure to maintain investment in products and marketing.
   – Complacency.
   – Changes in strategy.

You may have grouped causes under the headings of the different areas of the organisation's environment: macro, micro and internal.

- Avoiding wear-out:
  - Market-led (or customer-focused) culture.
  - Environmental scanning.
  - Effective planning.
  - Internal market audit.
  - Preparedness to recognise and see through change.
- Conclusion – a short concluding statement, perhaps linking back to the strategic management cycle and emphasising the role of control, feedback and use of analysis tools in evaluating the environment.

The 20 marks might have been allocated as follows: 4 for explaining what strategic wear-out is; 6-8 marks for the causes; and 8-10 marks for the ways to avoid it and a conclusion.

Syllabus area – 3.4.2 (strategic wear-out and renewal).

## Question 5.

The examiner has specifically asked for a **report** on **organisational buying behaviour** and approaches to **segmenting organisational markets**. Your 'customer' is the new Marketing Director, someone from a consumer marketing background, who, you can assume, is aware of the basic principles but wants to see how they are being applied in your company, an IT equipment and service supplier. This helps you to focus your answer rather than writing generally.

It helps to plan your answer to this type of question carefully before you start writing to prevent time running away with you. Remember that you have about 30 minutes to plan and write your answer.

Your answer may have contained some of the elements shown below:

- Introduction – what the Marketing Director has asked you to do and how your report is structured. Ideally you should link the question to the Director's experience by saying that the **segmentation process** is the same but that the key difference is the **DMU**.
- Organisational buyer behaviour – explain the make-up and behaviours of the DMU and the effects it has on the buying process (making it more complex).

324

- Segmentation and criteria – cover the two main approaches to segmentation and the criteria used to segment:

  - **Macro**: sector, size, location, or end use.

  - **Micro**: DMU, decision process, buying function, attitude to innovation, decision criteria, or personal characteristics of decision makers.

- Conclusion – you might suggest that both are valuable approaches but require different levels of knowledge and information. In practice a **'nested' approach** may provide the most effective approach for the company. (You may suggest that this is the approach the company already uses.)

Of the 20 marks, you might expect: 6-8 marks for explaining organisational buyer behaviour, its complexities and differences from/similarities to consumer segmentation; about 10 marks for macro and micro segmentation and criteria; and 2-4 marks for explaining the 'nested' approach.

Syllabus area – 3.2.1 (customer analysis) and 3.4.3 (segmentation).

## Question 6.

The examiner is looking for candidates to demonstrate their understanding of **scenario planning** by **evaluating** its use by an electricity supplier and **comparing** it to traditional **econometric models**. It is not enough to describe scenario planning or explain how it is carried out.

Your answer must link scenario planning to the electricity company by quoting examples or showing how it would fit into the forecasting activities you could envisage a company like this using.

Your answer may have followed a structure as follows:

- Introduction – what scenario planning is, why it is different from other forecasting techniques and its use in organisations as they face increasing uncertainty.

- Stages – a brief account of the stages that an electricity company might use when conducting scenario planning:

  - Identify change drivers relevant to the company/industry, e.g. competitive supply, government regulation, climate change, etc.

  - Develop a few possible 'scenarios' and refine down to about 2-4.

  - Define the scenarios.

- Identify the issues and assess the likely outcomes.

Note: there is no attempt to allocate probability to any scenario occurring.

- Benefits – for the electricity supplier:
  - Focus on issues critical to the future of the company.
  - A framework for understanding events and contingency planning.
  - Identifies possibility of discontinuous events (e.g. another oil shock).
  - Places strategic issues on management agenda.

- Conclusion – a concluding statement comparing scenario planning with econometric models, which tend to contain few simple variables and 'continuous' trends and are deterministic ($a * b$ always $= c$; so long as you know values of $a$ and $b$, you will always know $c$). Scenario planning has the great advantage that it allows for discontinuities and a broader spectrum of uncertainty. In practice, the electricity company is likely to use both.

The 20 marks are likely to be allocated as follows: 4 marks for explaining what scenario planning is; 4 marks for how scenario planning is used; 8 marks for its benefits to the company; and 4 marks for the comparison with econometric models.

Syllabus area – 3.3.3 (techniques for developing a future orientation).

## Question 7.

The examiner has specifically asked for a **report** on **establishing a control system** for a sportswear manufacturer. Your report also has to cover the **potential problems** such systems can create. You are working in the role as a **Consultant**, so the language you use in your report should reflect this role: Consultants advise and recommend; Managers make decisions.

Your answer may have covered the following points:

- Introduction – a brief explanation of the purpose of a control system to a sportswear manufacturer, to put the rest of your answer in context.

- Control system principles – including:
  - Involvement of staff.
  - SMART target setting.

- Focus on sources, not symptoms.
- Measure effectiveness, not efficiency.
- Management by exception.
- Action trigger.

■ Problems created:

- Costly/time-consuming to report and review.
- Stifle innovation and creativity.
- Further costs/resources required to take action.
- Tend to measure symptoms, not underlying causes.

■ Conclusion – a short concluding statement, perhaps with a recommendation to pilot a simple monthly control system monitoring key financial and budgetary performance indicators to start with, and use this to identify and assess the problems it may create.

The 20 marks may be allocated as follows: 10-12 marks for the underlying principles and 8-10 marks for the problems they cause.

Syllabus area – 3.5.2 (key elements of control).

# Appendix 5

# Assessment guidance

**The method used for assessment of candidates at Diploma level is Examination.**

The Chartered Institute of Marketing has traditionally used professional, externally set examinations as the means of assessment for the Certificate, Advanced Certificate and Postgraduate Diploma in Marketing.

The information in this appendix will:

- Provide hints and tips to help you prepare for the examination.
- Manage your time effectively in preparing for assessment.

## Examinations

Each subject differs slightly from the others, and the style of question will differ between module examinations. All are closed book examinations apart from **Analysis and Decision** (see below).

For all Diploma examinations, the examination paper consists of two sections:

### Part A – mini case, scenario or article

This section has a mini case, scenario or article with compulsory questions. You are required to make marketing or sales decisions based on the information provided. You will gain credit for the decisions and recommendations you make on the basis of the analysis itself. This is a compulsory section of the paper designed to evaluate your practical marketing skills.

### Part B – examination questions

You will have a choice from a number of questions, and when answering those you select, ensure you understand the context of the question. Rough plans for each answer are strongly recommended.

The examination for **Analysis and Decision** takes the form of a Case Study. This is mailed out 4 weeks before the examination and posted on the CIM student web site (www.cimvirtualinstitute.com) at the same time. Analysis and preparation should be completed during these four weeks. The questions asked in the examination will require strategic marketing decisions and actions. The question paper will also include additional unseen information about the Case Study. The traditional form of the examination is an open book examination. However, CIM is piloting a 'closed book' form, which centres can elect to undertake by registering with CIM. Further details can be found in the Companion for the Analysis & Decision module or obtained from CIM.

## CIM code of conduct for examinations

If being assessed by examination you will receive examination entry details, which will include a leaflet entitled "Rules for Examinations". You should read these carefully, as you will be penalised by CIM if you are in breach of any of these rules.

Most of the rules are common sense. For example, for closed book examinations you are not allowed to take notes or scrap paper into the examination room, and you must use the examination paper supplied to make rough notes and plans for your answer.

If you are taking the **Analysis and Decision** examination, ensure that you do take your notes in with you, together with a copy of the Case Study.

## Hints and tips

There are a number of places you can access information to help you prepare for your examination, if you are being assessed by this method. Your tutor will give you good advice, and exam hints and tips can also be found on the CIM student web site (www.cimvirtualinstitute.com).

Some fundamental points are listed below.

- Read the question carefully, and think about what is being asked before tackling the answer. The examiners are looking for knowledge, application and context. Refer back to the question to help you put your answer in the appropriate context. Do not just regurgitate theory.

- Consider the presentation style of your answer. For example, if you are asked to write a report, then use a report format with number headings and not an essay style.

- Structure – plan your answer to make it easy for the examiner to see the main points you are making.

- Timing – spread your time in proportion to the marks allocated, and ensure that all required questions are answered.

- Relevant examples – the examiners expect relevant theory to be illustrated by practical examples. These can be drawn from your own experience, reading of current journals and newspapers, or just your own observations. You could visit

"Hot Topics" on the CIM student web site to see discussions of topical marketing issues and practice.

## Managing your time

What is effective time management? It is using wisely one of your most precious resources, **TIME**, to achieve your key goals. You need to be aware of how you spend your time each day. Set priorities, so you know what's important to you, and what isn't. You need to establish goals for your study, work and family life, and plan how to meet those goals. Through developing these habits you will be better able to achieve the things that are important to you.

When study becomes one of your key goals you may find that, temporarily, something has to be sacrificed in favour of time needed for reading, writing notes, writing up assignments, preparing for group assessment, etc. It will help to "get people on your side". Tell people that you are studying and ask for their support – these include direct family, close friends and colleagues at work.

Time can just slip through your fingers if you don't manage it, and that's wasteful! When you are trying to balance the needs of family, social life, working life and study, there is a temptation to leave assignments until the deadline is nearly upon you. Don't give in to this temptation! Many students complain about the heavy workload towards the end of the course, when, in fact, they have had several months to work on assignments, and they have created this heavy workload themselves.

Knowing how to manage your time wisely can help you:

- Reduce pressure when you're faced with deadlines or a heavy schedule.

- Be more in control of your life by making better decisions about how to use your time.

- Feel better about yourself because you're using your full potential to achieve.

- Have more energy for things you want or need to accomplish.

- Succeed more easily because you know what you want to do and what you need to do to achieve it.

## Finally…

Remember to continue to apply your new skills within your job. Study and learning that is not applied just wastes your time, effort and money! Good luck with your studies!

# Index

See also the Glossary on page 267.

You may find referring back to the Learning Outcomes and the Summary of Key Points at the beginning and end of each Session will aid effective use of the Index.

Only where subjects are relevantly discussed or defined are they indexed.